Paul Robert Hanna

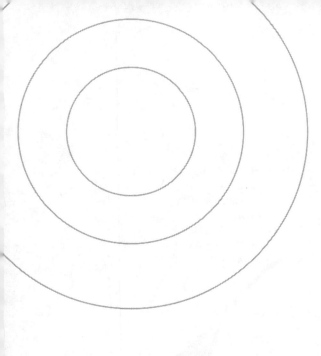

PAUL
ROBERT
HANNA

A Life of Expanding Communities

Jared R. Stallones

HOOVER INSTITUTION PRESS

Stanford University   Stanford, California

www.hoover.org

Hoover Institution Press Publication No. 495
Copyright © 2002 by the Board of Trustees of the
    Leland Stanford Junior University

First printing 2002
08   07   06   05   04   03   02   9   8   7   6   5   4   3   2   1

Manufactured in the United States of America
The paper used in this publication meets the minimum requirements
of American National Standard for Information Sciences—Permanence
of Paper for Printed Library Materials, ANSI Z39.48-1984. ⊗

Library of Congress Cataloging-in-Publication Data
Stallones, Jared.
    Paul Robert Hanna : a life of expanding communities / Jared R. Stallones.
        p.   cm.
    Includes bibliographical references (p.) and index.
    ISBN 0-8179-2832-4 (alk. paper)
    1. Hanna, Paul Robert, 1902–88   2. Educators—United States—Biography.
I. Title.
LB875 .H222 S72   2002
370′.92—dc21
[B]   2001039664

To Jan, Lindsay, and Cameron
for all their sacrifices

Contents

Acknowledgments

This work would not have been possible without the help and guidance of Dr. O. L. Davis Jr., Dr. Eugene L. Johnson, Dr. David B. Gracy III, Dr. Mary S. Black, and Dr. Norman Brown. Their encouragement and advice are deeply appreciated. The cooperation of Mrs. Aurelia Hanna and John P. Hanna was also invaluable. Their willingness to share their family stories of Paul Hanna added depth to my understanding of him. Thanks to all of Paul Hanna's former students and colleagues who spent time helping me understand the complexities of this educational leader. Many thanks to Gerald Dorfman, curator of the Hanna Collection, for all of his encouragement and kindness. A special debt of gratitude is owed to Don, Sharla, David, and Zachary Ekvall, who gave of their time to allow me the freedom to complete this book. Finally, this project would not have been possible without the support of John Raisian, director of the Hoover Institution.

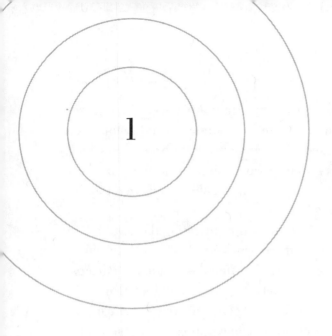

Introduction

Social studies education plays a crucial role in preparing American children to take on the duties of citizenship. In a liberal democracy, however, tensions exist between the needs of individuals and those of the greater society. These tensions are evident in public education every time a teacher encounters difficulty interesting students in the prescribed curriculum. Paul Robert Hanna struggled throughout his career with these often conflicting needs as he sought an appropriate balance for the foundation of social education in the schools. The models he developed went far beyond the traditional approaches to the social studies.

Hanna's solution, first reached in the 1930s and refined in many applications throughout the remainder of his career, replaced the traditional approach to American schools' social studies programs in the elementary grades with a new curriculum design. Instead of deferring until the upper elementary grades a thoughtful introduction to several social sciences, or offering only history and geography as discrete subjects, Hanna incorporated Harold Rugg's integrated secondary social studies approach in his design for the elementary social studies curriculum. Hanna believed that the social sciences could be employed to help students understand the development of the social, political, and economic systems in which they lived. Deeper understanding would empower them to effect change through democratic means that would benefit them as individuals and society as a whole.

Hanna's work took many forms, from educational research and consultations with schools and governments here and abroad to helping establish professional organizations as forums for discussion of the role of education in society. His consistent focus throughout his career, however, was development and refinement of the "expanding communities" design for elementary school social studies instruction. Promulgated in several major textbook series published by Scott, Foresman and Company for almost forty years, the expanding communities design profoundly changed how social studies was taught in schools both in the United States and abroad.

Surprisingly, given his long career and major contributions to education, no comprehensive biography of Hanna exists, although three dissertations have focused on aspects of his work. Robert E. Newman Jr. (1961) studied *Building America*, a monthly magazine series designed to help secondary students investigate social problems facing the United States. Hanna proposed this series to the Society for Curriculum Study and chaired its editorial board from the magazine's inception in 1935 to its demise in 1948. At its peak, *Building America* enjoyed a monthly circulation of more than a million copies. Norman Miller (1967) focused on the way in which Hanna's expanding communities curriculum design treated one international community, the Atlantic nations. Martin Gill (1974) focused on Hanna's long and successful partnership with the textbook publishing house of Scott, Foresman and Company. Through Hanna's social studies textbook series, published in multiple editions by Scott, Foresman, his expanding communities design achieved its widest dissemination and revolutionized the way social studies was taught at the elementary level. Daniel Tanner estimated that Hanna's textbooks were among the most widely used in U.S. schools (1991, 43).

Despite Hanna's impressive impact on American educators, professional historians of education have ignored him. David Tyack (1974), for example, did not mention Hanna in his landmark work on American schooling, even though he surely was aware of Hanna's work because they were colleagues for a time at Stanford University. Herbert Kliebard (1986) also failed to include Hanna in his discussion of the Depression-era shift in progressive education from a child-centered to a social reconstructionist approach to the school curriculum. Kliebard ignored Hanna in his discussion of the Virginia Curriculum Study's role in this shift, even though Hanna was directly involved in that landmark work. Lawrence Cremin overlooked Hanna's contributions in both his history of Teachers College (1954), where Hanna studied and taught for eleven years, and his study of American schooling in this century (1961). More recently, Tanner and Tanner (1990) continued this pattern of neglect. Even books on the elementary curriculum, wherein Hanna reasonably might be emphasized, routinely ignore his role. For example, one recent work described the rationale for an integrated approach to the social studies this way:

> The integration of information gives students and teachers an opportunity to plan a program in which the barriers between areas of study begin to dissolve and the possibilities for experiencing real-life situations are greatly increased . . . societal conditions are explained not only in greater depth but in a context that is meaningful in relation to contemporary living (Reinhartz and Beach 1997, 275).

This statement succinctly describes the approach that Hanna pioneered more than sixty years ago, but Hanna is not mentioned or referenced in the text.

Possible reasons for this neglect of Paul Hanna's contributions are discussed in Chapter Eight, but the ultimate effect of excluding Hanna from historical memory is that an important part of education history remains unknown. Hanna's role in the debates about progressive education and social reconstruction in the 1930s, his role in the creation of several important organizations for professional educators, his formulation of a new curriculum design by which social studies is taught, his part in the development of school systems abroad, and his many other activities combine to support serious investigation of his life and work.

ORGANIZATION AND SOURCES

The organization of the following pages is somewhat unconventional and bears explanation. Chapters Two, Three, and Four of this book are organized chronologically. They describe Paul Hanna's personal growth and career, from its beginning in the small towns of the rural Midwest to its peak as he became the leading figure in elementary social studies education. These chapters unfold the personal expanding communities of influence Paul Hanna achieved throughout his life.

Chapter Two portrays the significant formative influences of Hanna's early years. Paul Hanna was born on June 21, 1902, in Sioux City, Iowa, the first of three children born to George Archibald Hanna and Regula Figi Hanna. His father was a Methodist minister much influenced by the theology and practices of the Social Gospel movement, whereas his mother held to a more traditional form of religion. The interplay of these two belief systems powerfully affected the young Paul Hanna. While attending public schools in several Midwestern communities, Hanna decided to pursue a career in higher education. Toward this end, he earned a Bachelor of Arts degree in philosophy from Hamline University in 1924.

Chapter Three details Hanna's eleven years of association with

Teachers College at Columbia University. Following his graduation from Hamline, Hanna went to Columbia in order to continue his studies in philosophy. He intended to study under John Dewey, but Dewey was detained in China that year. Consequently, he turned for mentorship to William Heard Kilpatrick of Teachers College (Hanna 1973a). This change in advisers influenced Hanna to shift his attention from philosophy to education.

Hanna was a student at Teachers College from 1924–1929, earning both his M.A. and his Ph.D. degrees. From 1930–1935, he served as an assistant professor on the Teachers College faculty. During these years, Hanna worked with many individuals who were then or later became leaders in American educational thought and practice. He worked with Jesse Newlon and Harold Rugg at the Lincoln School from 1928–1935. William Kilpatrick invited him to attend the legendary bimonthly dinner discussions that Kilpatrick hosted. Hanna benefited from participation in the ongoing debates of John Dewey, George S. Counts, John L. Childs, Rexford Tugwell, and their colleagues. Other far-ranging discussions of education and social conditions occurred later as Hanna helped plan and teach the College's Education 200F course in foundations of education with Harold Rugg and William Heard Kilpatrick. Hanna was profoundly influenced by the educational and social thought of these leaders in American education. During this time, too, he was invited by his former Teachers College classmate, Hollis L. Caswell, to consult on the landmark Virginia Curriculum Study. This project prompted Hanna to develop a scope and sequence for the social studies curriculum that came to fruition in the Hanna textbook series.

In 1935, Paul Hanna moved his family across the country to begin a new phase of his career at Stanford University. Chapter Four describes his long career at Stanford and the opportunities that opened to him there. Among these opportunities was his involvement in building a first-class education school. During World

War II, he and his students developed a program for democratic education that became a model for schooling in Japanese-American relocation centers (Hanna 1942g), and from Stanford, Hanna began his consulting work abroad in 1940. His work overseas accelerated throughout the 1950s and 1960s under the sponsorship of the United Nations Educational, Scientific, and Cultural Organization (UNESCO) and the United States Office of Education, and it influenced nations in Europe, Africa, Asia, and Latin America. In 1954, he established the Stanford International Development Education Center and served as its director until 1968. Paul Hanna was named the Lee L. Jacks Professor of Child Education in 1954 and held that chair until he retired in 1967 (Nelson 1988, 413).

Beyond his work in education, Hanna was instrumental in building the reputation of Stanford University by forging partnerships between the university and governments (Lowen 1997; International Cooperation Agency 1957). After his retirement, he endowed and devoted the final years of his life to establishing the Paul and Jean Hanna Archival Collection on the Role of Education in Twentieth-Century Society at the Hoover Institution on War, Revolution and Peace at Stanford University. He sought to create a unique archival collection and research program on the relationship between education and society. It has become the largest collection of its kind in the world.

Other facets of Hanna's life and interests blossomed in California. He and his wife, Jean, raised their three children and collaborated on textbook projects. In addition, Hanna and his wife, Jean, wrote articles and textbooks on spelling instruction. Together they oversaw the construction of a Frank Lloyd Wright-designed house overlooking the Stanford campus. With Stanford colleagues, Hanna launched a forestry business that involved him in serious conservation efforts both locally and nationwide.

Chapters Five, Six, and Seven deal topically with specific major aspects of Hanna's career. Chapter Five traces the development of

Hanna's thought on matters of social and educational concern, from his doctoral dissertation in 1929 to his final publication in 1986. Most of Hanna's writing focused in one way or another on his analysis of modern social, political, and economic institutions and ways in which schools could be used to help children learn to mold these institutions to their own needs. Although life experiences altered Hanna's view of just what those needs might be, his main thrust remained remarkably consistent. He felt that the key to constructive democratic change was providing children with sound information from the social sciences and experiences in democratic practices. His major works in these areas, as well as those of his critics, are cited and discussed in the chapter.

Hanna wielded considerable influence on American education through his work within a number professional organizations for educators. Chapter Six discusses his role in founding and leading several of these organizations. The crisis of the Great Depression mobilized many progressive educators to address the schools' responsibility to the larger society. Some in the Progressive Education Association (PEA) opposed this emphasis and held to individual child interest as the sole basis for curriculum decisions. Hanna and others were appalled at this position and, after attempts to modify the PEA's position, broke with the organization to found new groups. The John Dewey Society and the Association for Supervision and Curriculum Development were two that Paul Hanna had a leading role in establishing.

Chapter Seven details the development and extent of Paul Hanna's consulting work overseas. Hanna found a ready audience for his ideas on community schools and democratic education overseas in the years following World War II, under the auspices of the United States Agency for International Development, UNESCO, and other agencies. His efforts brought him international prominence. Perhaps more important, Hanna's work in East Asia, Africa, Europe, and Central and South America deepened his understanding of other cultures and the impact of social, political, and economic institutions on the lives of people. It also gave him a stronger sense of the interdependence of nations. Both of these understandings profoundly affected his work in the United States.

The final chapter of this book analyzes and places in context Hanna's various contributions to American education. It also elaborates on the reasons for his neglect by educational historians and argues for more attention to educational biography. Taken together, these seven chapters provide a richly textured analytical narrative of Hanna's life and of his role in the development of twentieth-century American education.

THE NATURE OF BIOGRAPHY

Thousands of pages of writings by and about Hanna were analyzed for this work, and dozens of his former colleagues, students, and family members were interviewed. Yet even with so rich a variety of sources from which to craft Hanna's story, it can only be a construction of reality. What perspectives of Hanna's life are missed because friends, family members, former students, and colleagues were unavailable or declined to contribute to this volume? As Edward Carr wrote,

> The facts are really not at all like fish on the fishmonger's slab. They are like fish swimming about in a vast and sometimes inaccessible ocean; and what the historian catches will depend partly on chance, but mainly on what part of the ocean he chooses to fish in and what tackle he chooses to use—these two factors being, of course, determined by the kind of fish he wants to catch. By and large, the historian will get the kind of facts he wants. History means interpretation (Carr 1967, 26).

Inevitably, some sources slip by the hook of even the most diligent biographer. A life as long and fruitful as that of Paul Hanna presents the biographer with a daunting mass of information that leads in dozens of intriguing directions. From this jumble of events, experiences, and personalities, he must craft an orderly narrative that makes sense of a complex life. Obviously, in this process, some information receives more attention and some less. A special difficulty lies in describing the subject's life with sufficient richness to offer a true portrayal without devolving into irrelevant minutiae, or in attaching more importance to events than the subject did, thus distorting their influence on the subject's life. Portraying the life of Paul Robert Hanna presents just this dilemma. For instance, in recent years historians of curriculum have given much attention to the Virginia Curriculum Study. Consequently, this biography devotes more space in the story of Hanna's life to that study than he himself might have.

The biographer's task becomes even more delicate, because sometimes his subject distorts events, personalities, and even his own importance. Sometimes his recollections are faulty. Sometimes he lies. Nevertheless, the biographer must allow his subject to tell his story in his own way. Novelist Arthur Golden observed that using autobiographical material "is like asking a rabbit to tell us what he looks like hopping through the grasses of the field. How would he know? If we want to hear about the field, on the other hand, no one is in a better circumstance to tell us—so long as we keep in mind that we are missing all those things the rabbit was in no position to observe" (Golden 1997, 1–2).

The biographer's subject has a voice, and that voice must be allowed a hearing so that the reader may see the "field" from the subject's point of view. On the other hand, the biographer is obligated to add some analysis or include the voices of observers with conflicting viewpoints to help portray how the "rabbit" appears from afar. It is the intention of this biographer to let Paul Hanna tell about his "field" in his own words as much as possible. To do otherwise is to use Hanna's life as a foil for expressing only the biographer's point of view. At the same time, the biographer intends to share his own view of Hanna, knowing full well that it is filtered through his own experiences. Hopefully, the result is a reasonably faithful portrayal of Paul Hanna's life and contributions within the context of his time.

CONCLUSION

Paul Robert Hanna had an immense impact on education in the United States and abroad. His analysis of modern culture and his indictments of its schools still ring true. Throughout a career of more than fifty years, his diverse interests and contributions included significant roles in major professional organizations for educators, a curriculum design that became the standard for elementary school social studies instruction, the construction of a Frank Lloyd Wright-designed home, new formulations of the community school concept for international development education, the production of dozens of textbooks in social studies and spelling, and the creation of an important resource for research in the instrumental uses of education.

This great volume of work would not have been possible without Hanna's unique combination of personal characteristics. He possessed tremendous energy, an ability to organize and motivate others, and lofty visions of the social good that education can produce. At the same time, he could be stubborn, arrogant, and self-important. The development of Hanna's personality and intellect is the subject of Chapter Two.

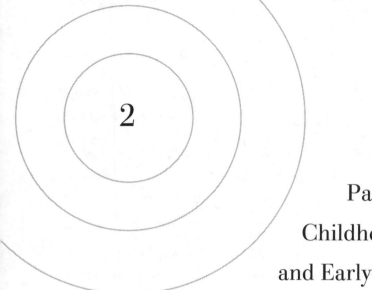

Paul Hanna's
Childhood, Youth,
and Early Adulthood

Powerful influences worked in Paul Hanna during his childhood and young adulthood to develop a unique combination of idealism and pragmatism. During these formative years Hanna also developed his lifelong interest in education, philosophy, government, and foreign cultures. The unique blend of traits and interests that came together in Hanna made possible his later development of the expanding communities curriculum design for social studies, his founding role in important professional organizations, his formulation of various instructional approaches to encourage democratic education for citizenship in the schools, his studies of school systems abroad, and his many other projects in education and in business. Paul Hanna's early life and school experiences prepared him for his role as a leader in education, both at home and abroad, throughout the middle decades of the twentieth century.

CHILDHOOD

Paul Robert Hanna was born in Sioux City, Iowa, on June 21, 1902, the first of three children born to George Archibald and Regula Figi

Hanna. Scholarly pursuits had brought the young family to Sioux City, where George Hanna was preparing for the Methodist ministry at Morningside College. A career in the ministry was something of a departure from family tradition. For generations, the Hannas had pursued business and industrial interests in Ohio. However, George Hanna's branch of the family frequently departed from family tradition (Hanna 1982a, 2).

The first of Paul Hanna's ancestors to strike out on his own was his great-grandfather, George Washington Hanna. Described as "an adventurer . . . 'a boomer,'" in 1849 George Washington Hanna left friends and family in southern Ohio and northern Illinois for the Territory of Iowa to the west (Hanna 1982a, 4). With his wife, Mary Melrose Hanna, and their eleven children, he settled on pleasant ground along the Cedar River in the northeastern quadrant of Iowa. According to family lore, Mary Hanna was fascinated by the life of Napoleon Bonaparte. She chose the name Waterloo for their settlement, possibly to indicate the end of their journeys, as its European namesake was the end of Napoleon's (Hanna 1982a, 3). Paul Hanna so admired the pioneering spirit of his predecessors that he used their story in one of his later textbooks (Hanna 1943b). Memorial markers now stand at the site of the original Hanna homestead in Waterloo.

Apparently, George Washington Hanna's children shared his wanderlust. When they were able, they "scattered across the country and abroad" (Hanna 1982a, 3). Paul Hanna's grandfather, Wesley Hanna, moved to Laverne, Iowa, to work for one of his brothers in a bank. He was "a man of ideas but a poor businessman" (ibid., 5). As a consequence, he encouraged his son George to consider a career of service instead of business. Thus, Paul Hanna's father prepared for ministry in the United Methodist Church.

The late nineteenth century was a time of great upheaval in many Christian churches. Traditional Christian beliefs were challenged on all sides by Darwinism, by Charles Lyell's geological evidences for an old earth, and by the European innovation in theology known as higher biblical criticism. Perhaps the most immediate challenge for the Church was addressing the rapid pace of change in American social, political, and economic institutions resulting from industrialization and urbanization. Church historian Bruce L. Shelley observed that Protestants reacted in two ways: "One party chose to embrace the changes as blessings sent from God; another chose to resist the changes as threats to the Biblical message" (1995, 392). Those who welcomed the changes adopted liberal theologies and formed the core of the Social Gospel movement, a faith-based effort to alleviate the ill effects brought on by change in American society. Those who resisted the changes tended to turn inward, focusing on salvation of the individual. This group formed the core of the Fundamentalist movement (ibid.). Both points of view were represented in the Hanna household, and Paul Hanna grew to reflect a blend of them.

One of the hallmarks of Paul Hanna's personality was the interplay between idealism and pragmatism that enabled him to envision what education could be, but kept him rooted in reality so that he could pursue the possible. George Hanna was an idealist, and his idealism most often took the form of activism for social reform. His son recalled, "I do not remember his preaching very much about life in the hereafter or the miracles of the Old and New Testament. Rather his texts were usually related to the social, economic, political, and moral missions and problems of our time" (Hanna 1982a, 6).

Hanna's father's sermon preparation reflected his concerns. "He read widely in the social sciences and humanities. I think more so than he did . . . theological literature" (Hanna 1973a, 10). On at least one occasion, George Hanna's views encountered strong opposition. "I recall, while I was in the middle elementary grades, that he was threatened by the Ku Klux Klan because of his preachment for the equality of races, sexes, etc. It was a frightening experience but my father never seemed to be deeply disturbed by such threats to his social philosophy" (Hanna 1982a, 6).

Nor was George Hanna's activism merely talk. He often organized efforts to improve conditions for workers, youth, and the poor in the communities he served. Paul Hanna described his father as a progressive thinker and recalled many conversations concerning the ills of society and how they could be alleviated. Hanna attributed profound influence on his own later thought and attitudes to his father (Hanna 1973a, 10).

Regula Figi Hanna had a different outlook from that of her husband. Whereas he was idealistic, she was more practical, and her pragmatism added another dimension to her son's personality. She was born Regula Figi, the daughter of Swiss immigrants, from whom she absorbed the verities of Calvinistic determinism. Paul Hanna recalled that ". . . she believed there was a certain fate . . . that certain things were as they were and couldn't be changed" (Hanna 1982a, 7). She was also quite conservative. Paul Hanna's son, John, recalled that at his sister's wedding reception, his job was to keep his teetotaling Grandmother Hanna away from the alcoholic punch that was served (John Hanna 1998). She would have disapproved.

Regula Figi Hanna grew up on a farm in Renwick, Iowa, on which she learned the habits of hard work and saw profound patterns in nature. She frequently spoke to her son about the value of experience in education. He recalled that she expressed regret for "the children of my time who had to learn these things out of books rather than from actual first-hand experience" (Hanna 1982a, 7). His mother's conviction that experience was the best teacher influenced Paul Hanna's philosophy of life and education.

Paul Hanna often observed the tension between his parents' competing views of life. In his view, his father embraced change, believing that it provided opportunities for people to improve their situations in life. His mother, on the other hand, believed more firmly that God guided the affairs of men. She was uneasy with too much social activism, because that might represent interference with God's will (ibid.). He attributed the greater influence in his own development to his father: "I suppose in another generation, back a generation, I would have been a minister or a missionary" (Hanna 1973a, 22).

Hanna's reaction to his parents' faith was not unusual. Historian Robert M. Crunden (1982) drew a connection between the Protestant traditions in the midwest and progressivism in American society. He argued that by Hanna's time, "the ministry no longer seemed intellectually respectable and alternatives were few. Educated men and women demanded useful careers that satisfied demanding consciences" (Crunden 1982, ix). They entered politics, social work, journalism, and academia.

Along with his father's sense of social justice, Hanna also recognized the value of his mother's practical nature. He recalled, "She always applied the brakes to my father's flights of fancy. My mother would take a realistic and practical slant and often would prevent Father from making unsound moves" (Hanna 1973, 10). One effect of his parents' differing personality styles on Paul Hanna was that he developed a visionary outlook, but one that was tempered by consideration of practical realities. For example, in a discussion with his father about the biblical parable of the lost sheep, Hanna argued that the shepherd should not sacrifice the good of the many for the sake of the individual.

> I thought he had better sacrifice the one sheep and make sure the wolf didn't get the ninety-nine in the fold. Father and I would argue about this. He tried to get me to see what the New Testament was trying to say by way of concern for the lost soul, for the underprivileged, etc. And I was more concerned for the welfare of the majority, but I think again this was Father's way of getting me to develop consideration for all points of view (Hanna 1982a, 9).

This anecdote points to the divergence in thinking between father and son brought about by the twin influences of the ideal and the practical. The ability to blend these two outlooks formed the foundation of Paul Hanna's worldview.

As Paul Hanna grew older, his world expanded to encompass more people and wider experiences. The work of a Methodist minister often entails frequent moves. After leaving Sioux City, George Hanna moved his family to Nebraska for a year, then to Minnesota (ibid., 2). The family moved several more times during Paul Hanna's youth, as his father was assigned larger and larger pastorates. Paul Hanna spent the rest of his youth in various communities in central Minnesota.

Regula Hanna taught her son to read at home, but the first record of his formal schooling is a third grade report card from a public school in Annandale, a small community in south central Minnesota not far from Minneapolis. Young Paul's report card recorded that he earned excellent marks in all subjects during the 1910–1911 school term (Annandale Public Schools 1911). No social sciences appear in the categories on the report card. The early decades of the twentieth century were a time of much discussion and study by scholars as to the proper placement of the social sciences in the grade levels. Apparently the Annandale school followed the pattern advocated by the Madison Conference of 1892, first introducing history in the upper elementary grades (Saxe 1991, 47). Hanna later identified the lack of social science instruction in the earliest grades as a weakness in the elementary school curriculum.

An occurrence in 1911 displayed two of Hanna's hallmark traits, his love of learning and his stubborn determination to achieve despite the odds. His eyesight was always poor, and at the age of nine he visited an eye doctor. The doctor prescribed glasses, telling the young Hanna that he should give up any idea of ever getting much of an education and should pursue a career in which he would not be required to read much. He advised him to become a farmer, and the school's principal agreed. Hanna was bitterly disappointed, because learning and scholastic pursuits were already important to him.

Late in life he recalled his early love of learning: "I found science and history and geography fascinating" (Hanna 1982a, 11). His parents encouraged Hanna's interest by the value they placed on formal education. He recalled that while his mother was concerned "that I brought home good report cards, that I had a good deportment record, et cetera, Father was interested in what concepts and values I was getting through my school" (ibid.). The intellectual atmosphere of the Hanna home also stimulated his passion for ideas. He recalled that "we always had literature in the house. He [Father] read to help himself prepare his sermons. I was subject to much of that literature together with his weekly sermons" (ibid., 8).

The news that he might not be able read much must have been a bitter blow to a young boy who was already perusing his family's bookshelves, as well as the public library. He recalled weeping, but he also remembered that "this did not shake my interest in education or in a life of the mind . . . It never really influenced me . . . I didn't pay any attention" (ibid., 10). His father was supportive. Hanna recalled that, "Father said if you want to be a scholar, be a scholar, there are other ways of compensating" (ibid.). Indeed, his weak eyesight never impeded Paul Hanna's scholarship or other pursuits.

Report cards from Hanna's fourth grade year have been lost, but for grades five through seven, 1912 through 1915, Hanna attended the public schools in Paynesville, Minnesota. Paynesville is eighty miles northwest of Minneapolis. Again, his report cards show high marks, especially in history and geography, which first appear as distinct courses on the fifth grade report (Paynesville Public Schools). During these years, Hanna became aware of how the traditional curriculum could interfere with natural student interest.

When Hanna was ten years old, in fifth grade, he acquired some magnets with which he experimented at home. Thrilled by his discoveries, he brought some of the equipment to school one morning to share with his classmates and teacher. His classmates gathered around his desk before school to see what he had, but when the teacher entered she dispersed the students, confiscated the magnets, rapped Hanna's knuckles with a ruler, and publicly lectured him on the impropriety of bringing his toys to school (Hanna 1974). The incident made a deep impression on the sensitive and serious-minded Hanna, and he grew to resent the disparity between the wonder and excitement of learning through real life experiences and the often dull curriculum of the school.

During these formative years, the Hanna family expanded. Russell G. Hanna was born in 1907, and Geneva R. Hanna in 1914. They were so much younger than Paul that he did not recall specific instances in which they engaged in the types of lively debate with their parents that he did, but judging from their later careers they certainly received similar intellectual encouragement (Hanna 1982a, 9). Russell Hanna graduated from the University of Minnesota as an electrical engineer and enjoyed a distinguished career with Bell Laboratories. In retirement, he devoted his energies to church work and community leadership. Geneva Hanna, later Geneva Hanna Pilgrim, followed her brother Paul into education. She earned her Ph.D. degree from Northwestern University and served for years on the education faculty of the University of Texas at Austin. She also held various leadership positions in professional organizations. Later in life, Paul Hanna visited his siblings as often as his busy schedule permitted. He always spoke proudly of their accomplishments. Nonetheless, the difference in their ages meant that Paul Hanna enjoyed the undivided parental attention given an only child during his formative years.

In 1915, the Hannas moved from Paynesville fifty miles northwest to Glenwood, Minnesota. Paul Hanna attended the schools there from eighth grade through the beginning of his senior year in high school. His eighth grade report card reflected lower marks than normal, possibly due to the dislocation of moving. His marks were a mixture of As and Bs, with a C in spelling. Regula Hanna must have been concerned. He took routine courses including arithmetic, English grammar, history, reading, writing, and manual training. His highest marks, not surprisingly, were for the trait of "industry" (Glenwood Schools 1916). An incident that occurred in Paynesville exemplified his industriousness.

At the age of fourteen, Hanna found a magazine advertisement for a self-improvement course. The ad promised that those who completed the one-year correspondence course would substantially improve their personal efficiency. The course cost the princely sum of $100, an amount that Hanna had managed to save by doing odd jobs, but he determined to spend it all on the course. His mother thought the idea was silly, but his father supported him as long as he saw it through to the end. Hanna registered for the course. Each week, for a year, he received a new lesson in the mail. They included instruction and exercises in planning, time management, and self-evaluation. He surprised and delighted his parents by completing the entire course. He recalled it as "a profound experience. . . it probably had as much influence on my work habits as anything that I ever did" (Hanna 1982a, 13). Hanna's capacity for managing multiple projects and using his time efficiently became a trait that evoked much admiration from his colleagues later in life. His determination to master these skills as a fourteen-year-old boy certainly set him apart from his peers.

At the end of his eighth grade year, Hanna also set himself

apart from his classmates by announcing an unusual career goal. He would become a university president. Hanna had been profoundly influenced by periodic visits to his home by church officials, bishops, and other highly educated individuals. One he recalled especially was Samuel F. Kerfoot, the president of Hamline University. Hanna remembered being "fascinated by his range of knowledge, his depth of experience and his wonderful human qualities. I wanted to be a person like Kerfoot and thought that to be a university president was possibly the answer" (ibid., 15). When the guidance counselor at Glenwood High School interviewed entering freshmen about their future plans, Hanna told her of his ambition. Unfortunately, the information slipped out and Hanna endured much kidding from neighbors in the rural community. Nevertheless, he held fast to his goal. This dogged determination and self-confidence in the face of obstacles were traits that served Hanna well later in life.

Hanna spent the years from 1916 to 1920 in high school. This period was a happy time for him. He formed close friendships with two boys, Celius Doherty and Wallace Royster, and they played chess together almost every afternoon (ibid., 13). Chess became a lifelong passion of Hanna's; as an adult he collected rare and antique chess sets. More than just chess, however, the boys shared dreams of glorious success. They made a pact, duly written out and signed in blood, to return to Glenwood twenty-five years after graduation and provide "our former classmates a big thrill on seeing the three who had achieved so much" (ibid.). Children who feel a bit on the outside of their social group, as these studious chess-players must have in their small agricultural community, often harbor such ambitions. Although the three never fulfilled their pact, each accomplished a great deal. Wallace Royster became a top official in the U.S. Department of Labor, and Celius Doherty became a piano instructor at the Juilliard School of Music. During Hanna's tenure at Stanford

University, he arranged for Doherty to perform a concert there for the Students' Association.

Hanna proved himself an able high school student. In ninth grade, he took courses in English, Latin grammar, elementary algebra, physical geography, and botany (Glenwood Schools 1917). In his second year, he took English, a Latin course entitled "Caesar," plane geometry, and ancient history (Glenwood Schools 1918). His junior year was his last complete year at Glenwood High School. That year, he took English, higher algebra, solid geometry, chemistry, and modern history. He also was active in journalism and debate (Glenwood Schools 1919).

At the beginning of Hanna's senior year, his father was assigned to pastor a church in Alexandria, Minnesota, a few miles to the north. The Hannas considered leaving Paul in Glenwood to complete high school there, but finally decided that he would go with the family, even though he would have to enter Alexandria High School a month into the fall term (Hanna 1982a, 13). When he arrived, Hanna discovered that his new school had neither a debate team nor a school yearbook. These deficiencies gave Hanna an opportunity to exercise his organizational and leadership skills, "I persuaded my new classmates that a big and prestigious high school, as I perceived it in Alexandria, could not be without an annual and a debate team" (ibid., 14–15). He and his new friends organized a yearbook staff and published Alexandria High School's first annual. They also persuaded one of the teachers to serve as debate coach. Hanna and two others entered the state debating competition, where they advanced to the final rounds. Again, Hanna's supreme self-confidence empowered him to enter a new school as a senior and organize extracurricular activities to suit himself.

Hanna's report card from his senior year in school showed only partial coursework because of his midterm transfer from Glenwood. It revealed, however, that he took both American history and civics that year, rounding out his secondary school introduction to the social sciences (Alexandria Public Schools 1920). The social science courses that Hanna took in high school—physical geography in ninth grade, ancient history in tenth, modern history in eleventh, and American history and civics in twelfth—display a sequence based on the school system's assumptions about knowledge growth and cognition. Despite Hanna's attacks on those assumptions later in his life, the sequence of coursework remains remarkably unchanged to this day.

Paul Hanna graduated from Alexandria High School on the evening of Friday, June 4, 1920, a few weeks before his eighteenth birthday. Because the high school curriculum was more widely differentiated in those days, he shared the accomplishment with twenty-six other graduates in the general course of study. These students had prepared to enter the job market or go on to higher education. Twenty students graduated in the commercial course, a special curriculum designed for those pursuing careers in business. Seven graduated in the normal course, preparing to teach in the lower schools (Alexandria High School 1920). Hanna had no doubt about his future. He would attend college at the school headed by Samuel F. Kerfoot, the man he so admired. He would attend Hamline University in St. Paul, Minnesota.

Hamline was a natural choice for other reasons, as well. Founded in 1854 by Methodists, it was Minnesota's first university and awarded the first bachelor's and master's degrees granted in the state. Hamline had a long heritage of preparing leaders in Minnesota's legal, medical, and political communities. The university's distinguished past likely appealed to Hanna's sense of history and status. Moreover, it must have appealed to his budding progressivism and sense of social justice. Hamline had been one of the first universities in the United States to admit women. Its stated mission was to prepare young people to "make the world a better place" (Hamline University 1999).

HANNA AT HAMLINE UNIVERSITY

Attending Hamline University represented another expansion of Paul Hanna's community, and it impacted him in several important ways. First, he had the opportunity to view firsthand the duties of a university president, which caused him to rethink his career goal. Second, he again fell under the sway of an influential mentor. Third, Hanna's years at Hamline afforded him the opportunity to refine further his leadership skills and to achieve success in a larger venue than he had up to then. Perhaps most important, Hanna met Jean Shuman at Hamline. She came to the University from Marshall, Minnesota, and she became just as energetically involved in the social and intellectual life of Hamline as Hanna did. They encountered each other in clubs and organizations, and they fell in love. Hanna eventually proposed, and Jean became his life partner and collaborator in numerous projects.

Among the first people he met with after arriving on campus was President Kerfoot. Hanna explained his aspiration to become a university president, and Kerfoot was delighted. He agreed to provide Hanna with experiences that would teach him all that such a career involved. For the next two years, Paul Hanna accompanied President Kerfoot as he went about his duties. He acted as Kerfoot's secretary and chauffeur as he traveled throughout the region raising money, recruiting students, and meeting with school administrators. When the winter weather made travel too difficult, Hanna observed Kerfoot's administration of the university.

Hanna gained a good sense of Kerfoot's responsibilities in the areas of curriculum, faculty relations, and the work of the trustees (Hanna 1982a, 16). President Kerfoot maintained a grueling schedule, but it did not deter Hanna from his goal. As his freshman year came to a close, Hanna wrote to William J. Davidson, executive secretary of the Commission on Life Service of the Methodist Episcopal Church, asking how he might prepare himself to lead a university. Mr. Davidson's advice included ". . . a Doctor of Philosophy Degree in Education, specializing in School Administration. . . . and at least ten years of professional teaching in a Department of Education at some first-rate college or university" (Davidson 1921). Hanna determined to follow his advice.

At the same time, other career options opened to Paul Hanna. The need to earn money to help pay his college costs prompted him to exercise his latent entrepreneurial skills. During the summer and fall of 1921, he sold books door-to-door in rural communities throughout the region. Judging from the correspondence between Hanna and his supplier, the R. C. Barnum Company of Cleveland, Ohio, he had some success and took pride in his developing salesmanship skills (Hanna 1921). His business acumen and willingness to shoulder responsibility did not go unnoticed by others. Hanna's repayment of a small bank loan before it came due brought this praise from an official of the bank: "So many young men in these times think more of joy riding and other amusements than meeting their obligations and it is indeed a pleasure to find one like yourself that attends to his business as he should" (unsigned note 1924). Hanna also found an opportunity to hone his public relations skills by writing brief articles on the activities of Hamline students for publication in their hometown newspapers (*Greater Hamline Liner* 1924).

Not all of Hanna's extracurricular activities in his early years at Hamline were devoted to earning money or assisting President Kerfoot. In the fall of 1920, Hanna worked in the national presidential election as head of Hamline's Young Republicans Club (Hanna 1982a, 18). This activity afforded him the opportunity to know and become known by professional politicians in the state capital and cemented his lifelong affiliation with the Republican Party. Later in life, Hanna became highly skilled at moving in the halls of power. Typically, he recalled working with influential business leaders and government officials as "a good experience" (ibid., 19).

Some of the relationships Hanna developed through his extracurricular pursuits at Hamline became important lifelong connections. An example is his friendship with Dison Po, a visiting student from China. Po's spoken English was not good, so Jean Shuman tutored him. Paul met Po through Jean, and the three became good friends. When Po returned to China, he served as an adviser to Chiang Kai-Shek and later became the first governor of Taiwan under the Kuomintang government. Later, when Paul Hanna was involved in international educational consulting, the Hannas visited Taiwan as Po's guests, and he provided an entree to educational leaders there (ibid.).

Hanna also made important connections with his own heritage during his college years. His uncle Phillip and aunt Emily Hanna employed him as a live-in "companion-cook-chauffeur-yardman, et cetera" (ibid., 4) during the summers of 1923 and 1924. Spending time with these living bridges to his own past gave him a deeper, more immediate understanding of the importance of history to individuals and nations than could be gleaned from books. Hanna recalled, "These two summers were great because I learned so much of the life of my ancestors" (ibid.). Phillip Hanna had served as Consul-General to Mexico, and in that capacity accepted the surrender of Puerto Rico from the Spanish in 1899. Hanna recalled, "I used to sit up well into the wee hours listening to Uncle Phil tell me stories of his experience with Pancho Villa and taking the surrender of the Spanish in Puerto Rico" (ibid., 4–5).

The most important alliance that formed at Hamline was his romance with Jean Shuman. Both were "joiners," as the 1924 edition of Hamline's yearbook, the *Greater Hamline Liner*, reveals. The photographic portrait of Paul Hanna that year shows a thin-visaged young man with a confident gaze peering out from behind round-framed glasses. The activities listed beneath his name include, "Beta Kappa, [president of the] Student Council, chairman of the Student Chapel, Kappa Delta Rho President, Hamline Players treasurer, YMCA Cabinet, Apportioning Board, Oracle Staff Exchange Editor, Liner Staff, Spanish Club, Debate, Extemporaneous Team, Junior Play" (*Greater Hamline Liner*, 116). These activities reflect an ambitious, self-assured, and energetic Paul Hanna.

On the next page of the annual is a photo of a dark-haired, round-faced Jean Shuman with an intelligent look in her large eyes. She is listed as a French major. Her activities include, "Sigma Delta, YWCA Cabinet, Class Secretary, Hamline Players, French Club, Le Cercle Francais Secretary, Student Council, *Liner* staff, Junior Play" (ibid., 117). Obviously, two such dynamic people sharing so many interests were thrown together time and again on the small Hamline campus. Mutual admiration quite naturally grew into a deeper attachment.

Of all his extracurricular activities, Paul Hanna particularly valued his involvement with the University's debate team. He joined it during his first year at Hamline and teamed up with the captain of the high school team that had beaten Hanna's high school in the state finals the previous year. They proved to be a formidable pair, winning three collegiate debates in 1920, and continuing this success over the next few years (Hanna 1982a, 19). Debating buoyed Hanna's self-confidence and honed his public speaking skills, but more important, it drew him deeper into philosophical reflection. Although the debate topics were policy questions, the debates often cut to the philosophical heart of the questions. Hanna recalled "experiences in that debate team which were philosophical" (ibid., 18).

Paul Hanna had displayed a philosophical turn of mind from early childhood, but by his third year at Hamline he made it the focus of his academic studies. One reason was his disillusionment with his previous career choice. Reconsideration of the tedium of fund-raising and travel that Hanna had witnessed in assisting President Kerfoot convinced him that he no longer wanted to be a university president (ibid., 16). Still, he knew he wanted to be a scholar in the field of philosophy. Once again, Hanna's career goal was swayed by a scholar he admired: "The choice of field was undoubtedly due to the influence of Gregory D. Walcott whom I chose as my major professor" (ibid.).

Professor Walcott was a popular figure at Hamline. The 1924 *Liner* displayed the students' affection for him in the dedication: "[To Gregory Walcott] who has so royally given of his store of wisdom and courtesy we dedicate this volume" (*Greater Hamline Liner*, 1). No doubt Hanna had a hand in this tribute. Walcott was a generalist in philosophy who had great faith in the efficacy of the scientific method applied to any discipline. His talent lay not in original research, however, but in teaching. Hanna remembered that ". . . his courses really pulled the heart out of each of the great philosophers and you understood what that philosophy was about . . . he was a student of philosophy and an interpreter, a purveyor of the great philosophers" (Hanna 1974, 57).

Walcott not only influenced Hanna's choice of academic concentration, but he also offered Hanna a framework in which to incorporate all his previous learning. That framework took shape in Hanna's senior year at Hamline while he was pursuing an honors degree in philosophy. The plan required that he read 100 "great books" and take Walcott's senior seminar entitled "Creative Realism." The course traced the history of thought from the earliest ideas about the origins of man to the present. Hanna described it as "a magnificent summation to one's undergraduate education. My previous courses in economics, political science, sociology, anthropology, history, geography, et cetera, all came together and made unified sense through this reading which I did and in the final course which I took" (Hanna 1973a). The profound impact that this synthesizing and integrating approach to scholastic material had on Paul Hanna later emerged in the rationale and execution of his expanding communities curriculum design and other curriculum innovations.

In 1924, Paul Hanna graduated magna cum laude from Hamline University with an A.B. degree in philosophy. The next step in his plan to become a professor of philosophy was graduate study. As the summer of 1924 ended, Paul Hanna prepared to move to New York City to attend one of the key centers of philosophical thought in America, Columbia University.

CONCLUSION

At each point in Paul Hanna's early life, key figures exerted influence that shaped him in profound ways. His father was the formative figure in his childhood, and he adopted the idealism and humanitarian outlook of the liberal churchman. Assessing his father's impact later in life, Hanna declared, "I think it's a rare privilege to have grown up as a P.K. [Preacher's Kid]" (Hanna 1982a, 17). Of course, the influence was primarily intellectual, not spiritual. Hanna described his church experience as a youth as largely custodial: "I swept out the church, I reorganized the chairs for preschool, made sure the hymnals were in place, and I would help get the church heated up for Sunday, or a prayer meeting, or whatever it was. Somehow I was never interested in attending prayer meetings or in partaking of the ceremonial aspects of the church" (ibid., 8).

A countervailing influence in Hanna's early life was his mother. She represented the values of a more traditional faith and a more conservative social philosophy than those of her husband. Her world view influenced Paul Hanna as well. The result of these earliest associations was a synthesis in Paul Hanna that allowed him to dream great dreams, but also realistically to assess their chances before committing his resources to them. Together, Hanna's parents provided an environment that nurtured his sense of self.

In school, home, and church he learned the value of perseverance and hard work. He also developed a healthy skepticism for the opinions of "experts," and learned to ignore them when he thought better of their advice. This critical turn of mind would benefit him later as he pioneered new approaches to the social science curriculum in the schools. The most profound impression left by his early schooling, though, was the betrayal Hanna remembered feeling when the school curriculum did not take advantage of his natural interest in learning about the world. This disdain for traditional methods of instruction became a focal point of Hanna's educational philosophy in later years.

High school provided Paul Hanna with many opportunities to try new things, and he usually succeeded. Success built his self-confidence and perhaps contributed to a certain arrogance that often accompanies early success. During these years, he discovered debate as a natural outlet for his intellectual powers. High school also allowed him to move into positions of leadership, both formally and informally. He discovered that he could organize and persuade others to accomplish worthwhile ends.

At Hamline University, Hanna made firm career decisions and fast friendships, and he began a relationship that ran deeper than friendship. There, also, he plumbed the roots of his own heritage and gained the sense of himself as part of a larger whole that a deep study of history can provide. Most significantly, he discovered at Hamline the power of integrating diverse subject fields into a coherent whole. Integration of the social sciences formed the foundation of Hanna's later curriculum innovations.

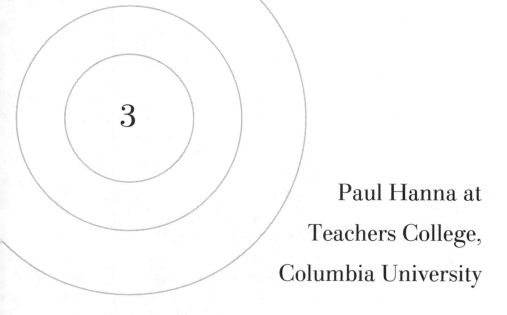

3

Paul Hanna at Teachers College, Columbia University

Paul Hanna arrived in New York in the fall of 1924. His previous education had developed his inquisitive mind and laid the foundation for his future scholarship. His negative experiences with traditional schooling developed his bias toward experiential education, and his studies at Hamline University provided him an intellectual framework into which to place elements of his previous learning. At Teachers College, Columbia University, Hanna's assumptions and abilities were challenged by his interactions with some of the leading thinkers in American education. In his decade there as a graduate student and a faculty member, Hanna embarked on a new career and began his family. He began to formulate his view of the roles of schools in democratic societies and, in the process, rejected traditional schooling. He pioneered work on the curriculum design for which he is best known—the grand scope and sequence that came to be called *expanding communities*—and entered into a life-long relationship with a major textbook publisher, Scott, Foresman and Company, to develop it. At Teachers College, Paul Hanna's

own community expanded to embrace school issues on a national
level.

THE EARLY YEARS AT TEACHERS COLLEGE

Hanna's mentor at Hamline University, Gregory Walcott, knew
William Heard Kilpatrick of Teachers College. Kilpatrick arranged
for Hanna to serve as an assistant to John Dewey while he pursued
his Master of Arts degree in philosophy. Professor Dewey was scheduled to return from China for the 1924 fall term, but the Chinese
government persuaded him to prolong his stay through the end of
the year. Hanna found himself without the mentor for whom he had
hoped. Kilpatrick agreed to employ him as an assistant, and the
change in plans altered Hanna's life. His focus gradually shifted
from Columbia University to Teachers College, and from philosophy to education.

Assisting in Kilpatrick's classes, Hanna met school superintendents who had enrolled in the courses. They expressed surprise at
Hanna's ambition to become a professor of philosophy, asking
"How are you ever going to earn a living?" (Hanna 1974, 58). Their
concerns caused Hanna to worry that, as a philosopher, he might
not be able to afford marriage and a family.

Beyond these practical considerations, Hanna found that as he
spent time around the educators at Teachers College, he became
increasingly intrigued with the problems and promise of the impact
of schools on society. Hanna recalled that ". . . by Christmas time
the die had pretty well been cast" (ibid., 59). He moved from Columbia to Teachers College and changed the focus of his study to
school administration, even though he had never taught in or administered schools.

The Teachers College Hanna found had an enrollment of nearly
7000. By far, most of these students came from Northeastern states,
with nine percent from the South, five percent from the West, and

sixteen percent joining Hanna in coming from the Midwest. Students were transient; fifty-seven percent attended only part-time. New York was an expensive city in which to live in those days, as it is now. Fully half of the single men in graduate study had to work to meet expenses, and another forty percent incurred debt to pay for college (Cremin, Shannon, and Townsend 1954, 257–259).

The leading figure in the field of school administration at Teachers College was George Strayer (ibid., 57). Professor Strayer had come to school administration with a background in science. He pioneered the use of scientific school surveys as a tool for administrators, and, over the years, he turned his department at Teachers College into a survey workshop for his students (Burlbaw 1989, 90). Fully half of their program was devoted to the collection and analysis of data for one of Strayer's ongoing school surveys (ibid.). He wrote that surveys facilitated the "analysis of a total situation into the many problems which demand solution" (Strayer 1925, 822). Hanna completed a Master of Arts degree in school administration, under Strayer's supervision, in 1925.

Even during this early phase of his studies in education, Hanna began to formulate his view on the roles of schools in society. This view became the underlying motivation for all of his major contributions to education. One student of Hanna's expanding communities curriculum design claimed, "Hanna's design was based on his conception of the proper relationship between education and society" (Gill 1974, 1).

Hanna represented a bridge between two major educational trends of his time. Social efficiency educators viewed the schools as tools for preparing children to fit neatly into their future roles as citizens and workers in an industrial democracy (Kliebard 1986, 28–29). The curriculum of such schools must be based on the needs of society. Some progressive educators, on the other hand, thought that schools should serve the present needs of children exclusively. In their conception, the curriculum derived solely from the interest children showed in the world around them (ibid., 190). Hanna's involvement in the ideological struggle between these two camps is detailed later in this chapter and in Chapter Six, but an early version of his thinking on the matter appeared in a paper he wrote for his Philosophy of Education class. He wrote, "Democratic education so manages the educative process that each individual, irrespective of social position, will receive that particular education which will be of most profit to himself and to his community" (Hanna 1925). In this paper, Hanna revealed his view that education in a democracy must serve both the needs of society and those of the individual.

These considerations remained central to Paul Hanna's philosophy of education throughout his career and dovetailed with those of key figures at Teachers College. Dean William F. Russell characterized the intention of the founders of the College and their successors as "the improvement of the life of the people, with special emphasis on the underprivileged and the young; the use of education as a means of sectional and national reconstruction . . . and the guarding of the liberties of the people" (Cremin et al., 273). At Teachers College, Hanna found an institution supportive of his investigation of these concerns.

By 1925, Hanna had become deeply immersed in educational issues, but only at a theoretical level. He had no practical experience in the schools, and he realized his deficiency: "I didn't know about curriculum. I didn't know enough about instruction, learning, and teaching. These things I had missed in my Master's degree because I was still interested in philosophy, and I had added the superstructure within administration without anything to really administer" (Hanna 1974, 60).

His thesis advisers knew his deficiency, too. Hanna remembered that "they realized that I had never taught a day. They realized that my experience had not been in professional education and they wanted me to get my feet wet" (ibid., 61). Thus, when George Strayer learned of an opening for a superintendent of schools in West Winfield, New York, a village of 2000 near Utica, he insisted that Hanna interview for the position. Such was the influence of Strayer, as well as the state of superintendency, in those years that his endorsement of a young, untried candidate with no classroom experience gained Hanna an interview for the position. He must have made a strong impression on the West Winfield Board of Education, because he returned to New York with an offer of the position and a yearly salary of $2500. At twenty-six years old, Hanna made plans in the spring of 1925 to move upstate and gain practical experience before returning to complete his doctorate at Teachers College (Hanna 1974).

HANNA AT WEST WINFIELD

The condition of the West Winfield schools contributed to Paul Hanna's growing sense of what education should and should not be. Evidently, the previous superintendent had provided little leadership and the schools suffered from neglect (Gill 1974, 22). Hanna recalled his first visit to his new office: "I found a table in the center of the room piled so high with unopened mail that you couldn't put another piece of paper on top without it sliding onto the floor. There had been no attention on his part to curriculum, to staff, to student affairs" (ibid., 101).

The schools displayed a deplorable neglect of student interests. Hanna recalled that "there was not a single athletic team, nothing in publications or forensics. It was a dead school" (ibid.). Hanna understood that although student interest was not an adequate foundation on which to build an entire curriculum, interest was a necessary factor in motivation. He swiftly added cocurricular activities to the school program in an effort to increase its relevance to students.

West Winfield High School became a center of activity. Hanna incorporated his recollections of school activities that had appealed to him as a youth with Kilpatrick's and Dewey's ideas on experiential learning, which he brought from Teachers College, to enhance the school program. With the help of sympathetic faculty members, Hanna organized athletic teams, debate teams, a school newspaper, and a yearbook and launched school-based community service projects (ibid., 23). The fruits of these efforts appear in a description of some of these activities in the 1927 edition of the high school annual:

> In West Winfield high school French, learned in the classroom, becomes the official spoken word in the club known as Le Cercle Francais. Parliamentary procedure studied in the English classes becomes something alive in the Hi-Y Club, Young Farmers' Club, and others. The Young Farmers' Club very practically tests the principles taught in agriculture. English reaches a fuller expression in the debates, plays, and declamation contests held throughout the school year (*The Tournament* 1927, 20).

The West Winfield graduating class of 1926, the first over which Paul Hanna presided, consisted of twenty-one students. Thirteen graduated from the general high school program, and eight more graduated from a teacher certification program that extended one year beyond high school (*The Tournament* 1926, 7). In this small student body, Hanna's personal qualities of enthusiasm and energy became infectious. One student recalled, "One day they've got us doing track for physical education and we couldn't believe it but there was Mr. Hanna high jumping! He jumped higher than any of us could and from that day on we'd try anything he asked us to . . . Such zeal!" (Griffin 1974).

Hanna's willingness to poke fun at himself was a welcome contrast to the aloofness of his predecessor and helped to endear him to the students (ibid.). Page 38 of the 1927 *Tournament*, West Winfield's yearbook, pictured a skinny Paul Hanna and another young man in running shorts over the caption, "Columbia Track Team."

In addition to adding cocurricular activities, Hanna enhanced the academic program at West Winfield High School. He taught biology, economics, and physics himself, although his college degree was in philosophy. As in taking a superintendent's position without having teaching experience, Hanna's willingness to teach high school classes without formal preparation displays an astonishing level of self-confidence by today's standards. However, the high school faculty consisted of only six teachers, so some of them must have taught subjects for which they were less-than-thoroughly prepared (*The Tournament* 1926, 3). Hanna's innovative methods engaged the students and helped make up for deficiencies in his subject preparation. His physics classes were especially memorable. The 1926 *Tournament* includes in a timeline for the year, "Dec. 8— The queer experiment to determine the velocity of sound was tested . . . Apr. 23—Prof. Hanna shocks the Physics class by means of a small wire on the seats" (ibid., 46–47).

Despite his own efforts, Hanna observed "the inadequacy, the inappropriateness, the lack of match between the curriculum and what these children were interested in or what their lives were like. There was no relevance whatsoever" (Hanna 1974,103). He organized students to survey community needs, and he sometimes interrupted the regular schedule so that students might take advantage of community events. One student recalled being enlisted to speak before a hastily called assembly of the high school student body about his experiences exhibiting a prize steer around the state. Hanna "turned the whole thing into a discussion of the future for scientific improvement in animal husbandry . . . [he was] always looking for ways to include our own experiences into the curriculum" (Griffin 1974).

Faculty members were perhaps more difficult to charm than were the students, especially considering Hanna's youth and scant teaching experience (Gill 1974, 22). His master's degree from the highly esteemed Teachers College may have impressed some teachers, and his energy and enthusiasm may have impressed others. He certainly represented a refreshing change from the inactivity of his predecessor. In addition to his teaching duties, Hanna served as principal of the elementary and high schools and school board secretary. He also substituted for teachers who were absent in every grade, kindergarten through high school (Hanna 1974, 101). Through this broad variety of experiences, he gained invaluable insights into the practical world of the classroom.

As principal, Hanna held weekly faculty meetings at which he introduced new curriculum concepts (Gill 1974, 25). These meetings did not always communicate what he intended. For example, one meeting designed for the elementary teachers featured a graduate from New Jersey State Teacher's College who was acclaimed as the college's outstanding student in elementary and primary level art instruction. She was scheduled to demonstrate a model art lesson for third graders as Hanna's teachers observed. Instead of the exciting experience of helping children explore their own creativity that Hanna expected, the teacher set up a factory-style assembly line with the students performing merely mechanical tasks that resulted in thirty identical "works of art." Hanna was embarrassed. He did not want his teachers to imitate what he considered to be dull instructional techniques. He felt that instructional activities requiring little independent, creative thought were unprogressive and undemocratic. Hanna blamed himself for not thoroughly previewing the presentation and never again scheduled a meeting for which he did not know the exact content in advance, even to the point of holding pre-meeting rehearsals (ibid., 25–26).

Despite such minor embarrassments, the students and the school board appreciated Hanna's efforts. His students dedicated the 1926 school yearbook to him with many affectionate comments (*The Tournament* 1926, 2). At the end of the 1925–1926 school year, the West Winfield school board rewarded his work by renewing his contract and increasing his annual salary to $3000 (Gill 1974, 24). This good fortune enabled him to return to Minnesota in the summer of 1926 to marry Jean Shuman, his sweetheart from Hamline days.

The young couple returned to West Winfield for the 1926 fall term, and both threw themselves into the work of modernizing the school curriculum. Jean taught high school English and organized a drama club. She also helped students with public speaking and served as an adviser for the 1927 yearbook (*The Tournament* 1927, 40).

The Hannas worked as a team to make the schools more responsive to the students, but roadblocks to change remained. Hanna was disappointed that many teachers did not respond to his attempts to introduce new teaching methods in the schools (Gill 1974, 26). He also lamented the fact that West Winfield certified teachers with so little preparation beyond high school (ibid., 25). By the winter of 1926–1927 the Hannas were weary of their effort. At one point, both suffering from head colds, they met in Paul's office and decided that the time had come for a change. In February they traveled to New York City and arranged to return to Teachers College for the 1927 fall term, Paul to pursue his doctorate and Jean to pursue a master's degree in English (Hanna 1974, 105).

In his two years at West Winfield, Paul Hanna gained what he desired and needed. He now possessed some practical experience as a schoolman that would inform his efforts as he wrestled with curriculum questions in the coming years. He also had tasted success as an educational leader and had felt the satisfaction that comes from impacting the lives of individual students. W. F. Griffin, a West Winfield student during Hanna's superintendency, later chaired the education department at Colgate University. He recalled that "Mr. Hanna was one of the strongest influences in my life, and planted the idea of pursuing a career in education. What a marvelous man" (Griffin 1974).

Perhaps the most important thing Paul Hanna gained from his time at West Winfield was a growing concern about school curriculum. He had rejected the traditional curriculum in favor of one that focused on students' natural interests, but, with practical experience, he perceived problems with that approach to curriculum building as well. The weakness of the traditional approach was its lack of relevance to students and, therefore, its failure to enlist their natural curiosity in the learning process. The weakness of the interest-centered curriculum was that it failed to direct what content should be taught. It seemed that the school could either interest students or inform them, but not both. Hanna decided that he needed to study curriculum. He sensed that if West Winfield was any indication, "curriculum was sadly in need of complete modification" (Hanna 1974, 104). In the summer of 1927, the Hannas moved to New York City to embark on the next phase of their life together.

RETURN TO TEACHERS COLLEGE

Paul Hanna determined to pursue a doctorate with an emphasis in curriculum, but his restless mind could not be so constrained. For his advisers, he chose scholars in supervision, curriculum, and subject matter education. Milo B. Hillegas taught courses in elementary and secondary supervision, James R. McGaughy taught curriculum courses, and Clifford B. Upton and John R. Clark taught courses in mathematics education (Cremin et al., 103). Hanna created a customized degree program. He recalled

> taking all I could handle in both [curriculum and elementary education] . . . I realized that it was curriculum focused in the elementary school years I wanted to get a hold on . . . I took a number of courses in elementary school mathematics, curriculum and instruction . . . in the social studies, social sciences, reading . . . I was literally bridging these two fields . . . curriculum and elementary education (ibid., 62).

Despite his academic commitments, Hanna found time to tinker. He invented a mechanical device to help children calculate sums, and he filed a patent application for it on November 26, 1927. The device was designed to relieve children of the tedium of memorizing endless computation tables, so that they could focus on the patterns underlying arithmetic calculations. Nothing ever came of his invention, but it demonstrated Hanna's commitment to educational approaches that stress students' thinking through subject matter concepts rather than simply learning skills.

Hanna's knowledge of elementary education deepened through his work at the Lincoln School, beginning in 1928. Lincoln was the brainchild of Abraham Flexner, as a forum for experimentation (Cremin et al. 1954, 110). The school was organized as a unit of Teachers College in 1917, with twenty-five teachers and 116 students in grades one through five. A large grant from the General Education Board provided the funding (Rugg 1941, 185). At Lincoln, teachers created their own materials and textbooks and devised their own curricula, often integrating different subjects within one unit of study (ibid., 111). They also developed their own methods of assessing student achievement (Reich 1996, 33). One instructor characterized the faculty's approach as, "Try anything once and see if it works" (ibid.). By the late 1920s, Lincoln was a beacon of child-centered progressive education.

In 1928, Teachers College employed Jesse Newlon, one of the most prominent school superintendents of the time, to replace Otis Caldwell as head of Lincoln School (Cremin et al. 1954, 113). Newlon represented a tradition of superintendents as curriculum makers. As superintendent of the Denver Public Schools in 1922, he had pioneered an innovative curriculum development project that directly involved Denver's teachers. Up to that time, curriculum development primarily had been the domain of *experts*.

Upon his arrival at Lincoln, Newlon realized that he needed an assistant. Through the good offices of Strayer and Nickolaus Engelhardt, Hanna gained an interview with Newlon. In Hanna's words, ". . . it was love at first sight . . . he was a great 'father figure' and we were just like father and son" (Hanna 1974, 62). Hanna became Newlon's executive assistant on December 5, 1928, the beginning of a long and fruitful association.

Hanna first worked with Newlon on a reorganization of the administration of the school. The two then launched a study of the school curriculum (Gill 1974, 31). This effort proved to be one of the key events in shaping Hanna's thinking about the purposes of education. Hanna's first impression of the Lincoln School's curriculum was that the concept of basing lessons solely on child interest had run wild there. As he described it, "There was no continuity whatsoever in the curriculum. It was what each of the teachers decided that he or she wanted to do" (ibid., 64). He was not critical of the quality of instruction, however. In fact, Hanna described Lincoln's teachers as "magnificent . . . I would just as soon that my grandchildren . . . be under these stimulating and magnificent people . . ." (ibid.). The problem lay with letting children's immediate interests shape the curriculum. Hanna feared that "It was quite possible for a child progressing through the grades for thirteen or fourteen years in the Lincoln School and [sic] study nothing, say, but science, or nothing but sculpture . . . There was no general or common core to prepare one for a broad view of life . . ." (Gill 1974, 104–105).

Another member of the Lincoln School staff shared Hanna's reservations about the foundations of its curriculum. Harold Rugg first came to the Lincoln School in 1919 as an educational psychologist specializing in testing (Rugg 1941, 189). He also served as a professor of curriculum at Teachers College. With each Lincoln teacher assessing student progress in his own manner, there was no standard of comparison. One author claimed that ". . . because Lincoln was Lincoln, its students found themselves guinea pigs for every new testing technique that came down the pike" (Reich 1996,

34). It was to bring some order to this chaos that Rugg was brought to Lincoln.

Rugg shared Hanna's concern about the curriculum at the school. In 1928, he coauthored a book that was critical of the extremes in child-centered progressive education. He complained that the curriculum in schools like Lincoln was fragmented and failed to give students a clear picture of the world. He observed that "We find interesting separate units of work devoted to a study of Holland, China, the desert life of the bedouins. These have been selected, however, largely in the expressed interests of a few children or the personal interest of the teacher. They do not represent integral units in a carefully designed scheme for the curriculum of the whole school" (Rugg and Shumaker 1928, 123).

Out of his concern for a more orderly approach to curriculum development, Rugg developed innovative materials for junior high school social studies instruction. These materials began as pamphlets first distributed to schools through subscription in 1922, and grew into a popular textbook series published by Ginn and Company (Rugg 1941, 206). Rugg's pamphlets pioneered both an integrated approach to presenting social science information and the use of scholarly work in the social science fields to determine content. In these books, Rugg addressed what he saw as the premier educational need in the United States: "an honest and intelligible description of our social order" (ibid., 210).

Hanna admired Rugg's attempts to integrate the previously segregated fields in social science and his efforts to ensure the intellectual integrity of the subject matter (Gill 1974, 37). Rugg's approach to curriculum making seemed more rational than blindly following student interest. Moreover, as he observed Lincoln teachers planning curriculum, Hanna began to question whether or not they were following student interest or creating it. Hanna observed that the same inquiries repeated themselves year after year after year in specific classrooms. Teachers apparently assumed that cer-

tain interests were innate to certain age groups, but Hanna sus-
pected something else was at work. He theorized that the teachers
communicated their interest in certain topics to the students and
then read it as the children's own (Hanna 1974, 100). This assumption was borne out by his observations of a third grade teacher:

> Miss Keeler's youngsters always had culminating experiences in
> which they invited the kindergartners and 1st and 2nd graders to
> come and share their marvelous and exciting experiences. The
> glass showcases in the halls were always filled with the things that
> Miss Keeler's group were [sic] doing on Manhattan Indians or the
> Dutch colonial settlement. So there was an expectation on the part
> of the children. It was Miss Keeler, in her class, who set the
> interests in the youngsters who came to that 3rd grade. Miss
> Keeler would never acknowledge this (ibid., 105).

Harold Rugg had observed much the same behavior in Lincoln
School teachers (Rugg 1928, viii).

Rugg left the Lincoln School in 1928 and Jesse Newlon employed another curriculum authority to help Hanna in his study of
the curriculum (Gill 1974, 33). He was L. Thomas Hopkins, a professor of education at the University of Colorado who had worked
with Newlon on the Denver Curriculum Project. In Hanna's view,
Hopkins represented the other end of the curriculum spectrum from
Lincoln—traditional education. For him, curriculum making was
a methodical, scientific process centered on discerning what content
students needed to know (ibid., 65). Child interest was not a major
concern.

Hanna and Hopkins worked as a team with the faculty to try to
find some middle ground between the traditional and child-centered
approaches. Just as Hanna had at West Winfield, the two men held
weekly faculty meetings and enlisted the help of other members of
the Teachers College community (ibid., 105). Hanna worked on this
project for three years, but the teachers remained "under the impression that there was something inborn in children . . . intrinsic

. . . and we were never able to get any kind of curriculum consideration" (ibid., 106).

Despite his failure to persuade Lincoln's teachers to look beyond the child as a basis for curriculum making, Hanna benefited greatly from his work at Lincoln. The experience helped move him further along in his thinking about the purpose of the curriculum and curriculum development processes. Thus far, he had rejected traditional instructional methods as irrelevant to the lives of students, and he was moving closer to rejecting child-centered progressivism as lacking direction. Hanna began to consider other foundations for curriculum making, such as social utility.

An early expression of Hanna's interest in the social utility of the schools was his involvement with adult classes at the Lincoln School. Convinced that the school could provide greater service to its community, Hanna helped form a Parents' Recreation Club at Lincoln. Under his supervision, this group surveyed all parents of Lincoln School children about their hobbies and interests. Analysis of the responses prompted the school administration to open the school to the public. Each Tuesday night from 7:30 until 10:00 p.m., adults attended seminars and classes, used the art studios and dramatic facilities, conducted experiments in the science lab, and exercised in the gymnasium and the pool (Hanna and Gucker 1930, 66). This curriculum consisted of "anything that takes their fancy in the realm of modern experimental education" (*World* 14 January 1929). Concepts developed during this work formed a foundation for some of Hanna's later efforts in the development of community schools here and abroad.

The Lincoln School afforded Hanna some of his first opportunities to publish his ideas. He was reluctant at first, but his mentor, Newlon, urged him, "Boy, you have got to write . . . to get your name in print" (Hanna 1974, 69). Lincoln students compiled stories, myths, and legends of flight that were compiled in a volume entitled *Wonder Flights of Long Ago* (1930). For this collection,

Hanna appeared as the second editor behind Mary Elizabeth Barry. He also was assistant editor of the Lincoln School Curriculum Research Studies, a compilation of lessons prepared by various Lincoln teachers. Hanna authored the promotional brochure for the series. It indicates his understanding of the importance of student interest in motivating learning. He wrote that, "The theory underlying the unit of work curriculum recognizes the dynamic effect on the learner when he engages in a series of related activities in which he personally feels a purpose, an adventure, a meaning" (Hanna 1932a).

INFLUENCES ON HANNA'S THOUGHT
REGARDING THE ROLE OF THE SCHOOL

Paul Hanna completed his Ph.D. degree in 1929 and joined the faculty of Teachers College as an assistant professor. The title of his dissertation was "Arithmetic Problem Solving: A Study of the Relative Effectiveness of Three Methods of Problem Solving." However, Hanna soon focused on broader curriculum questions than the study of specific instructional applications. The Great Depression caused many educators to rethink the role of schools in society. Social reconstructionist educator Henry Harap recalled, "Many people thought that we were on the brink of an economic disaster . . . It was a time of a terrific awakening of the schools to their educational responsibilities" (Harap 1970, 157). It was a unique time in which scholars of curriculum went far beyond advocating certain instructional methods or new subject matter offerings and questioned the basic assumptions upon which their ideas were founded. Hanna found a stimulating environment in which to investigate the proper balance between child interest and social needs in the curriculum of the school.

Discussion of the school's role in society took place in both formal and informal settings at Teachers College. William Heard

Kilpatrick organized a bimonthly dinner and discussion group that met off and on from 1928 through 1938. Joining Kilpatrick as regular attendees were Newlon, Rugg, and Professor George S. Counts, as well as John Dewey, political science professor Rexford Tugwell, Dean William F. Russell, and others (Cremin et al. 1954, 144). These scholars represented a wide variety of disciplines. Harold Rugg described them as, "canvassing informally, without programs planned in advance, the roots of every phase of our culture. In hundreds of hours of friendly argument we dug to the social foundations of education" (Rugg 1941, 155). Hanna's entree to these meetings was through his association with Newlon and Rugg. As a junior participant, he listened more than he spoke, but he benefited from his observations of these great minds as they, "revolutionized our personal understandings and our theories of society and the culture" (Rugg 1952, 225).

Rugg's recollections emphasized the harmony of thought reached by discussion group participants (Rugg 1941, 155). Hanna, on the other hand, recalled considerable disagreement (Hanna 1973). Perhaps Hanna's relative inexperience in academic argument caused him to perceive these discussions as more heated than did other participants. The discussion group considered all means of social change and the school's role as an agent for change. Some adopted Marxian interpretations of the Great Depression, but most of the social reconstructionists rejected Marx (Cremin et al. 1954, 253). In 1932, George Counts published his landmark *Dare the School Build a New Social Order?* In it, he argued that teachers should be the instruments of social change leading to social perfection. Dean Russell took issue with him, arguing that such utopianism plays into the hands of both fascists and communists (Cremin et al., 252).

The dialogue in the Kilpatrick discussion group had a profound influence on Paul Hanna's thought. He summarized selected writings on methods of social change as a talking paper and distributed his findings among his colleagues. In the introduction to that work, Hanna eschewed both those who would attempt to halt all social change and those who see it as inevitable, but uncontrollable by human means—those who would simply let it take its course. As an alternative, he advocated planned social change. He wrote that this approach "would direct and control the change so as to move at varying speeds toward selected goals" (Hanna 1932b, 1). He then selected quotations from writings by agents of change classified by their ultimate goal—a classless society or one that retains class distinctions—and by methods advocated for change, including "by education and propaganda." He concluded by declaring, "Today we need to be students of the methods of social change as at no time since the days of the American Revolution . . . We hope the study of the 'readings' presented will be of aid in formulating the method of social change which is undoubtedly crystallizing in the contemporary American scene" (ibid., 8).

Hanna's study of revolutionary writings led him to another conclusion. He observed that firebrands are often martyred. He thought that working within accepted mechanisms for change was more effective than revolutionary action. He wrote, "If you really want to affect institutions and individuals, you have to work within the framework. You have to support the establishment and work to change the attitudes, understandings, and so forth . . . That is, it is the evolutionary concept, not the revolutionary concept in which I believe" (ibid., 109). Although his association with the Teachers College *radicals* would later turn suspicion on him, Hanna's insistence on working *within the framework* eventually allowed him to exert great influence on the attitudes and understandings of generations of schoolchildren.

Another literary outgrowth of the discussion group meetings was the Progressive Education Association journal, *Social Frontier*. Hanna served on its board of directors along with Kilpatrick, Counts, Rugg, Newlon, and others (Johnson 1977, 70). They believed that the schools ill-served the dawning age with their out-moded, individualistic emphases (Cremin et al. 1954, 146). Hanna perceived that "the age of individualism in economy is closing and that an age marked by close integration of social life and by collective planning and control is opening" (*Social Frontier*, 4). The periodical was developed to provide a forum for "the development of the thought of all who are interested in making education discharge its full responsibility in the present age of social transition" (Cremin et al., 146). Hanna's orderly mind was drawn to the concept of scientific social planning (Johnson 1977, 67). Others in the group became more critical of American education as a result of their discussions (Cremin et al. 1954, 145).

Another significant result of the discussion group's deliberations was the merger of six departments of Teachers College into one, the Division of Social and Philosophical Foundations (ibid., 145). Until that time, "history, psychology, philosophy, sociology, and economics of education, and comparative education, had been laws unto themselves, each professor teaching what he wanted to teach" (Rugg 1952, 225). Rugg, the great curriculum integrator, described this academic segregation as "the chronic and besetting sin of academic life" (ibid.). Members of the discussion group concluded that separate fields of educational study shared the common mission of providing depth of understanding for teachers and administrators at all levels (Cremin et al. 1954, 145). In 1934, the departments of history of education, educational sociology, educational psychology, educational economics, philosophy of education, and comparative education joined to form the Division of Social and Philosophical Foundations. The introductory Education 200F course, required for all Teachers College master's degree students, sprang from that union of departments in 1934.

The innovative Education 200F course, a year-long class in the foundations of education, was both a result of debate and a forum for further debate. Each section of the class enrolled nearly 500 students taught by six professors, one of whom chaired the panel (ibid., 152). Hanna, Isaac Kandell, and others took part in course preparation and teaching on the faculty committee chaired by Kilpatrick. Each week, Hanna, Kilpatrick, and the others met to plan, then to teach their class as a panel. These meetings took place in the midst of the vigorous debates within Kilpatrick's discussion group and in the academic journals. For example, Kilpatrick and educational psychologist William C. Bagley sharply opposed each other over the nature of the curriculum. Kilpatrick, representing the progressive social reconstructionist view, wrote that the future was unsettled, uncertain. Therefore, no set subject matter could adequately prepare children for adulthood. The better approach, he argued, was to teach children problem-solving skills through real-life experiences (Kilpatrick 1934). The curriculum that would best prepare them for their roles as citizens in a developing democracy would be drawn primarily from present conditions, not the past.

Bagley opposed many tenets of progressive education (Cremin et al. 1954, 48). He responded by pointing to two fallacies in Kilpatrick's argument. The first was the assumption that more traditional subject matter consisted merely of memorized facts, instead of deeper understandings. The second was the assumption that instrumental knowledge was the only worthwhile knowledge, and he disputed both of these positions (Bagley 1935). Isaac Kandel joined Bagley's side, arguing that rejection of the traditional was anti-intellectual, irrational, and antidemocratic (Kandel 1933).

Cremin described Education 200F as a stimulating experience for students (Cremin et al. 1954, 147). Hanna's recollections confirmed Cremin's description: "We had Kandell who was on the extreme right and we had Kilpatrick who was on the extreme left. All six of us would sit on the platform of Horace Mann School [auditorium] and each of us would have a certain part in lecturing to the two hour section . . . . This was a fascinating experience" (Hanna 1974, 67).

Once each week, all of the 200F faculty panels met together under Rugg's chairmanship to plan the course. Hanna recalled that a wide range of views was represented. "There were reactionaries, conservatives, there were radicals, there were those who wanted to go communist right now! In that kind of a discussion group you had an exciting exchange" (ibid., 70). Certainly, the topics of discussion were not limited to curriculum and instruction. Hanna recalled his attendance at meetings in which the social problems of the Depression were discussed. "He [Harold Rugg] might take a half-hour to make the key issues of what the Depression was doing to the family, to the neighborhood, and so forth. And then it would be open for discussion" (ibid.). In these wide-ranging discussions the strong views of influential men were reasoned, debated, and defended over and over again, and Hanna's view of education and its role in the wider society was challenged and refined.

The effect of this rich intellectual ferment on Hanna's thinking was the realization that the schools, and especially social science instruction, had failed to prepare children for productive lives in a complex, democratic society by failing to provide them with solid, accurate information about the origins and nature of their social, economic, and political worlds (Hanna 1973a, 23). Schools had also failed to guide children in putting their social education to good use. This failure was not just irresponsible, but also dangerous; democratic government in the United States was under attack from both the right and the left. Hanna was concerned that the Depression encouraged ". . . all kinds of wild ideas about how you change society through revolution—through evolution—whether you become technocrats or communists or whatnot" (ibid., 23–24).

Hanna saw some hope in Harold Rugg's approach. Influenced by Rugg, Hanna believed that adequate social education required instruction in all the social sciences. He thought that "the separate subjects—history and geography—were inadequate for living in a modern society in which knowledge of economics, political science, sociology, et cetera were just as important as history and geography" (ibid., 4). Moreover, Rugg's arguments and Hanna's own experience at West Winfield convinced Hanna that "there was little or no scholarly underpinning in the study of the social sciences in high school curriculum." Hanna believed that these ideas could be translated to the lower schools, as well. He resolved to restructure the teaching of social science topics in the schools through a new curriculum of integrated social sciences, but he had not yet settled on a design for this new curriculum. He developed that design in his work on the Virginia Curriculum Study.

THE VIRGINIA CURRICULUM STUDY

State and school curriculum reform projects had become a fixture in American education by the early 1930s (Cremin et al. 1954, 81). A rising leader in these efforts in the South was Hollis L. Caswell (Seguel 1966, 147). Caswell had been Hanna's classmate and friend at Teachers College. In fact, Paul and Jean Hanna had first introduced Hollis and Ruth Caswell to each other, and the four remained close in the years after graduation (Hanna 1973a, 78). Caswell studied educational administration with George Strayer and became thoroughly versed in the theory and practice of school surveys. His graduate studies had prompted his increased concern about the impact on students of a school system that advanced the goals of society without regard to the needs of individual students (Fraley 1981, 96).

In 1929, Caswell joined the faculty of George Peabody College for Teachers in Nashville, Tennessee. He worked on curriculum revisions in Alabama and Florida, but was not pleased with the results. He believed that those revisions had failed to institute changes that would produce true democratic conduct in youth (ibid.,

97). When Sidney B. Hall, a former colleague of Caswell's at Peabody and the new State Superintendent for Public Instruction for Virginia, called him to help in a revision of Virginia's school curriculum, Caswell responded. The project, which began in 1931, required three years to produce a tentative course of study, followed by six years of experimentation to implement it (ibid., 99).

The Virginia Study broke new ground. It was one of the first to involve teachers intimately in the curriculum-making process. Most curriculum projects at the time employed experts in school administration or in the academic subjects to produce courses of study for teachers to follow (Seguel 1966, 149). Caswell believed that teachers were the key to any curriculum reform. He wrote, "The individual classroom teacher is the final arbiter of the curriculum" (Caswell 1977). In order to involve teachers, Caswell distributed to them a brief study guide describing the process of curriculum development, and he invited teachers to attend seminars and discussions at six study centers around the state (Seguel 1966, 148).

The Virginia Study stood alone among curriculum revisions of its time in that it introduced an innovative structure for organizing the curriculum. Caswell was dissatisfied with his previous efforts at curriculum reform and wanted to develop something more appropriate for a democratic society (Fraley 1981, 97). Instead of the traditional subject matter divisions, the Virginia curriculum was organized around a number of basic human activities, functions carried out by all people throughout time and space (Seguel 1966, 153). These activities constituted the scope of study across the grade levels, and the sequence of study was organized around centers of child interest (ibid., 154).

Caswell invited Hanna to work with him in Virginia and the two proved to be a formidable team. At least one history of the Virginia Study attributed development of the scope of study to Caswell and the sequence to Paul Hanna (Seguel 1966). Others portray Hanna as merely a "consultant for social studies" (Burlbaw 1989;

Fraley 1981), if they mention him at all. Paul Hanna's version of events claims for himself much greater involvement in the process of devising the core curriculum for the State of Virginia.

In Hanna's version, he developed a plan to survey the thousands of teachers involved in the activity of the study centers, in order to assess students' natural interests in the social sciences (Hanna 1973a, 5). He planned to have the teachers develop social studies units based on their students' interests, teach them, and then report to him on the results. Once the reports were collected, they were divided by grade levels, with each grade level's reports further divided by topic. Hanna anticipated that once the reports were sorted, one topic would stand out in each grade level, representing the natural interest of school children of that age. Hanna believed that, "If the pupil interest theory of curriculum development were correct, then this procedure should give us some evidence that such natural interest did in fact exist in youngsters and from such evidence we could provide instructional guides for teachers and learning materials for pupils in the social studies" (ibid.).

The reality was quite different. When the reports came in, they revealed no natural pattern of interests.

> We had no bell-shaped curve of piles of papers, each pile representing a topic like "the Mailman," or "the Fireman" or "the Aviator." Instead we had piles of reports from the first grade through the elementary school that had no pattern. We found a stack of reports on aviation units in every grade. As many teachers reported units on aviation in the first grade as reported them in any other grade. . . . Indians! We found as many Indian units in the first grade as we found in the fourth or the seventh grades (ibid., 6).

This disturbing result prompted Hanna to jettison innate child interest as the principle around which to organize the curriculum, but he had nothing to take its place. Hanna was at a loss because he had promoted his survey as the tool that would "give us a struc-

ture as to how we could build the curriculum in the social studies"
(ibid., 7) and it had failed. He returned to New York in late spring
of 1933, desperate to find a framework for the social studies curriculum.

Hanna already had determined that the traditional disciplinary
divisions of the social sciences were too artificial to describe for
children all of the social, economic, and political interactions in the
real world, but his attempts to devise a design for integration had
been thwarted. At the time, Hanna was reading a two-volume study
that impressed him: "President Hoover's magnificent reports [*Recent*] *Social Trends* and [*Recent*] *Economic Trends*" (ibid., 131).
These documents appealed to him because of their systematic approach to social change. "The great engineer, Herbert Hoover, saw
that we had to have national planning and he ought to take broad
base studies of what society was at that time—what our objectives
and long-range goals were, and then set up an educational system
that would move us in the direction of those desirable goals" (ibid.).

Hanna was particularly taken with a chapter that grouped basic
human activities into broad categories such as communication,
transportation, and health. He decided to adopt those categories as
organizing principles for the scope of content for the Virginia curriculum. He employed twenty-three chapter headings from Hoover's work on a vertical axis and used the various grade levels on
the horizontal axis. Hanna recalled, "So I took some 23 chapter
headings out of *Recent Economic and Recent Social Trends* [sic] and
made them the columns of my big wall chart and made the grades
the rows and crossed the grades or levels of schools with these 23
categories of basic human activities" (ibid.). The interaction of these
two axes became the scope of the social studies curriculum for
Virginia. The centers of student interest, such as home and school
life, community life, and pioneering activities comprised the sequence.

The scheme was too complicated, however. Hanna recalled,

"When I went down and presented my huge chart, they [sic] covered a whole side of the library wall of the Department of Education in Virginia. I couldn't even remember what was on it" (ibid., 8). He had to condense it and make it more useful for teachers. He could simply fall back on the traditional social science categories of economics, political science, and so on, but he feared that it would "scare most teachers not having had anything in these fields." It would also violate what Hanna had come to believe about the importance of integration. He determined to use more familiar, accessible terms, "like transporting, communicating, education, or recreating" (ibid.) for the vertical axis representing the scope of study.

For the other axis, the sequence of study, Hanna modified a design that had existed since at least the turn of the century. Charles McMurry advocated a plan in his *Special Method in History* (1903) in which children studied first the history and geography of their family and community, then of their state and region, and then of the nation. By the time of the Virginia Study, nearly half of the curriculum guides in use in the schools employed some version of this "widening horizons" design (LeRiche 1987, 148).

Hanna borrowed this pattern. In his plan, the earliest grades would be exposed to how the basic human activities were carried out in the contemporary home and local community. Grades three through nine followed a sequence of study loosely based on the history of man's conquest of his environment through technological advances. Grades ten and eleven focused on the effects of social change and planning (Fraley 1981, 104–107). Hanna thought "This was a much better sequence for allocating what you would do in grade one to three than had been this [earlier] one" (Hanna 1973a, 8). Although it would undergo considerable refinement in the years to come, the basis for Hanna's expanding communities curriculum design found its genesis in the Virginia Study.

Hanna's version of the Virginia Study story has a number of

flaws. In the first place, Hanna seemed to claim that the innovative design of the Virginia curriculum grew out of his search for an appropriate structure for the social studies curriculum. In fact, Caswell himself viewed the traditional curriculum divisions as inadequate for the proper preparation of children for life in a changing industrial democracy. He too was looking for a more comprehensive organizing structure for Virginia (Burlbaw 1989, 242).

The biggest problem with Hanna's version of events in Virginia is that it portrays him as the prime innovator behind the project. In truth, many brilliant scholars and teachers worked together to produce the innovative Virginia curriculum design. Caswell led the project, and Hanna's account of it stands alone in diminishing Caswell's role.

Two reasons may account for the discrepancies in Hanna's story. One is that most of Hanna's accounts of his work on the project were recorded in interviews conducted late in his life. Aside from the normal reconstruction of memory over time, Hanna's version was clouded by a break in his friendship with Caswell. An incident occurred in 1964 in connection with their work together on the World Book Encyclopedia, in which Hanna felt Caswell misrepresented himself and embarrassed Hanna. The friendship that had lasted nearly forty years was severed. Sadly, Hanna reported that "Now Caswells and Hannas exchange Christmas cards only . . . We just don't see each other" (Hanna 1973a, 79). The rift lasted more than ten years. During that period, Hanna omitted Caswell's contributions from the version of the Virginia story he recounted in interviews. Consequently, the interviewer's questions focused on Hanna's, not Caswell's, role in the Virginia Study.

Still another factor may account for the exaggerated role Hanna assigned himself in the development of the Virginia curriculum design. The design fundamentally became the one that he employed in his development of commercial social studies textbooks for forty years following the Virginia Study. His textbooks became so popular that his name was linked to the design indelibly. Late in life, he may have had a greater interest in underscoring that link than he had in historical precision. Whatever the reasons for the different versions of events in Virginia, the Virginia Curriculum Study represented the genesis of Hanna's best-known contribution to curriculum.

LEAVING TEACHERS COLLEGE

In the summer of 1930, Hanna taught summer courses at Washington State University. Hanna and his wife toured the region during the summer. They were especially intrigued with the easy lifestyle of northern California and the beauty of the Stanford University campus. Paul Hanna recalled, "The campus was such a pleasing contrast to our urban environment of New York City. As we walked about, we dared to think wistfully of some day living on this beautiful campus" (Hanna 1976, 1). Four years later, when an offer came to teach a summer course at Stanford University, they were already favorably disposed toward that part of the country.

Hanna understood that the summer teaching assignment was, in part, a prolonged interview for a permanent position, and he was not an unknown quantity at Stanford. He was acquainted with Stanford president Ray Lyman Wilbur and other faculty members: "[Grayson] Kefauver, who was one of my very good friends and . . . who lived just above us at Columbia, had come out the year before as the new Dean [of Education] to follow Cubberley . . . Harold Hand and I were very close friends" (Hanna 1974, 139–40).

Jean Hanna particularly impressed Jesse B. Sears, one of the "grand old men" in the Stanford School of Education. After chatting with Mrs. Hanna for nearly a half hour at a cocktail party, Sears declared, "I am not sure that I want to invite that radical husband of yours to join the Stanford faculty, but I will tell you one thing, I am all out for you!" (ibid., 138). The offer of a permanent position to Paul Hanna followed soon after.

In considering the job offer, Paul Hanna followed the sort of deliberate process that characterized major decision making throughout his life. He asked his mentors for their opinions, and thirty-six people in all responded to his requests for advice. His senior colleagues at Teachers College advised him to make the move. They believed that in their shadows at Teachers College he would be too reticent to challenge them and fully develop his own ideas. They told him to "take this Stanford position where you will be confident enough and forced by the circumstances to speak up. To write. To take leadership. You will not do that as long as you remain here" (Hanna 1973a, 69). Hanna recognized the validity of their advice. He accepted Stanford's invitation and, in the fall of 1935, he joined the Stanford faculty as an associate professor of education.

CONCLUSION

Paul Hanna's years at Teachers College had crystallized his thinking on the relationship between the school and society. There he formed the foundation for his later production of textbooks and other activities. At Teachers College Hanna developed a rich network of friends and colleagues with whom he learned and grew, debated the great issues of the day, and taught groundbreaking courses. The next stage of his career, his more than three decades at Stanford University, saw his own community of influence expand. From Stanford—through his teaching, writing textbooks, involvement with professional organizations, and consulting work with school districts in the United States and abroad—Hanna's ideas reached a worldwide audience.

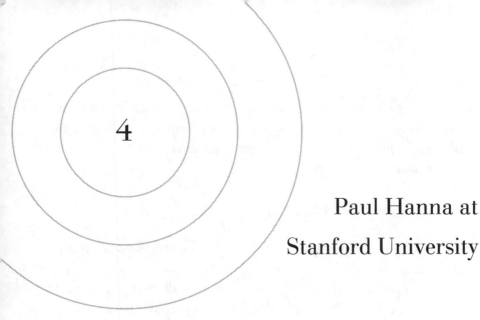

Paul Hanna at
Stanford University

At Stanford University, Paul Hanna became a leading figure in American education. There he solidified his growing academic reputation and parlayed that reputation into entrepreneurial efforts that benefited both the university and himself. He established himself as a writer and developer of school textbooks and as a consultant to school systems across the United States and around the world. Sometimes those interests overlapped. His entrepreneurial skills helped shore up Stanford's shaky finances during the war years and enriched both the Hannas themselves and the friends that he brought into his business endeavors.

While at Stanford, Hanna became intrigued with the instrumental use of schools to promote democracy on a global scale. He served as a consultant to governments in many foreign countries and founded an institute to study education as a tool in international development and to prepare policy makers in its use. Ironically, this scion of democratic education came under fire from forces on the political right wing for his associations with progressive educators at Stanford and Columbia Universities. Hanna's career on the Stanford faculty spanned three decades, and his association with the school lasted even longer. It culminated in significant bequests to various units of the university, although, curiously, not to its School of Education.

HANNA AND STANFORD

Hanna first taught at Stanford during the summer session of 1934. Late that summer, his wife Jean joined him in the West, and the two made favorable impressions on the Stanford faculty. The mild climate and relaxed lifestyle of California impressed them as well. "We found it a paradise in contrast to New York City" (Hanna and Hanna 1981, 17). When the offer of a permanent job followed in early 1935, Paul Hanna gladly accepted. In June of 1935, Paul and Jean packed a trailer, loaded their three small children and dog into their Chrysler Airflow, and headed for California.

Stanford University at that time had a mixed reputation. Its nickname was "the Harvard of the West," but the appellation was not entirely complimentary. It was widely known as California's "country club university" (Davis and Nilan 1989, 221). A 1931 *Time* magazine article referred to Stanford as "predominantly a rich man's college" (1931, 40). The article emphasized the upscale facilities of the university, including "one of the finest Pacific Coast golf courses, two lakes, a polo field . . ." (ibid.). Regarding the student body, the article claimed that "more than half own automobiles. Some fly their own planes" (ibid.).

Stanford students were politically conservative. Straw polls revealed that an overwhelming majority of students preferred Republican to Democratic candidates in presidential elections throughout the 1920s and 1930s. Students preferred Stanford alumnus Herbert Hoover to Franklin Delano Roosevelt by a three-to-one margin in 1932 (Davis and Nilan 1989, 219).

The Depression accelerated the narrowing of Stanford student demographics (ibid., 218). The university served an increasingly homogeneous conservative, Protestant, Anglo-Saxon student population drawn from middle and upper socioeconomic backgrounds. The student tuitions imposed in 1920 to support university expansion had become a necessary funding source that further limited diversity in the campus population (ibid.). Stanford's academic reputation suffered a blow in 1934 when the school's academic council decided that students unable to maintain an adequate level of scholarship would not be dismissed. Instead, the university would rely on students' common sense to know when to disenroll. Critics suggested that this change in policy demonstrated that tuition was more important than scholarship (ibid., 220). These factors served to diminish Stanford's academic reputation; a national survey of academic institutions ranked Stanford twelfth. In a humiliating turn, the same survey placed the University of California at Berkeley, Stanford's arch rival, in fourth place (Embree 1935).

Despite its somewhat exaggerated reputation for lavishness, Stanford remained one of the premier universities on the West Coast, particularly in the field of education. The School of Education at Stanford had been led by Ellwood P. Cubberley since 1898. Under his guidance, the school became an important center of educational thought. When Cubberley retired in 1933, he was followed as Dean by Grayson Kefauver of Teachers College, who continued to build a first-rate faculty and program. When Paul Hanna joined the Stanford faculty in 1935, he had good reason to be optimistic about the university's prospects.

THE TEACHER EARLY IN HIS CAREER

At Stanford, Hanna employed the teaching methods that he had found effective at Teachers College. He preferred a seminar format designed to foster investigation, discussion, and debate among his students, similar to what he had experienced in planning the Education 200F course at Teachers College. He often enlisted students in his own textbook and curriculum projects. This approach is not surprising considering his foundational belief that education is best achieved through real life experience, but it seemed exploitative to some students (Douglass 1998). However, the majority of Hanna's students who were interviewed by this author remembered him as an engaging and stimulating teacher with a strong but winning personality.

The first classes Hanna taught after joining the Stanford faculty were three seminars during the 1935 summer session. Throughout his career at Stanford, Hanna taught most of his courses during summer sessions. Summer courses were especially suited to Hanna's seminar style, because most of his students were experienced school administrators continuing their education while holding jobs in the schools (Mayhew 1974, 30). In fact, Stanford University consistently conferred many more Doctor of Education degrees, those preferred by educators planning careers in school administration, than it did Doctor of Philosophy degrees in education (ibid., 32; Stanford University 1952).

One of the 1935 summer session courses, a seminar in elementary school curriculum labeled Education 256, illustrates Hanna's teaching style. Hanna's colleague and friend, Harold Hand, taught a companion course: Education 331, Seminar in Secondary Education (Hanna 1935c). The two young faculty members planned their seminars in tandem, and they jointly wrote the syllabi. The seminars met together for orientation on the common problems of curriculum development in the elementary and secondary schools. Students then met with Hanna or Hand and developed individual curriculum inquiries based on their own interests. For the balance of the course, students pursued their projects. No grades were assigned, but a plus or minus was given based on criteria established by the student and the instructors in their planning conferences. Mandatory meetings of the whole group occurred each Monday.

Attendance at other meetings was optional when individual topics proved interesting to the students. Even these seminar topics were chosen by a vote of the students (ibid.).

This course represented an early attempt by Hanna, with Hand's involvement, to design a course unfettered by imposing authorities such as those at Teachers College. Nevertheless, it retained several features of significant Teachers College courses. Hanna and Hand expected their students to display a high level of competence. Although no specific prerequisites were listed in the syllabus, a section in the document entitled "assumptions" states that the seminars were planned for

> mature students who have previously made a systematic study of curriculum development . . . have reasonably adequate backgrounds in educational sociology and psychology . . . reasonably adequate conception[s] of the nature of the learning experience and of the guidance service which the school should provide . . . [and] some one or more problems which [they] want to work out, preferably for a specific educational situation (Hanna 1935c).

The syllabus advised students who did not meet these criteria to enroll in another course. In addition, students were advised that as part of their individual project planning sessions, the instructors would probe their knowledge of such areas as educational sociology and psychology (ibid.).

Another imprint of Teachers College influence on Hanna's seminar was the assumption of the school's dual role in meeting the needs of both individual learners and the larger society. The syllabus included the assumption that "all students will possess a reasonably adequate understanding of the social and individual needs which the school should attempt to meet" (ibid.). These needs were not detailed, but neither was the mission of the school left open to debate: the school was to serve both the individual and society. This assumption remained a constant theme in Hanna's writing and teaching throughout his career.

Perhaps the most direct connection of Hanna's seminar to his experiences at Teachers College was his description of the instructional personnel. He and Hand listed themselves as chairmen of the seminars, whereas other teachers were described as "seminar staff" (ibid.). Perhaps Hanna attempted to replicate on the West Coast the incredibly rich experiences that he and his students had enjoyed as participants in the Teachers College Education 200F course. Hanna cotaught courses with Hand for several years thereafter.

Another summer course taught by Hanna in 1937 displayed many of the same characteristics. Education 256, The Curricula of Modern Elementary Schools, was a general survey of three approaches to curriculum organization: the traditional approach, with subjects taught as distinct courses of study; the broad fields approach, with subjects grouped as social sciences, general science, and so forth; and the integrative activity approach, with subjects taught in integrated units (Hanna 1937a). The integrative activity approach apparently drew heavily on Hanna's own experience, because the Lincoln School and the Virginia state curricula were listed as examples to be studied. The course evidently was designed for school administrators, because discussion of each curriculum approach included consideration of how to organize a staff to meet school goals (ibid.).

The syllabus offered students considerable latitude in how to approach their study. It contained a seven-and-one-half-page bibliography from which students were to pick their own readings. Hanna advised students to read "those particular aspects of the problem which interest [them] most" (ibid.). He required them to submit a bibliography of materials read during the course, but no annotations were requested beyond what they "may care to keep for [their] future reference" (ibid.). Hanna did not require a term paper, but he had no objection to students organizing their studies around such a project if they so desired. Assessment was individualized and very subjective, based on student participation in class discussion, individual conferences, and "the keenness of the reaction to the reading" (Hanna 1937a).

Despite the elements of student choice, the organization of the 1937 summer course displayed far more structure than did the one taught two years earlier. A curriculum dictated by Hanna replaced a purely student-generated one. Although he offered students considerable latitude in their choice of reading, they picked from an approved reading list. No such list accompanied the 1935 syllabus. These differences indicated a further departure on Hanna's part from the idea of student-designed curricula, in favor of the idea of a common core of concepts essential to each discipline. This change in his approach roughly paralleled his struggles within the Progressive Education Association dealing with similar curriculum issues. Hanna's gradual change to a more structured approach also may reflect his internalization of the conservative, traditional environment he encountered at Stanford. He also may have determined that education courses should be as soundly ordered as courses in other academic disciplines.

During the 1930s, Hanna developed many new courses and taught a wider variety of courses than he would in later years, including one-time offerings such as Silent Reading to the Upper Elementary and Secondary Schools (Stanford University 1936) and Natural Science in the Elementary and Junior High School Curriculum (Stanford University 1938). Evidently, Hanna was not shy about teaching courses outside of his immediate areas of expertise.

Hanna also maintained his heaviest teaching load during those years. Stanford operated on the quarter system, and Hanna taught an average of ten courses a year. During the academic year 1938–1939, the busiest of his career at Stanford, Hanna taught thirteen courses (Stanford University 1938). Some of these courses were offered year after year, including his Seminar in Elementary School Administration and his Seminar in Elementary School Curriculum (Stanford University 1935). Throughout his career, he taught ad-

ministration and curriculum courses more often than he taught any
others.

During Hanna's first two years at Stanford, the School of Education conferred three Ph.D. degrees and fourteen Ed.D. degrees.
Hanna's first doctoral advisee was Cecil W. Mann, who wrote a
dissertation entitled, "The Education System of the Colony of Fiji"
(1936). Apparently, Hanna had an interest in international education even at this early stage of his career. Mann's dissertation was
the only one that Hanna supervised during this time.

HANNA TURNS WEST

In March, 1938, Hanna was invited to head the elementary education program at Teachers College, Columbia University (Russell
1938). This position was possibly the most prestigious in its field.
In addition, Teachers College offered him a salary of $7000 per
year, nearly a $3000 increase over his Stanford salary. To apply
even more pressure, his former Teachers College colleagues show-
ered him with telegrams in which they urged him to return. For
example, Dean William F. Russell wrote, "We want you to throw in
your lot with us," and asked Hanna to "tell Mrs. Hanna for me that
Mrs. Russell and I particularly want her to come down" (ibid.).

The job offer was tacit acknowledgment that Hanna had become
the outstanding figure in the field of elementary education. His
mentor, Jesse Newlon, articulated its significance when he wrote,
"I am very confident that you will make a most important contribution to American education wherever you may work . . . . My
eagerness for you to come here was evidence of my realization that
you have come to full maturity and a place of leadership" (Newlon
1938a).

Newlon also warned Hanna that ". . . Stanford is likely to fold
up educationally and . . . all important contributions are going to
be limited to Teachers College" (Newlon 1938b). This view reflected

a common attitude among easterners toward educational institutions in other regions, particularly on the West Coast, but it spurred Hanna to write Grayson Kefauver about the future of the Stanford School of Education. Kefauver urged Hanna to stay at Stanford, but his letter must have been small comfort. He wrote it from Austin where he was interviewing for the presidency of the University of Texas (Kefauver 1938). Retired Stanford Dean of Education Ellwood P. Cubberley even weighed in on the matter. He wrote to Stanford President Ray Lyman Wilbur of Hanna's concern that

> The president and trustees be willing to support Dean Kefauver in enabling him to retain the present rather remarkable group of young teachers he assembled here . . . . Hanna said that if he felt sure that this group could be held together, and augmented as vacancies occur, he had no doubt we could equal any place in education within the next decade, and under such circumstances he would want to remain. If, on the contrary, the group . . . was to be continually raided by other institutions and men were lost because the university would not or could not make such conditions as to keep them here, then he would prefer to leave now (Cubberley 1938).

Hanna did not allow the prestigious weight of the Teachers College name and the flood of flattering telegrams to cloud his thinking. He followed the same deliberate decision-making process he had employed in the past. He consulted with colleagues whom he knew and trusted. Willis Scott of Scott, Foresman and Company argued, "Of course, from our standpoint as publishers, you would be in a much more prominent position there at T.C., and you would be able to exert much more powerful influence at T.C. than you can at Stanford" (Scott 1938). Genevieve Anderson, his coauthor on the Scott, Foresman textbooks, sent a telegram warning that the Hannas would have regrets if they turned down the position (Anderson 1938).

The most influential input into Paul Hanna's decision, however, was that of his wife, Jean. In a note to her husband dated simply

"Monday," she reassured him that she understood what the invitation from Teachers College meant to his career, but she relayed her conviction that, ". . . we shall have a greater degree of happiness if we remain here" (Jean Hanna 1938, undated). She expressed her concern that "The strain of building up the Elementary Department there together with the necessary coordination with Lincoln and Horace Mann will put a strain on you that your health won't stand" (ibid.). She listed ideas for strengthening the education program at Stanford and asked, "Will the results be any more valuable for Education than if you remained here and helped to establish a strong, influential school of education on the West Coast?" (ibid.). She argued also for quality of life: "What became of all the talk of living the good life when we deliberately and willfully turn our backs upon and choose the worst sort of environment . . . . Our professional life is so short! And then what?" (ibid.).

Jean Hanna saved her most powerful argument for last. She wrote that they had a duty to support the philosophy of architecture they had adopted in 1935, when they had engaged Frank Lloyd Wright to design a home for them. A move now, she argued, would be ". . . a blow to Wright's living architecture. When the most beautifully livable of all homes couldn't keep us from the siren call of the big invitation!" (ibid.) Beyond their obligation to Wright's architectural philosophy, the Hannas had very real financial obligations to Scott, Foresman and Company. Paul Hanna's publisher had arranged loans to help the Hannas build their dream house. Besides, in the spring of 1938 they had only lived in their new home for a few months, after years of anticipation.

Whether or not his wife Jean's arguments were those that swayed him, Hanna decided to remain at Stanford. He relayed his refusal to Dean Russell on April 27, 1938. Many at Teachers College and elsewhere did not understand the reasons for his decision, attributing it to simply ". . . too much house" (Hand n.d.). With this decision, Hanna turned his back on the East Coast educational establishment in favor of the promise of the future represented by Stanford University and the West. Some educators, then and since, have taken him less seriously because of his choice, but Hanna always considered it to have been the right one (Hanna 1974, 139).

HANNA AND HIS FAMILY

The Hanna family thrived in California. Lula Shuman, Jean's mother, moved to the area, and other family members visited often. The Hannas' focus, though, was on their children. Colleague Richard Gross recalled Hanna as being "highly concerned with his family" (Gross 1998). As evidence, he pointed to Hanna's Frank Lloyd Wright–designed home, known as the Hanna-Honeycomb House. Wright designed the structure to change according to the growth of the Hanna children. For instance, a room that originally served as the children's playroom was converted to a dining room as the family's needs changed. The children's bedrooms became a spacious master suite once the children were grown and moved away. Other needs were considered, as well. Wright originally suggested that the two boys, John and Robert, share a room, but their parents insisted on their need for privacy and independence. They also insisted that their daughter, Emily, have her own bathroom, despite the increased costs of building additional rooms (Hanna and Hanna 1981, 92).

The Hannas shared aspirations for their children and worked as a team to see them fulfilled. Paul and Jean attended Methodist worship services only rarely, although they did see to it that their children received a Sunday School education (John Hanna 1998). John Hanna believes that his parents' nonchalance toward religious matters was a reaction against their childhoods as children of clergymen. Although rejecting their parents' lifestyles of faith, the Hannas embraced their work ethic and they expected their children to do so as well. They always worked industriously around the house, whether in the yard or in their study and their children naturally picked up this ethic. Family discussions centered on social and political issues and they rarely included talk of money or religion. John Hanna does not recall that his parents ever argued so that their children might hear (ibid.).

The Hannas placed a high priority on their children's educations and devoted considerable resources to them. Emily Hanna, born in 1932, attended the Castilleja School, an exclusive private school for girls near the Stanford campus. She graduated in 1948 and went on to Claremont College and Stanford for her college study (ibid.). Paul Hanna served on the Board of Trustees of Castilleja from 1957–1981, and he endowed the Hanna Family English Chair there with a $100,000 gift in 1982 (Castilleja School 1982).

Both of the Hanna boys attended the Menlo School, a private school in the Stanford area. Richard Gross, later a colleague of Hanna's on the Stanford faculty, was a social studies instructor there. He remembered teaching Robert, the youngest Hanna child, born in 1934. He recalled Robert as a shy boy (Gross 1998). After high school, Robert attended the University of Colorado. Never particularly interested in academic pursuits, he became the showman of the family (John Hanna 1998). Taking the stage name "Dusty Russell," he formed a traveling stunt show known as the World Champion Auto Daredevils in the 1960s and 1970s. After the troupe dissolved, he settled in Vancouver, Washington, where he became a successful businessman (ibid.).

John Hanna, the eldest child, was born in 1930. After attending the Menlo School, John enrolled at Andover. Although he excelled academically, he and his father did not always share priorities in that regard. John Hanna recalled that he had fallen behind in school at Andover, due to illness. Spring break lay just ahead and he planned to go on a trip with some school chums. His father advised him to stay at school and use the vacation week to catch up on his studies, but Hanna went with his friends instead (ibid.).

John Hanna was admitted to both Harvard and Stanford Universities. His father wanted him to attend Harvard, but John chose Stanford. Paul Hanna was fond of telling people that John argued, "Why should I go to the Stanford of the East when I could go to the Harvard of the West!" John Hanna subsequently graduated from the Stanford Law School and became an invaluable legal adviser to his parents in later years (John Hanna 1998).

These few family anecdotes illustrate the high expectations Paul Hanna held for his children. He expected them to adopt a positive work ethic and to excel at their various endeavors. He also generously provided for their formal educations. No record exists that he perceived any inconsistency in sending his children to private schools while his consulting and publishing work focused on public schools.

THE TEACHER LATER IN HIS CAREER

Hanna gradually moved toward a more structured approach in his teaching in the years following his decision to remain at Stanford. Part of this shift was due to the atmosphere at Stanford, but part was due to his growing prominence in his field and his increasing conviction in the correctness of his own ideas. Despite the shift in style, students continued to enjoy his seminars. Forbes Williams recalled, "He was very democratic except that you never for a moment forgot that he was running the seminar. He liked people to express their ideas; he never put you down" (Williams 1998). In later years, Hanna gathered small groups of eight or nine graduate students and assistants for informal discussions. Although these meetings were not part of the formal course requirements, preparation often was necessary. One participant recalled that Hanna set up debates between students to stimulate the flow of ideas (Rusteika 1998). Although these discussions were informal, "attendance, though he never did say it, was mandatory. . . . A command from Paul Hanna, if you worked for Paul Hanna, was next to God. At the same time, nobody that I know of, including myself, ever objected to those [seminars]. We looked forward to them" (Williams 1998).

The purposes of these meetings ranged from gleaning feedback on one of Hanna's ideas to listening to visiting scholars. Hanna's worldwide network of colleagues afforded seminar attendees unsurpassed learning opportunities. Williams, for example, recalled a day-long affair that began with a spirited discussion with the superintendent of schools of New Delhi, India, in the morning, and concluded with similar interaction with the superintendent of the New York City schools in the afternoon (ibid.). Former Hanna student George Rusteika reported that Hanna frequently shared his own experiences in international education in these seminars (Rusteika 1998).

The years surrounding World War II marked an interlude in Hanna's teaching career as he directed his energies and time toward securing government contracts for Stanford University. Stanford records reveal that he served as adviser on two doctoral dissertations in 1941 and four in 1942, but none in 1943 and only one in 1944 (Stanford University 1952). He taught fewer courses during these years than he had in the previous decade, averaging only nine per academic year. During 1941–1942, Hanna's sabbatical year, he taught only two courses, both summer seminars (Stanford University 1941). He followed a similar pattern in 1942–1943, when he was most deeply engaged in lobbying work in Washington, D.C., on behalf of the University (Stanford University 1942). Many of the new courses Hanna offered in the 1940s were simply revisions of courses he had developed during the previous decade. For example, Curricula of Modern Elementary Schools, developed in 1936, became Curriculum of the Elementary School in 1943, and Individual Study in Elementary Curriculum and Instruction became Individual Study in Elementary Curriculum, Instruction, and Supervision.

The war years also shifted Hanna's focus from domestic to international education, and he was frequently away from campus in the 1950s. He taught an average of just five courses each academic year during his heaviest involvement in consulting work in the Philippines. As usual, most of his courses were concentrated in the summer sessions. Richard Gross took one of Hanna's courses in the years soon after the war, a lecture course in elementary curriculum. He recalled it as a well-organized and somewhat demanding class. He thought that it "covered the field adequately," but was not especially inspiring, and he noticed that Hanna made liberal use of teaching assistants to operate the course. Gross identified I. James Quillen, not Hanna, as the best teacher he had at Stanford (Gross 1998).

As Hanna gained prominence in the field of elementary education, he received invitations to teach at other prestigious institutions. The courses he taught there revealed a stronger trend toward structured presentations. They also served as opportunities for the entrepreneurial Hanna to promote his own concepts of curriculum. For example, in the summer of 1958 he taught a course at the Harvard University Summer School entitled Social Studies: Curriculum in the Elementary School. The course syllabus listed topics to be covered, and they read like an outline of Hanna's critique of modern society and the role of the school in addressing it.

> The critical imbalance of our time—the lag of the social sciences and humanities behind advances in science and technology; the need for the social studies curriculum to prepare tomorrow's citizens for creative effort toward cultural imbalance; the design of the social studies curriculum with the "expanding communities of men" and the "basic human activities" as the two dimensions (Hanna 1958b).

The course required considerable writing on the part of the students. Assessment was based on a midterm exam, a final exam, and a term paper, a dramatic change from the days when Hanna assigned only plus/minus grades and had "no objection" if students wished to write a term paper. Students were expected to engage in "wide reading" from the list of items Hanna had placed on library reserve in Lawrence Hall. Hanna's reading list was revealing. The entire first page was devoted to a group of Stanford doctoral dissertations that Hanna had sponsored, on generalizations in the social sciences. He also included his own essay, *Society-Child-Curriculum*, and two of his school textbooks, *At Home, At School*, and *In the Neighborhood*. Hanna had moved from teaching a variety of schemes for curriculum organization to advocating only his own.

Although Hanna dictated the reading list and topics for the course, his methods of instruction and evaluation still permitted wide student choice. In addition to required readings from two textbooks, he permitted students to choose selections from his reading list based on their own interests. His testing also allowed students some latitude in responses. The midterm exam was an essay about his *Society-Child-Curriculum*. For the final exam, students had their midterm exams returned to them, and Hanna asked them to evaluate their own examinations in terms of content and presentation. They then were asked to make any changes to their original statements that they wished, and to explain the reasons for those changes. Some very focused short-answer questions followed, but the last question asked students to write an editorial reacting to a proposal that the school teach geography as a separate subject, beginning in the fourth grade (Hanna 1958b).

The following summer, Hanna returned to Harvard to present his controversial proposal for a national curriculum commission. He spoke at the Advanced Administrative Institute on the topic, "A National Curriculum Center: Threat or Promise? (Harvard University 1959).

Hanna's teaching load did not grow lighter in his last decade on the Stanford faculty. During the 1960–1961 school year, for instance, Hanna taught three courses during each of the fall and winter terms, including courses in elementary school social studies, elementary school curriculum, and general curriculum development. During the spring term he taught four courses, including two graduate courses in elementary school curriculum, instruction, and supervision, and he taught two courses during the summer of 1961 (Stanford University 1961). In a testament to his tremendous energy, he taught the summer session while suffering from hepatitis (Hanna 1961d).

Hanna maintained a similar courseload for the following year. In 1961–1962, he taught three courses each term. Most were similar to the ones he had taught the previous year, but he added a course in elementary school supervision and administration with a field experience component. During the summer session he taught the same two courses he had taught in the summer of 1961 (Stanford University 1962).

Hanna taught a reduced courseload in the school years 1962–1963 and 1963–1964, teaching only two courses each term. He taught only one course during the summer session of 1963 and none during the summer of 1964. All of these were graduate courses (Stanford University 1963; 1964). The reduced load for the 1962–1963 school year was due to the fact that Hanna served as acting dean that year, while I. James Quillen was on sabbatical leave (Hanna 1962a). Reasons for his reduced teaching load the following year are unclear. Hanna taught an average of seven courses each academic year during the 1960s. His heaviest teaching load was in the year of his retirement, 1967 (Stanford University 1966).

During the 1960s Hanna developed new courses that reflected his interest in international education. In 1961, he offered a course entitled Seminar in Comparative and Overseas Education (Stanford University 1961). In 1964, he developed Comparative Education (Stanford University 1964), and in 1966 he offered an International Development Education Seminar (Stanford University 1966).

As Hanna gained both national and international prominence during the 1950s and 1960s, his relationships with his students changed. In earlier times, students and faculty had played together in a recreational softball league (Davis and Nilan 1989, 77). Hanna described the warm camaraderie and good-natured teasing between students and faculty in games organized by Harold Hand. He recalled that the faculty team "could expect to be worked over at every game by a determined student team" (Hanna 1976, 5). Few of the faculty players could compete with the students, so there was a standing practice of collusion with the umpires. Sometimes a faculty player would be allowed to bat out of turn, to help another around the bases. Then the crowd erupted into screams of "pseudo protest that the faculty was being pampered by a prejudiced umpire. But by fair or foul means, the faculty did win as many games as they lost" (ibid.).

By the 1950s and 1960s, however, the nature of faculty–student relations at Stanford had changed as a result of the university's increased enrollment and rising national reputation (Lowen 1997). Hanna's own growing reputation and his advancing age also were factors in the changed nature of his relationships with students. Former students remembered him fondly, but they also held him somewhat in awe: "not fear, but awe" (Gross 1998). For instance, former student Forbes Williams reported that his first meeting with Hanna in the early 1960s was interrupted by a telephone call from the United States ambassador to the United Nations. Williams was impressed (Williams 1998). Hanna's students took pride in his prominence. For example, Williams recalled that Hanna's students basked in the reflected glory when he was the sole American educator invited to an exclusive conference at Lake Como, Italy (ibid.).

Hanna's students also benefited from his prominence and his network of former students and professional colleagues. Many reported that their connection with Hanna led to employment. Harold Drummond, who served as Hanna's personal secretary in the immediate postwar era, reported that Hanna recommended him, at different points in his career, to friends at Allyn and Bacon publishers for work on geography textbooks, to Teachers College colleague Hollis Caswell for a position on the editorial board of Childcraft Books, to other colleagues at the National Society for the Study of Education as a writer on community schools, and to those at George Peabody College for Teachers for a faculty position there. He also recalled that his work as Hanna's secretary itself was invaluable: "It was a wonderful learning experience, for I got to know through correspondence almost every leader in American education. When I met them later, most of them would greet me with, 'Oh yes, I know you—you were Paul Hanna's secretary'" (Drummond 1997).

Richard Gross was not one of Hanna's advisees, but Hanna was responsible for his first faculty appointment. In 1950, Florida State University had just expanded its progr,m and was seeking new faculty. Search committee members there had exhausted funds set aside for interview visits without finding a suitable candidate, and they called Paul Hanna for a recommendation. He suggested that they talk with Gross, and he was hired sight unseen. Florida State University again figured in a 1967 recommendation Hanna wrote to R. Freeman Butts, enlisting his help in gaining a position there for Richard King. He wrote, "If you would put in your word to [Associate Dean of Education, Philip] Fordyce, I think the chances are very great that Tallahassee will make him an offer right away" (Hanna 1967a).

Hanna recommended former doctoral advisee Robert Newman to the editorial board of *Weekly Reader Magazine* as a writer and several others to Houghton Mifflin as textbook authors. Long after his retirement, he continued to help people in this manner. In 1975, Donald Foster, a 1959 doctoral advisee of Hanna's, wrote to express thanks for Hanna's support of Foster's application for an administrative position at the East–West Center in Hawaii. He reminded Hanna, "You've given so much to so many" (Foster 1975).

For all the help he could offer, some students found Hanna's networking distastefully self-serving. For example, George Rusteika recounted an instance in one of Hanna's informal seminars when a student asked him how he had gained such international prominence. Hanna proceeded to relate a detailed list of image-building activities to pursue, including joining the *right* organizations and getting to know the *right* people. The discourse made him sound "like a real manipulator" (Rusteika 1998). Many of the students left the meeting discouraged by the level of personal politics involved and wondered if they could adjust to academic life as Hanna portrayed it.

Other aspects of Hanna's personality and career also bothered his students. For example, Malcolm Douglass remembered Hanna as "a fairly distant guy" (Douglass 1998b). Harold Drummond, among others, noted that Hanna "was out of town a lot" (Drummond 1997). His absence from campus was also a sore spot between Hanna and faculty colleagues, but Hanna was not unique. Visiting scholar Edgar Wesley was amazed at the tendency of Stanford faculty to leave campus for long periods during the school term. Richard Gross explained that Stanford paid low salaries but allowed faculty members generous time for consulting, saving university funds and increasing Stanford's prestige at the same time (Gross 1998).

Some students were unaffected by Hanna's travels. Malcolm Douglass somewhat sarcastically counted himself "lucky that Hanna was on campus throughout my work" (Douglass 1998b). Others were more generous. Forbes Williams reported that Hanna was

> always available to his graduate students. If you had a problem you could stick your head in the door and say, "Mr. Hanna, what do you think about this?" and he'd say, "Well, sit down for a minute" and we'd talk about it. He was very approachable. Whatever his activities were . . . it never seemed to me, from my personal

viewpoint, to detract from my ability to work with him or ask him
questions or get advice and counsel (Williams 1998).

Some graduate students objected to Hanna's using them as
cheap or free labor in his own business undertakings. For example,
several members of the education faculty were partners with Hanna
in a Christmas tree farm. Malcolm Douglass reported that these
men often employed their graduate students to cut and load trees
for customers. He termed it a "sort of enslavement" (Douglass
1998b). John Hanna also recalled working alongside his father's
students on the farm (John Hanna 1998). Students may have
thought that helping in this way, although not required, constituted
one of those *Hanna commands* that was *next to God* or a way to
ingratiate themselves with one of the *right people*.

Perhaps more seriously, some graduate students criticized him
for assigning them to work for him on his various textbook publishing projects without pay or acknowledgment (Williams 1998).
Douglass (1998a), for example, recalled that Hanna, "did a lot of
consulting through his students." Hanna had a longstanding consulting career with state and local school authorities. This consulting sometimes was done in conjunction with his work on the Scott,
Foresman textbook series. Before coming to Stanford, Hanna had
served as a consultant to the Chicago Public Schools in 1932 and
worked on a State of Arkansas curriculum revision in 1933.

On the West Coast, Hanna expanded his consulting work. In
1935 he undertook a Virginia-style study of the Santa Barbara city
and county schools. One result was a scope and sequence plan for
Santa Barbara that closely followed that of Virginia, including elements reflecting Hanna's interest in community schooling. During
the same year, Hanna worked as a consultant to the Fresno, California, Schools and served on the Curriculum Scope and Sequence
Committee for the State of California.

As his national reputation grew, Hanna expanded his work to

other regions. In 1937 he worked in Michigan with the Flint, Grosse
Pointe, and Detroit schools, and two years later he led a landmark
curriculum study in the San Diego public schools. As late as 1975,
Martin Gill wrote to Hanna, "I was in Los Angeles this summer for
a bit of consultation work that brought me to the office of the
Superintendent of Schools. You may chuckle to know that the mere
mentioning of your name still causes the red carpet to unroll" (Gill
1975). This author experienced the same phenomenon in 2001.

Certainly, Hanna did not do all this work on his own. Douglass
claimed that "Paul was the senior consultant and he would blow in
and blow out at a very handsome fee and the rest of us were left
there to do the work. As I understand it, he had a lot of that going
on" (Douglass 1998b).

Oddly, Hanna did not keep a list of his doctoral advisees, but
many former students remember a map that Paul Hanna kept in
his office showing where his students were employed. Each of his
students was represented by a small pin. The map was an impressive
display of the spread of Hanna's influence worldwide, and some of
his students considered their inclusion to be a badge of honor.
However, Douglass and some others referred to themselves deri-
sively as just "pinheads on his map" (ibid.).

Despite some negative experiences, most of Paul Hanna's students felt warmly toward him, and even his critics among them
found him "very stimulating" (ibid.). In fact, his captivating presentations were what attracted some of his students to Stanford in
the first place. Hanna seemed to have no need to recruit students.
His reputation and prominence were such that individuals sought
to study with him (Douglass 1998a). For example, George Rusteika
first encountered Hanna in 1948 at a teachers institute on international affairs. He had read some of Hanna's work during graduate study at the University of Chicago. Although Rusteika recalled
that he disagreed with the views Hanna presented at the institute,

he thought, "Here's a person I hope I can keep talking to because I'm learning so much" (Rusteika 1998). Ten years later, Don Foster heard Hanna at another teachers institute on world affairs. He knew of Hanna from the Hanna Series of textbooks, and he recalled being "captivated by Paul's seminars at our conference, and [I] followed him like a groupie afterwards" (Foster 1998a).

Evidently, Hanna's ability to captivate audiences translated to the personal level, as well. Foster declared, "I unabashedly respect and admire Paul, and often refer to him as a surrogate father" (ibid.). Forbes Williams reported that although "he had a million of them," Hanna's graduate students were extremely loyal and always wanted to do their best work for him (Williams 1998). He attributed this loyalty to Hanna's ability "to make you feel as if you were the only important person in the entire world when you were talking with him" (ibid.). Hanna also had an uncanny ability to remember names. Douglass remarked that he "could enter a classroom of several dozen students and within an hour or so, he would know all their names" (Douglass 1998b). Some of Hanna's personal magnetism was a matter of learned skills, but much of it grew out of his genuine warmth and interest in people.

HIS STANFORD COLLEAGUES

From his first days on the Stanford campus, Hanna encouraged improved relations between the School of Education and other academic areas, even in an environment notorious for its lack of collegiality (Gross 1998). True to his commitment to integration of subject matter, Hanna encouraged his students to add to the depth of their substantive knowledge by taking graduate courses in relevant academic departments. George Rusteika, Richard Gross, and Forbes Williams followed his advice, and each reported receiving warm welcomes across campus when they mentioned that they were

Hanna's students. Likewise, Hanna's network of colleagues in the social sciences—at Stanford and across the nation—enabled his students more easily to enlist the aid of social science authorities in their educational research. Williams, for example, established a nationwide jury of thirty or forty leading social scientists to evaluate his identification of social science concepts applicable to the elementary school curriculum. Williams recalled, "They were all friends of Paul Hanna! His name opened doors" (Williams 1998).

For all of his work to build bridges between social scientists and the schools, some scholars retained the attitude that Hanna had encountered when he first tried to employ authorities to help with his social studies textbooks in the 1930s (Hanna 1973a). Williams recalled an encounter with a leading anthropologist at Stanford's Cubberley Conference in 1964. The Conference brought school teachers and academic authorities together to help the teachers increase their substantive knowledge and translate it into useful curriculum elements. In the flush of goodwill surrounding the week-long meeting, Williams asked the anthropologist how many of his colleagues would be willing to give a year to work with teachers on similar projects. The anthropologist answered that they could be counted "on the fingers of one mutilated hand" (Williams 1998).

On the Stanford campus, Hanna constantly sought ways to improve programs in the School of Education. He pioneered a five-year elementary education certification program in his early years there. Students began the program in their sophomore year and were awarded a Master of Arts degree upon completion of their courses and fieldwork. The program became a model for others nationwide (Gross 1998). In 1955, Hanna founded the Stanford International Development Education Center (SIDEC) to study the uses of education as a tool for economic, political, and social growth in developing countries. Through these activities and others on behalf of Stanford, Hanna developed formidable influence across the campus. Unfortunately, his influence gave rise to both political and ideological conflicts with colleagues.

Fannie Shaftel was one of Hanna's doctoral advisees in 1948 (Stanford University 1948). She joined the Stanford faculty, and she and Hanna served together on many dissertation committees. Over time, however, relations between the two soured (Gross 1998). She declined this author's request for an interview about her work with Hanna. Richard Gross, a Stanford colleague of both Shaftel and Hanna, believed that their estrangement resulted from ideological differences (Gross 1998). Like Hanna, Shaftel was educated in the progressive tradition at Teachers College. She was an unabashed proponent of child-centered, problems-centered curriculum approaches at a time when Hanna was becoming increasingly focused on issues of content in the curriculum. She hoped that she would find an ally in Hanna, but was disappointed (ibid.).

Hanna grew skeptical of child-centered progressivism early on, believing that "what you teach should never be determined only by how children learn" (Rusteika 1998). After moving to Stanford, he increasingly focused on balancing children's perceptions of their own needs with his perceptions of society's needs as the key points of curriculum development. Shaftel, on the other hand, was process-oriented (Shaftel and Shaftel 1967, 8). In 1950, the two joined forces to produce a textbook in elementary social studies methods (Scott, Foresman and Company 1950). Shaftel did much of the preliminary work, but then Hanna sought to mold it to the expanding communities curriculum design (Gross 1998). She disagreed with Hanna's scheme, and the two could not come to philosophical agreement on an alternative approach (Gross 1998). The book was never completed.

The ideological estrangement between Hanna and Shaftel only deepened with time. According to Richard Gross, Shaftel came to feel that "Hanna had sold out" (ibid.). In response to a paper George Rusteika wrote, Shaftel said, "George, I'm disappointed. You seem to have taken the Hanna approach hook, line, and sinker" (Rusteika 1998). Still, she recognized Hanna's influence. When Hanna suggested to Malcolm Douglass that he ask her to serve on his dissertation committee, Shaftel made it clear that she disagreed with many of Douglass' and Hanna's curriculum assumptions underlying the research, but she agreed to serve and replied with resignation, "anything Paul wants" (Douglass 1998b).

Ideological disputes with colleagues also arose over a dissertation series on social science generalizations that Hanna proposed in the early 1950s (Rusteika 1998). He planned to develop a group of dissertations, each identifying generalizations from a different social science, but all using the same research design. Such a project had never been undertaken at Stanford before, and some on the faculty opposed the idea. Chief among the project's critics was Arthur Coladarci, the chairman of the committee for advanced graduate degrees (ibid.). This committee was charged to approve all dissertation research, and the chairmanship put Coladarci in a position to block Hanna's project. Nevertheless, through Hanna's persuasion and skillful enlistment of faculty members to serve on the various dissertation committees, many dissertations were completed as part of Hanna's project (Douglass 1998a). His success with this project was a measure of his influence and persuasive powers.

Throughout his career at Stanford, Hanna helped to raise funds for the university, and he was not above reminding his colleagues in the School of Education of his long service to Stanford. In 1951, for example, Hanna wrote a strong letter to Dean A. John Bartky, arguing for a salary increase for himself and his colleagues. Among his reasons were the rise in the cost of living since his last raise, and he claimed he had not received an increase since 1946. In the ensuing years, he argued, the Consumer Price Index had risen thirty-three percent, and "my current salary of $9000 represents in purchasing power the equivalent of $4850, or $400 less than I received from Stanford 14 years ago" (Hanna 1951). He also cited job offers he had received at much higher pay, although he stated, "I have no desire to leave Stanford" (ibid.). Hanna pointed to the relatively low level of salaries for the education faculty compared to those in other Stanford Schools. He wrote, "I note in the AAUP [American Association of University Professors] report that the top salary of full professor of $9000 in the School of Education is out of line with the top salaries in the Biological Sciences ($11,000), the Humanities ($10,000), the Physical Sciences ($12,000), the Social Sciences ($12,000), Business ($10,600), Law ($12,500), and Medicine ($10,000) (ibid.).

Hanna argued that such a salary relationship was out of line with the tuitions that the School of Education attracted to the University compared to those brought in by many of the other schools on campus, "When the substantial net gain to the University from tuition over budget from the School of Education is taken into account competitively with other schools, then it appears reasonable to expect the salaries in Education to be equally generous" (ibid.). He concluded with a pointed reminder of all the funds he helped bring in through his work with University Services and private donors (ibid.). No record exists to indicate whether or not Hanna's salary was increased.

Sometimes his disputes with other faculty members were not ideological at all, but only political. Early in his career at Stanford, for example, Hanna was instrumental in the initiation of a five-year teacher certification program in elementary education (Gross 1998). By the 1960s, however, his main interest had changed to international education. Stanford's system of funding faculty positions required cutbacks in other programs to free up resources for his growing international education program (Douglass 1998a). Richard Gross described the shock and dismay of some faculty members when Hanna proposed in a faculty meeting in 1967 that the entire elementary education program be abolished (Gross 1998).

Again, Hanna's influence helped carry the proposal and the elementary program was scrapped. George Wesley Sowards was a former doctoral advisee of Hanna's and his colleague on the elementary education faculty. As a result of Hanna's proposal, the salaries of Sowards and a number of other faculty members were defunded, and they were forced to seek positions elsewhere (ibid.).

Hanna was a supremely self-assured man, and his success in business and academic life only increased his self-assurance. Some on the Stanford faculty may have disliked this aspect of his personality, and others may have envied his international reputation. Richard Gross recalls hearing pointed remarks about Hanna's extended absences from campus due to his international consulting work (Gross 1998). Some may have envied his nationwide prominence resulting from an extensive and lucrative career as a consultant to school districts and state education agencies and his production of school textbooks. Some might even have envied his influence with elements of the Stanford administration gained through his long service to the University in fund-raising efforts. Predictably, Hanna's influence at Stanford declined steadily after his retirement in 1967, to the point that even his reminders of his long service and many contributions to the university could not always accomplish his goals.

FUNDING FOR THE UNIVERSITY

A large part of Hanna's career at Stanford included extraordinary success in attracting funds to the University, especially during the postwar era. Throughout the 1920s, Stanford came to rely on student tuitions in addition to Stanford family funds, for operational revenues (Davis and Nilan 1989, 218). This reliance made the University increasingly vulnerable to external economic forces. Despite Stanford's reputation as a school for economically privileged and socially elite students, the decade of the Great Depression showed how vulnerable the school had become to the vicissitudes of the market cycle (Lowen 1997, 26). Many students in the 1930s lacked even basic transportation. Hanna recalled that in his early years at Stanford, drivers customarily picked up "hikers between campus and downtown Palo Alto" (Hanna 1976). Certain street corners on campus and in the town became regular pickup points for students who did not have their own transportation.

By the mid-1930s, Stanford students began to receive support from the California State Emergency Relief Administration, and about twelve percent of all students were enrolled in federal work relief programs (Lowen 1997, 23). Still, the university found federal support for private higher education unpalatable and suspect. Like many private institutions, Stanford questioned the propriety of accepting government support. Reliance on government funds seemed to blur the traditional distinction between public and private education and to threaten the independence of the private university (ibid.). For Stanford, however, the issue included a personal dimension. Both Stanford president Ray Lyman Wilbur and trustee and former United States president Herbert Hoover intensely disliked and distrusted President Franklin Roosevelt, and they disdained his New Deal initiatives (Nash 1988, 124). They were intent on heeding James Conant's admonition that "[I]f and when private institutions pass under government control, [it will be] because they were forced there as a result of their begging policy for money" (Conant 1937). Wilbur and Hoover encouraged Stanford to seek funds elsewhere.

Licensing technological innovations to industry seemed a promising source of revenue. Although some at Stanford saw peril in becoming too closely allied with industry, others welcomed the opportunity. Notably, Robert Swain, chairman of the chemistry department, and Frederick Terman, chairman of electrical engineering, actively courted this type of industrial relationship (Lowen 1997, 36). The results were mixed. Stanford signed a potentially profitable agreement with the Sperry Gyroscope Company regarding a navigational device developed by Stanford scientists, but the agreement degenerated amid concerns over faculty autonomy, control of university research facilities, and how traditional university promotion policies might be altered by the influence of business (ibid., 37–42).

Paul Hanna became involved in fund-raising for the university early in his tenure at Stanford. In 1936, Paul H. Davis, a 1923 graduate of Stanford and the newly named general secretary of the university, saw entrepreneurial qualities in Hanna that could be put to good use. He prevailed on Paul and Jean to join the Stanford Associates in their fund-raising efforts (Hanna 1982b). Few stones were left unturned in the search for private support for Stanford. Faculty members and alumni approached the Rockefeller Foundation, the Carnegie Corporation, and other organizations and individuals with a variety of funding proposals (Lowen 1997, 29). The economic conditions of the Great Depression, however, saw a decline in the availability of private funds (Davis and Nilan 1989, 224). Neither support from industry nor private sources of funding provided the steady income stream that Stanford needed in the 1930s.

By 1940 the university was again in severe financial straits, but a new model of government support had evolved. Instead of distributing funds through grants to private institutions, the National Advisory Committee on Aeronautics had pioneered the use of contracts with individual researchers. In the words of one historian of university-government relations,

> To those such as [Stanford President Ray Lyman] Wilbur, who worried that government support for private institutions represented an encroachment by the state, the contract was a reassuring symbol of the marketplace. It suggested, in form if not in fact, that the university was not a supplicant to the government but that the parties involved had reached a mutual agreement (Lowen 1997, 47).

Moreover, the generous provisions for the university's overhead expenses in these contracts resembled *profit* for Stanford, another concept from the world of business with which Stanford trustees were most familiar.

World War II marked a philosophical watershed for Stanford, as it did for many other private universities. The growing conviction that war might be unavoidable made alliances with the government seem to be a patriotic duty. Indeed, many in the Stanford community were frustrated by President Wilbur's reluctance aggressively to seek out government research contracts in the days before Pearl Harbor. Hanna joined other faculty members in purchasing a full-page advertisement in the local newspaper to argue that Stanford should prepare to take part in the war against National Socialism (Hanna 1974). As he recalled, "This was serious, this was survival — we knew we had to defeat the Germans." In response, Hanna received a "most devastating letter from [Herbert] Hoover, as a member of the Board of Trustees, telling me to shut up" (ibid.). Hoover's violent opposition to any alliance between Stanford and the Roosevelt administration helps explain President Wilbur's reticence on the issue, but Hanna was adamant about the need to prepare for war.

As a member of the National Resources Planning Board from 1937–1939, Hanna came to believe that U.S. involvement in the war was inevitable. Hanna met with President Wilbur and recalled Wilbur's telling him, "'I just don't want anything to do with this, but I wouldn't restrict you'" (ibid.). Hanna took him at his word and met with Donald Tresidder, president of Stanford's board of trustees. As a result of their meeting, Tresidder appointed Hanna to chair the Committee on University Services to investigate further opportunities for the university to contribute to wartime research (Lowen 1997, 55). Tresidder was a businessman rather than an academic. He did not share the view that Stanford must maintain a pristine separation from government, and he saw qualities in

Hanna that he recognized from the business world. Tresidder later succeeded Wilbur as president of the university, and he and Hanna formed a firm bond of mutual respect.

As war seemed increasingly likely, the federal government authorized creation of the National Defense Research Council (NDRC) and the Office of Scientific Research and Development (OSRD) to coordinate federal government contracts for war-related research and training. The NDRC panel that let contracts was a clubby group of academicians, and personal and professional contacts were as important as merit in their decisions. The primary recipients of NDRC–OSRD contracts included the Massachusetts Institute of Technology and Harvard University, both of which had officers serving on the NDRC–OSRD review board. When Stanford officials saw that the California Institute of Technology and the University of California, their West Coast rivals, had been granted NDRC–OSRD contracts, they decided to take a positive step toward securing similar contracts themselves. Demonstrating that they understood the gamesmanship involved, Stanford trustees offered the university presidency to Vannevar Bush, head of the NDRC–OSRD board, when President Wilbur's retirement approached. Unfortunately, the offer was made on December 5, 1941 (ibid., 52), and events of the following days rendered Bush's consideration of such an offer impossible.

The U.S. declaration of war posed other setbacks for Stanford. Students left the university to enlist in the armed services, further cutting into revenue from tuitions (ibid., 49). President Wilbur advised them to consider an alternative course of action: "Be reluctant to drop out of the University. The government will pull you out if it wants you. An engineering student who can get a new idea that will make an airplane go twenty miles faster per hour is worth a hundred thousand men in uniform" (*Stanford Daily*, 10 December 1941).

Just as ominous for the long-term health of the university was the exodus of its professors to schools with more prestigious, better-funded war research projects. Frederick Terman, for example, left to head up the Radio Research Laboratory at Harvard. By January of 1942, Stanford had lost forty professors to war work at other sites (Walker 1942). With the defection of top faculty members and fewer opportunities for research, many of Stanford's graduate programs also threatened to fold (Lowen 1997, 54). Whatever reservations Stanford officials still held about federal funding of private universities were swept away by the winds of war.

Hanna's University Services Committee geared up quickly. It recommended that the university send representatives to Washington, D.C., to offer Stanford facilities for war-related research. To President Wilbur, this smacked of begging the federal government for financial assistance and he was reluctant to commit precious funds to the effort (ibid., 56). The committee argued that success in Washington could enhance the university's prestige, stem the flight of faculty and graduate students, and provide needed revenue (ibid., 55). Members also contended that helping the war effort through research and training was a patriotic act. Their arguments swayed Hoover and the other trustees, and with their plan approved, Hanna and Paul Davis left for Washington in late 1942 (ibid., 56).

In fact, Hanna had already engaged Stanford in wartime research for the federal government. Beginning in 1942, Japanese nationals and Japanese-Americans throughout the West were evacuated to relocation centers administered by the War Relocation Authority (WRA). Many of these evacuees were children. Hanna knew that nobody benefited if these children languished educationally for any period of time, so he offered the services of his summer session graduate class to the WRA (Hanna 1942g).

In early July, 1942, the twenty-five students in Hanna's Education 299b course—Curriculum Development—undertook the study of educational problems at the relocation centers to ensure that Japanese-American children and youth, "continue their growth toward American ideals during the war" (ibid.). The incongruity of that goal to a situation in which American citizens were deprived of liberty and property because of their ethnicity received no comment from Hanna's class. The study began with a review of background materials concerning "the problem of cultural absorption of an alien minority group" (ibid.). Officials from the western regional office of the WRA met with students on the Stanford campus, and together they decided to focus on the Tule Lake Center in far northern California as representative of the educational challenges throughout the system of WRA installations. Seventeen members of the class then visited the center for a two-day period. In a series of subsequent meetings and conferences with WRA officials, Hanna's class sketched out a sample curriculum for camp schools (James 1987, 38–39).

The result was a design that blended Hanna's ideas of the community school and his notions about an expanding communities scope and sequence. The final report to the WRA contained a scope and sequence diagram in which the scope consisted of eight *basic human activities:* production; public works; community service; transportation, communication and supply; maintenance and operation; community enterprise; placement and labor relations; and administration. The sequence involved a progression from grades K-12 of studying each activity in the context of an historical, political, geographical, or conceptual community. The overarching integrative theme for all grades was Adaptation of our Socio-Economic Arrangements to the Control and Direction of Technological Development. Each cluster of grades—primary, elementary, and secondary—had a subtheme. For instance, the subtheme for the secondary grades was "Improvement of human arrangements to make better use of scientific technics [sic]." The curriculum at each grade level was organized around a *center of interest*. For example, the eleventh grade center of interest was "Continuous improvement of living within the community and the region" (Hanna 1942g).

Despite the complex nature of the curriculum design, the recommended content was eminently practical, and it clearly reflected Hanna's interest in the community school concept. For instance, under the basic human activity entitled *public works*, first graders considered how the schoolyard could be "made more useful and beautiful." Under *maintenance and operation*, they were to consider, "How can we help each other at the mess hall?" (ibid., IV-8).

Hanna's attempts to balance child-centered and content-centered curriculum approaches were also reflected in the curriculum plan. The explanatory material in the document specified that the curriculum design should have two major divisions:

> 1. There should be provided experiences which are common to all youth. Common experiences should be provided throughout each of the twelve school years.
> 2. The curriculum should also provide opportunities for selective subject experiences which the learner feels he needs for satisfactory living now or in his preparation for future living (ibid., III-2).

A chart in the document suggested time allotments for each strand of the curriculum. Equal school time was devoted to *common experiences* and *selective experiences* through grade six, but from grades seven through twelve, more and more time was to be given to selective experiences, until they consumed up to seventy-five percent of the school day by graduation.

The reality of relocation center life entered into the planning process. Because the student body was a captive group, idle time could become a problem. Hanna's class proposed year-round schooling as a remedy.

One of the WRA's goals was to provide the evacuees with "educational opportunities which will equip them for their return to postwar society" (ibid., III-1). Much of the center's population had been engaged in agriculture before the war, but because evacuation had forced them to sell their farms at bargain prices, evacuees were unlikely to return to their previous ways of life. Vocational education, then, became a major component of the curriculum plan. Most of the vocational component was taught in a traditional manner during school time allotted for selective experiences. However, in keeping with Hanna's view of the community school, some vocational education was implemented through community service. Students observed and participated in the center's motor pool, farm, maintenance shops, and other facilities in order to gain knowledge and skills. Thomas James, in a critique of the vocational approach, pointed out that participation in these community activities was inadequate social education for children. He felt they did not reflect the world outside the centers, but only the administrative divisions the government had established to manage center life (James 1987, 39).

The curriculum model proposed by Hanna's class was adopted for the relocation center schools in the western region of the WRA, although it was not slavishly followed (Light 1947). The document that resulted from their study clearly stated that "intimate contact with each Relocation Center would be necessary to insure the practicability of the recommendations in each instance" (ibid.). Hanna and his students recognized that each center had unique circumstances.

The result of the curriculum plan was mixed. Although the goal that students in the centers develop "the attitudes essential to democratic participation in group life" was evidently realized in most of their lives, that influence was not enough to prevent strife in the centers. Tule Lake, in particular, the very center Hanna's class had studied, was the site of considerable violence between the evacuees and officials. In the final analysis, the peaceful continuation of life and education may have been an unrealistic expectation under such adverse conditions.

Following his work on the relocation center project in the summer of 1942, Hanna, along with Paul Davis, prepared to travel to Washington, D.C. to offer Stanford's research and training facilities for war-related work. Once there, the two realized that their task was more formidable than they had anticipated. They were in competition with representatives of dozens of other institutions. Davis minimized the intensity of the competition in a letter that assured Wilbur, somewhat disingenuously, that he and Hanna were not like the "desperate university presidents [who] . . . sat on every doorstep and with trembling voices pleaded for a handout" (Davis 1943).

Hanna and Davis realized that the only way to earn Stanford a hearing in the capital would be to establish a permanent presence there. They leased space for a permanent office in the American Council building, on Lafayette Square, across the street from the White House, in order to cultivate the personal contacts upon which their enterprise depended. From that base, the two hosted events for Stanford alumni holding high government positions in order to gain information and plan strategies for approaching various government agencies. Hoover and Frederick Terman arranged introductions to important officials, and Terman was especially helpful. Hanna recalled that his name was "an open sesame to all the scientific research groups" (Lowen, 57).

Hanna's interpersonal skills, entrepreneurial frame of mind, and tremendous energy proved to be a match for his new task. *Time* magazine labeled him "Stanford's ambassador to the U.S. Government" (1943, 25). His schedule was grueling, typically alternating two weeks in Washington with two weeks in California. During this time, he maintained a minimal schedule of classes. He did not serve as adviser for any of the seventeen doctoral degrees in education conferred by Stanford in 1942–1943, and served as adviser on only four in the years 1944–1945.

In Washington, Hanna approached government officials through high-level contacts he made as a member of the exclusive

Cosmos Club. He recalled, "Most of the leaders of the war effort would gather for lunch. I would listen and ask questions and find out where research or training needs . . . were . . . And then I would come back and write up a proposition and take it back [to the appropriate officials]" (Hanna 1986).

Aggressively lobbying the Washington bureaucrats benefited the university. By the end of the war, Stanford had inked twenty-five contracts with the NDRC–OSRD (Lowen 1997, 57). These alone were worth more than $500,000, of which Stanford received almost $125,000 in overhead expenses (ibid.). In addition, the Office of Strategic Services enlisted Stanford to study German food production and distribution capabilities (Nash 1988, 114). The Civil Aeronautics Administration contracted with the School of Education to produce a sourcebook for aviation education. That contract resulted in more than $25,000 for Stanford's general funds, as well as a position for Hanna on the advisory board of *Air Affairs* magazine (Hanna 1982b). Later, *Air Affairs* considered moving to Stanford with Hanna as editor, but that possibility never materialized. By war's end, Hanna and Davis were directly responsible for dozens of contracts between Stanford and agencies of the U.S. Government that were worth hundreds of thousands of dollars.

Hanna also continued his efforts to raise funds from private sources. A 1944 memo by Hanna described a meeting in Detroit with Fred Black about strategies for getting financial help from the Ford Foundation. Hanna detailed a plan to induce Edsel Ford's son, William, to enroll at Stanford prior to approaching the foundation. Hanna wrote, "Mr. Black suggests that we get former Hotchkiss boys who are at Stanford, or who have gone to Stanford, to work on this possibility. Also, the Hoover boys appear to be rather close to the Ford boys and might be of assistance" (Hanna 1944). In the postwar era, the Ford Foundation became a major donor to Stanford and other universities (Lowen 1997, 194).

As director of Stanford University Services, Hanna oversaw the university's training programs for military personnel. These programs included the Army Specialized Training Program, programs run by the Signal Corps and Women's Army Corps, language and cultural training, training in military government, and other projects (Hanna 1982b). By the end of the war, Stanford ranked second among American universities in the total number of military personnel on campus, and its enrollment reached an all-time high during the war (Lowen 1997, 53). Donald Tresidder attributed Stanford's strong financial position at the end of the war to the work of Hanna and University Services (Hanna 1982b). Hanna continued to benefit the university by negotiating private fund-raising efforts in the following decades.

Hanna personally benefited in a number of ways from his wartime activities on behalf of Stanford. First, he earned the gratitude of powerful individuals in the Stanford administration. Although their gratitude did not express itself in concrete terms, it enhanced his prestige among his colleagues. Hanna thought that his actions during the war obligated the university to him and he occasionally reminded officials of his work. Unfortunately, university officials did not always respond as Hanna wished, and later events embittered him toward Stanford.

A second benefit Hanna gleaned from his wartime work in Washington was the opportunity to interact with powerful people. He built a useful network of relationships among leaders in government and industry, but more importantly, he learned how those contacts could be enlisted in helping him complete projects. He applied that knowledge in the ensuing years as he worked with government officials, business leaders, and the staff of international organizations in educational consulting abroad.

Finally, Hanna's wartime work helped him develop a deeper understanding of the relationship between the university and the

government. He knew that partnerships between the two institutions could profoundly change university culture. In a 1964 memo
entitled "The University and the Government," Hanna asked a
series of probing questions about these relationships. He questioned
the nature of the research — operations, applied, or basic research —
that universities should offer government. He thought that each
kind carried different moral implications (Hanna 1964a). He asked
what restrictions government should be allowed to put on scholars'
dissemination of research results. He thought that the confidenti-
ality required by government for certain types of research ran
counter to the traditions of the university, and he wondered if universities should relax their admissions requirements for foreign
students attending school as part of a government contract (ibid.).
All of these questions had direct bearing on Hanna's work in international education through SIDEC in the 1950s and 1960s.

THE *BUILDING AMERICA* CONTROVERSY

The war years marked a turning point in American education. The
pragmatic mood of the country favored traditional over experimental approaches to instruction. A return to traditional interpretations
of American history was part of this pragmatism. One historian
asserted that many people "believed the schools, in their excessive
concern for well-rounded social development, were neglecting their
responsibility to train youngsters' intellects" (Graham 1967, 123).
In this atmosphere, progressive education and its products were
attacked indiscriminately. Paul Hanna and his *Building America*
series of magazines for schools became a target of these attacks.

Building America was begun in 1934 as a project of the Society
for Curriculum Study. Paul Hanna proposed to the society the publication of a series of monthly magazines, designed for use in the
classroom, to generate discussion of significant issues facing the
United States. They would follow a *social problems* approach, and

Hanna intended that teachers would use them to help students become more informed and to discuss policy alternatives. Hanna believed that teachers must be agents of change, writing that "The social studies teacher accepts the challenge that our culture may be improved by the process of analyzing the culture's shortcomings, projecting solutions, and taking the necessary action to translate plans into achievement" (Hanna 1938b, 143). Through social analysis and action, teachers would help prepare students for active citizenship as adults.

By 1946 the magazines were used in thousands of schools across the country, including hundreds of California schools (Newman 1961, 291). In that year, the California State Curriculum Commission proposed an appropriation of over $173,000 to bind twenty selected issues of the magazine into three volumes as supplemental textbooks for California seventh and eighth grade classrooms (ibid., 292). The State Board of Education initially supported the idea. Among the Curriculum Commission's goals for the adopted texts was that they "emphasize desirable social attitudes and ideals and loyalty to principles of American Democracy" (California State Board of Education 1945, 3). Another goal for the textbooks was that they "contribute to an appreciation and understanding of present day social and civic conditions and problems" (ibid.). Controversy surrounded the textbook selection process as camps formed around differing interpretations of the two goals.

Foremost among the groups opposing the adoption of *Building America* was the California Society of the Sons of the American Revolution (CSSAR). This group believed that *Building America* was part of a larger plot by communists to undermine American values and institutions. The Society's concern was first voiced at a Curriculum Commission meeting in mid-summer, 1946, by CSSAR representative Aaron M. Sargent, a San Francisco attorney.

Sargent's initial attack was not directed against *Building America* itself, but against the progressive education approaches mani-

fested in integrated social studies and child-centered methods. Over
the course of the summer, he broadened his attack to include *Building America*. In testimony before the State Board of Education on
July 30, 1946, Sargent questioned the efficacy of social studies in
the schools, compared to the more traditional single-subject curriculum. He claimed that social studies contributed to "illiteracy, civic
illiteracy, ignorance of our form of government," and he argued
that the study of current events, as presented by *Building America*,
was insufficient for teaching children about their government (California State Board of Education 1946, 5–6). He took a broader
swipe at some of the experiential methods of progressive education
when he described a typical field trip:

> In the activity program they go to the firehouse to see whether
> they think it is a good idea, if they like the firehouse. Those things
> are useful in developing interest in your government but you can't
> learn about our constitution that way. You have to study history,
> where history was made, the past, and the experiences of the past,
> and so on down the line. In other words, ladies and gentlemen,
> this [social problems] method has been producing a mass of doubt-
> ing Thomases, students without experience, who don't even have
> the stability of religious ideals, morals, patriotism, allegiance and
> loyalty to our government, which normally children should have
> (ibid., 6–7).

If Sargent had talked with Hanna, he might have found significant points of agreement. Hanna, too, objected to meaningless
activities in instruction, and later wrote, "Children learn *something*
and we are definitely concerned that this something be good subject
matter. I cannot agree with some who say that *any* content is of
equal value with *any other*, or that content generally must be sub-
ordinate to process [emphasis his]" (Hanna 1954, 273). Their fundamental disagreement centered not on whether students should
be presented with substantive material, but on the proper way to

prepare children for citizenship and the way in which American culture should be portrayed.

Sargent's testimony before the Board of Education continued with a criticism of how world affairs were taught. "We find that the facts regarding the rest of the world are generally being taught before the facts of our own country are being taught. There is a definite attempt here to slide in some of this world citizenship, this half-baked, undigested material" (California State Board of Education 1946, 7).

Here, Hanna and Sargent parted company. Hanna passionately believed that American schoolchildren should understand their roles in communities larger than just the nation, and his concern rendered *Building America* vulnerable to Sargent's next attack. Brandishing a volume of the proposed text, Sargent asked,

> What do you suppose is in it? There should be something about America, shouldn't there? Let's open it. The first part of that book is about China, pictures, impressions, slick writing about China ... What is the next thing about building America? Russia. A long chapter about Russia ... the next section—Pacific neighbors, the East Indies; then some information about American possessions. Then there is something about Africa; American outposts; then there is a section on American and foreign trade, current events .... That is all there is about building America, just that (ibid., 7–8).

Apparently, Sargent missed the point that the proposed *Building America* textbook was intended as a supplement to a more traditional textbook. He proceeded to drive home the argument that a social problems approach alone was insufficient to teach American history and geography. He quoted from a 1943 state board document that rejected Harold Rugg's textbooks: "We do not believe in the study of problems as a satisfactory method of education for children of that age .... The pedagogical principles upon which these books are built disregard the fundamental fact that foundations of basic knowledge and skills must be laid before pupils are given the impression that they are ready to deal with contemporary problems" (ibid., 8).

Here was Sargent's main curriculum point: the need to return to a traditional organization of social science instruction in the schools. Discounting the history of curriculum reform which had led to the integration of social science content under the rubric *social studies*, he concluded by pleading with the board that, "if you here can conscientiously agree with us as to the apparent need of separating history and geography you will make another landmark in the educational history of California" (ibid., 9).

In Hanna's view, the traditional approach Sargent advocated had long since proved itself insufficient to meet students' modern needs. He wrote, "The typical curriculum of the traditional school has lacked vitality and meaning for children and youth. School tasks have become almost exclusively unrelated to the life of the community" (Hanna 1937b, 46).

The State Board of Education aligned itself with Hanna's approach to citizenship education. Some members of the board questioned Sargent's assertion about the civic and historical illiteracy of California's schoolchildren. Others took issue with his characterization of progressive education methods. All agreed to a formal reiteration of statements in the State Education Code underscoring the importance of instruction in civics and American history, focusing especially on the founding documents (California State Board of Education 1946). They emphatically refused to rule on the adoption of the *Building America* textbooks.

In August, 1946, Sargent renewed his attacks at the board's meeting in Los Angeles. In each community, competing newspapers allied themselves with one or the other side in the controversy. Polarization was especially keen in cities served by newspapers published by William Randolph Hearst's media empire.

In January, 1947, the state board voted unanimously to adopt the *Building America* series, but the appropriation to purchase the magazines was blocked in the state legislature by Senator Jack B. Tenney. Tenney followed the path of many prominent California politicians by advancing his career through McCarthyite investigations and pronouncements. He raised the stakes in the *Building America* controversy by instigating a full-scale legislative investigation in April of 1947 (Newman 1961, 370).

This move was precipitated by a formal petition for redress of grievances filed by Sargent on February 21, 1947. In it, Sargent maintained that, *"Building America* is a subversive publication in that it undermines principles essential to our form of government" (Sargent 1947, 2). Sargent outlined a number of grievances against the series, ranging from revisionist interpretations of American history to promotion of specific political policies. He warned that "adoption of *Building America* is part of a plan to enable radical educators to secure a monopoly over the subject content of courses in American history, civics, and American principles in the public schools" (ibid., 3–4). The "radical educators" were identified as "a group of left wing educators dominating its Department of Supervision and Curriculum Development" (ibid., 4). Sargent referred to the Department of Supervision and Curriculum Development of the National Education Association, an organization that sponsored the publication of *Building America* during this time.

Sargent called on the California State Assembly to take action. He asked that the assembly request a congressional investigation into the "interstate and international aspects of this situation" (ibid.). He also requested a suspension of the appropriation for the proposed printing and distribution of *Building America* and for a joint legislative resolution naming *Building America* "subversive, detrimental, propaganda, [and] dangerous," a publication to be banned from California's public schools (ibid., 5).

Sargent concluded by requesting a public investigation, into not just the immediate issue of using the magazine in public schools, but also the effects of "the so-called 'progressive' education method" in the schools, of individuals in the State Department of Education, and of "communistic and subversive teacher training programs being conducted by University Schools of Education and by State Colleges" (ibid.). This final request fed the hysteria reflected in a pamphlet entitled *Red-ucators at University of California, Stanford University, California Institute of Technology* (1950). The pamphlet listed faculty members at the three schools who belonged to purported communist organizations. Hanna was not among the three Stanford faculty members listed, but Lewis M. Terman was, apparently for his membership in the Consumers Union. Hanna was not singled out in the tract, but as chairman of *Building America*'s editorial board, he became a focal point of a subsequent investigation in the California Legislature.

The Senate Education Committee's investigation crystallized around the *Building America* issue entitled *Russia* that was proposed as part of California's textbook series. The editorial board of *Building America* did not shy away from controversial issues, but it miscalculated the mood of the times in presenting the Soviet Union in a somewhat sympathetic light. *Building America* was primarily a pictorial representation, and many were concerned about the pictures used to portray Russia, in which "all the Russian women are robust, sturdy, well-fed, well-dressed and appear to have been freshly scrubbed. Every field is lush with grain or corn; every barn is bursting with hay; the people are smiling and happy" (California Library Association 1948). Such a rosy portrayal was doubtless inaccurate, but so was the version the critics preferred. "None of these Soviet citizens appear to be afraid of the secret police, the purges, exile to the salt mines or Party discipline" (National Council for American Education 1948b).

In the supercharged atmosphere of the postwar era, a true portrayal of life behind the Iron Curtain was likely to be impossible. When the question arose in the committee as to where the favorable pictures came from, the Americana Corporation, *Building America*'s publisher, replied that they had indeed been supplied by "SOV-FOTO, the official and only source for pictures from Russia." In its defense, Americana stated that *"Building America* made an earnest effort to obtain photographs which would show existing poverty and distress. Such photographs were unavailable . . . I think everyone is well aware of the 'iron curtain' around Russia, and how difficult it would be to come out of Russia alive with the type of realistic photographs *Building America* feels should be included" (Newman 1961, 359). Apparently, Americana chose to use photographs it knew to be propagandistic rather than publish a text-only edition of its pictorial magazine. The question of whether or not the Soviets ought to be able to portray their nation as they pleased was not discussed. In the supercharged atmosphere of the committee hearings, such a question could not even be raised.

Ironically, the Soviet Union was no more pleased with the Russia issue than was the CSSAR. In a speech before the annual conference of California school superintendents in October, 1946, Hanna explained that the Russian consulate had protested *Building America*'s depiction of the USSR. In a swipe at both the Soviets and the CSSAR, he declared that "The truth must stand for children and youth to see no matter how deeply it may offend totalitarian states where freedom to speak the truth is denied" (*San Diego Journal* 5 October, 1946, 2). The State Board of Education decided in October to proceed with the adoption of the series, but with some revisions to address the complaints (Newman 1961, 360).

The investigation exonerated California's education officials, but it left a cloud over the *Building America* series and its proponents. Paul Hanna attended the hearings fresh from his service on behalf of the U.S. military government in Germany, but he was compelled to defend his patriotism (ibid., 352). Aaron Sargent testified on behalf of the CSSAR and claimed that the Stanford School of Education contained a "communistic cell closely linked with Columbia University." He labeled Hanna as "having leftist tendencies. I don't know how deep" (*Palo Alto Times* 7 April, 1947, 1).

As a result of the committee hearings, two pieces of legislation that aimed to change the California Education Code were introduced in the Legislature. One bill mandated a *back to basics* approach in the schools and limited use of the *social problems* approach to teaching the social sciences. It stated, "It shall be the primary function of the teacher to give effective instruction in fundamentals. Thorough instruction in fundamentals . . . shall be prerequisite to the participation by pupils in advanced courses, particularly in studies involving solution of social, economic, governmental and moral problems" (SB 1029, Sec. 1). The other bill allowed for the dismissal of an employee of a public school if he "advocates or is a member of an organization which advocates overthrow of the Government of the United States or of the State, by force, violence, or other unlawful means" (SB 97, Sec. 1). Both measures passed the California Legislature during the summer of 1947.

Many schools continued to use *Building America* despite the controversy (Newman 1961, 417). The U.S. Army used certain volumes in its education efforts in the occupied countries of Austria, Germany, Korea, and Japan (*Palo Alto Times* 31 March 1948, 2). The U.S. Navy ordered special sets as training materials for new recruits (Hanna 1974). Repackaged as *Your America*, the sets avoided the controversy surrounding the issue on Russia, but they did include such potentially controversial titles as Democracy and Totalitarianism, Roots of American Loyalty, and The Places of the Armed Forces in Our Democracy. The State of Georgia adopted *Building America* for its schools even in light of the California investigations (ibid.). Nevertheless, the controversy took its toll. California failed to fully adopt *Building America*, and the refusal of such a prominent state to place the magazine in its classrooms spelled its doom. It ceased publication in 1948.

Hanna remained strangely quiet throughout the *Building America* affair. His most eloquent defense of the series was made in a speech away from the government investigations:

> We do believe that strength sufficient to withstand the world pressure of communism will be enhanced if we are (1) realistic about our own achievements, and (2) know the strengths and weaknesses of our adversaries. To deny our youth a chance to study a balanced statement of the good and evil in our own nation and in the world is to render our future citizens weak and unprepared for the struggle of our time (*Palo Alto Times* 31 March 1948, 2).

He may have relied on the good sense of members of the California State Board of Education to see Sargent's attacks for what they were. Indeed, the board consistently supported *Building America* throughout the controversy. Hanna told Martin Gill that his friends on the board protected him during the hearings. He said, "I think they prevented any name calling" (Hanna 1973a, 40). He also did not take Sargent's charges very seriously (Newman 1960, 352). Unfortunately, when the hearings moved into the more politically charged atmosphere of the California Senate, neither Hanna nor his powerful friends could control the outcome. In the end, he chose to follow Ray Lyman Wilbur's advice to avoid confrontation (Hanna 1974, 109). Hanna might not have been able to prevent *Building America's* demise by assuming a more combative posture, but his decision to avoid the fight virtually ensured that the magazine would fail.

Hanna did not emerge from the investigations personally unscathed, either. His name was prominently connected with the magazine, which meant guilt by association in some quarters (Newman 1961, 432). In February of 1948, he attended a dinner in his honor given by the Americana Corporation. There he was introduced to "a little man who jumped up smiling and rushed toward us, extending his hand. The introduction was made but just the moment the little fat fellow heard the words *Building America*, he dropped my hand as though it had been molten iron and rushed away" (Hanna 1948).

On the heels of the controversy, Hanna was offered the deputy directorship of the Operations Research Office at Johns Hopkins University, a think tank organized to review promising research projects for the U.S. Army. The climate was such that California Superintendent for Public Instruction Roy E. Simpson found it necessary to emphasize in his recommendation letter that Hanna was "loyal to the United States. I have never discovered any reason that would change my opinion concerning his integrity of purpose in the democratic processes as they are generally practiced throughout the country" (Simpson 1948).

Nor did the controversy fade quickly. A 1953 booklet entitled *Communist-Socialist Propaganda in American Schools* dedicated an entire chapter to *Building America*. It rehashed the criticisms leveled against the magazines in California and claimed that "No single project of the National Education Association, or any of its divisions or departments, more certainly types the nation's greatest organization of educators as contributing to the cause of Communism-Socialism, than sponsorship of the textbooks *Building America*" (Kaub 1953, 63).

In 1961, Robert E. Newman recounted the controversy in a Stanford dissertation, History of a Civic Education Project Implementing the Social-Problems Technique of Instruction. Even then the subject inflamed passions. Newman recalled, "My jargon title of the dissertation was necessitated by the fears of some, when I wrote the dissertation, that its presence might stir up, anew, the conflict. . . . In order to get official permission to write the dissertation I had to do minor things like write the title without having the words Building America appear in it" (Newman 1969).

The *Building America* controversy may have contributed to Hanna's change in focus from domestic to international education.

He saw international education as a new, safer venue for his efforts to help students grow as democratic citizens.

INTERNATIONAL EDUCATION

Hanna claimed that his experiences with government work during the war ". . . broadened my horizons tremendously" (Hanna 1974, 142). More significantly, those experiences provided a venue in which he could continue to develop programs for citizenship education away from the intense scrutiny that had surrounded the *Building America* controversy. That venue was overseas, and it began with his war-related travel on behalf of the Coordinator for Inter-American Affairs (CIAA).

The CIAA was established under the authority of the Council on National Defense to coordinate the cultural and economic activities of U.S. Government agencies in Latin America. By 1940, growing U.S. concern over Nazi infiltration of Latin American economies brought the Coordinator under the direct purview of the President. On August 16, 1940, Franklin Roosevelt appointed Nelson Rockefeller head of the CIAA (Reich 1996, 187).

In late 1940, Paul Hanna met Rockefeller's newly appointed Coordinator of American Affairs, Robert G. Caldwell, at a dinner party for the Commissioner of Indian Affairs. Hanna was on sabbatical leave from Stanford, and during the course of the evening he described his upcoming trip to Central America to visit archaeological sites. The CIAA had been collecting firsthand information on Nazi incursions into South American culture, politics, and economies, so Caldwell asked Hanna to keep his eyes open and report on his impressions when he returned (Hanna 1974, 74). Hanna's trip became one of at least nine fact-finding missions authorized by the CIAA that year.

Hanna enjoyed the cloak-and-dagger mission. He characterized himself as "a first counter-espionage agent to find out what in hell

Germany was doing" (ibid.). Upon his return, he reported on German influences in the schools of the countries he had visited. The
report influenced the CIAA to alter the thrust of its efforts in Latin
America from parrying Nazi propaganda to aiding economic development, with education as a significant component (Reich 1996,
243). Hanna followed this trip with another in 1941–1942, from
which Stanford benefited by landing a small contract to update the
Latin American edition of *Who's Who* (Lowen 1997, 57).

From these missions Hanna developed the conviction that the
wider world should be included in his conception of expanding
communities and that education holds a pivotal role in national and
international development (Hanna 1974, 142). His growing interest
in international education coincided with the growing realization
among policy makers and average Americans alike that the postwar
world would not be one in which the United States could isolate
itself. International cooperation would be the commonplace.

Through international education, Hanna was able to wed his
interest in democratic education to his activities for Stanford's benefit. He took steps to position Stanford as a leader in international
education studies. Even before the war ended, Hanna planned a
conference at Stanford that would bring together top figures from
American universities, corporations, foundations, and government
to discuss programs of training, research, and service for the Pacific,
Asia, and Latin American regions (Hanna 1943). The conference
never took place due to lack of funds, but Hanna was undeterred.

In May of 1945, Hanna proposed the formation of a Stanford
Pacific Institute. Its fivefold purpose would include "teaching and
training personnel for duties in Far Eastern countries; [research to
make] relations with the Orient more effective and productive; collection of materials on the Far East; dissemination of information;
and promotion of international cultural relations" (Hanna 1945).
Part of the value of such an institute, Hanna wrote, would be "an
effective impact of American educational ideals and methods with

their emphasis on democracy and equality of opportunity." He felt that those ideals "can prove one of the great moulding forces in the future of the Pacific" (ibid.). The effect of such an institute would be that Hanna's ideas on education for democratic citizenship could be spread globally, as indeed they were in later years through his work with national and international agencies.

Hanna's work in international education gradually came to dominate his professional efforts. In the immediate postwar period, he traveled to Germany as an educational consultant to the Office of Military Government–U.S. (OMGUS) (Tent 1982, 262). He also spent time in Panama as a consultant to the U.S. Army in the Canal Zone (Newman 1961, 429). These efforts expanded into a series of contracts involving Stanford, the United States Government, and the Republic of the Philippines. Under the aegis of the Agency for International Development, Hanna administered multimillion-dollar contracts spanning the years 1951 through 1966 (Hanna 1982a). Stanford resources were devoted to helping the Philippine government rebuild the University of the Philippines' Colleges of Engineering, Business Administration, Education, and other institutions. Hanna made frequent trips to the Philippines and other regions of east Asia during this period, often staying for weeks or months. The overhead payments alone from these contracts amounted to more than two million dollars for Stanford (ibid.).

Hanna expanded his work in international education beyond southeast Asia with the development of the Stanford International Development Education Center (SIDEC). This institution was supported with grants from the U.S. Office of Education and private foundations. Its purpose was to study the "complex relationship between education and economic development and social and political change" (SIDEC 1967) Students came to SIDEC from around the world, sometimes with generous grants from their home governments (Foster 1998b). They often returned home to high positions in government (Foley 1997). Over time, these students formed a worldwide network of alumni loyal to both Stanford and Hanna. He was able to enlist their help in fund-raising efforts, arranging introductions with officials from their home governments, and establishing other important contacts overseas. These contacts and Hanna's growing international reputation led to consultations in Africa, Europe, and elsewhere.

SIDEC was not Hanna's only vehicle for bringing international education and increased funding to Stanford. In 1944 he was appointed to the W. K. Kellogg Foundation Advisory Committee on Education, and he served in that capacity for more than three decades. During that time, the foundation was involved in numerous international education projects centered at Stanford.

By 1955, Hanna was fully integrated into the network of international education leaders. In that year he was offered the directorship of the United Nations Educational, Scientific, and Cultural Organization's (UNESCO) Department of Education (Adiseshiah 1955). Hanna was chosen for several reasons. First, his network of friends and colleagues would enable him to enlist American scholars to support the work of UNESCO. Malcolm S. Adiseshiah, UNESCO's assistant director-general, wrote that American scholarship "should now be associated more closely with UNESCO's programme" (ibid.). Hanna was highly interested in the position. As was his practice with major career decisions, he sought the counsel of many friends and colleagues. Ultimately, he refused the post. The reasons he gave at the time included his ongoing administrative responsibilities on a number of overseas contracts and his publishing commitments at home (Hanna 1955). In addition, accepting the post would have required that the Hannas move to Paris and away from their lovely home. They looked forward to the last of their children leaving home and a fresh round of remodeling to plan and manage.

PHILANTHROPY

Paul Hanna's reputation as an educational leader at home and abroad rendered his fund-raising efforts on behalf of Stanford University more fruitful. Soon after their arrival on the Stanford campus, the Hannas joined the Stanford Associates organization in its fund-raising efforts. They were asked to cultivate two wealthy sisters, Margaret Jacks and Mary Jacks Thomas, both Stanford alumnae. The Hannas escorted them to numerous Stanford events, lectures, dedications, dramatic and musical performances, and commencements. An especially close friendship developed between the Hannas and Margaret Jacks. She visited the Hanna home on birthdays and holidays, and they were frequent guests at her homes in Palo Alto and Monterey. She and Jean Hanna took an extended trip together to visit Jacks' mother's birthplace in Oaxaca, Mexico (Hanna 1982a).

In 1957 the Jacks sisters drew funds from the estate of their sister, Lee L. Jacks, to endow two professorships in the School of Education at Stanford. Professor W. H. Cowley was the first David Jacks Professor of Higher Education, an endowed appointment named for their father, and Paul Hanna became the first professor to hold the Lee L. Jacks Chair of Child Education. Margaret Jacks later gave additional funds to enlarge both endowments (ibid.).

When Margaret Jacks died in 1958, she willed her $10 million estate to the university. At the time, it was the largest gift to the school since the original Stanford family endowment. Some of the bequest was used to rebuild the old physiology building, now Margaret Jacks Hall, and some of the funds endowed four more Jacks chairs in the School of Education (ibid.).

In 1943, the Stanford Associates asked the Hannas to approach Mrs. Myrna B. Martindale Freeman about establishing an appropriate memorial to her late husband, Dr. John Howard Martindale.

In visits to each other in their homes, they discussed archiving Dr. Martindale's papers and other ways of to memorialze him. In 1944, with input from the Department of Biology, Mrs. Freeman donated nearly $400,000 to establish the Myrna B. Freeman Scholarship Fund and the Dr. John H. Martindale and Myrna B. Freeman Institute of Biology (ibid.).

The general secretary of Stanford University approached the Hannas in 1967 with the need to renovate the organ and organ loft in the Memorial Church (ibid.). The Hannas were music lovers, and they especially liked organ music. They agreed to host a series of musical evenings at the Hanna-Honeycomb House for prospective donors (Hanna and Hanna 1981, 42). After each event, the Hannas personally contacted any guests that showed an interest in the organ project. Evelyn Almack Turrentine eventually donated $500,000 to the project (Hanna 1982a).

Late in his life, Hanna helped create the Associates of the Stanford University Libraries and he served as the group's first chairman. By inviting members to upgrade their membership classifications, Hanna helped raise more than $50,000 to support the libraries (ibid.).

The gifts to Stanford that gave the Hannas their greatest pleasure, however, were those that arose from their personal philanthropy. Paul Hanna recalled fondly the dedication, soon after his arrival at Stanford, of the Cubberley School of Education Building (Hanna 1976). Ellwood P. Cubberley had retired as Dean of the School of Education in 1933. During his long career, he had published a number of professional books that enjoyed solid financial success. He invested the royalties shrewdly and was able to donate sufficient funds for Stanford to build the new education building and to create a library fund, as well (Henderson 1952). Hanna took this act as his model.

Hanna's own publishing activity paid handsomely, but the business endeavors that enabled him to provide funds for Stanford and other benevolences were his real estate partnerships. In 1954, the Hannas and others purchased a tract of redwood timberland (John Hanna 1998). Paul and Jean had been interested in conservation at least since the days of Paul Hanna's prewar service as national director of the U.S. Council for Conservation Education. They had considered purchasing their own tract of forested land for some time, not simply for their own recreation, but also for conservation-oriented tree farming. The idea had first been proposed to Hanna at a Kiwanis Club breakfast by Ben S. Allen, a former Hoover administration official who was inaugurating a conservation education program in California. One evening, a dinner guest told the Hannas about a 1440-acre parcel of redwood growth for sale in the Santa Cruz mountains (Hanna 1957d). The Hannas approached their neighbors and education colleagues, I. James Quillen and William Odell, about forming a partnership to purchase and manage the land. Subsequently, the Hannas, Odells, and Quillens bought the property together, and Paul Hanna became the managing partner (John Hanna 1998).

After spending nearly every free weekend for two years camping on the site and trying to develop it themselves, the Hannas decided the job required professional management. They hired California–Pacific Forest Consultants to advise them. Under professional supervision, the forest land eventually became not just profitable, but also a model of managed timber harvesting. Additional tracts were purchased over the years by various combinations of the partnership. By 1971, their Gazos Creek Tree Farm consisted of 2464 acres of timberland in San Mateo County. Lumbering in redwood country had been a long-standing controversial issue in California, but Hanna received awards for ecologically sound practices, and San Mateo County used the Gazos Creek Tree Farm as a model for responsible timber management (ibid.).

The land was put to many uses. Cal-Pacific marketed its timber as logs, shakes, stakes, firewood, Christmas trees, and other products (Hanna 1957d). In 1966, Charles Taylor, Stanford's athletic director, established a summer camp on the property for children ages 9 to 16. Hundreds of children visited Chuck Taylor's Mountain Camp each summer and engaged in all of the typical camp sports and activities (ibid.). An additional tract known as the Blue Canyon Property was acquired in the Sierra Nevada Mountains to serve as a cut-your-own Christmas tree farm. Unfortunately, heavy snows forced its closure several years in a row. By the time more temperate winters returned, the stands had grown too big for Christmas trees and had to be sold as timber.

Paul Hanna began shopping for a buyer for the tree farms in the 1970s. His approach to pricing was unique. Instead of calculating the value of the land and timber and setting the price on that basis, Hanna calculated the value of gifts he wanted to bestow from sale proceeds and established his price from that number. He planned to endow chairs at both Hamline University and Stanford, as well as provide other gifts. The price he established was nearly twice the land's worth, but George Pope, a member of a family with timber interests in the Cascade Mountains of the Pacific Northwest, bought the property with cash. Pope lost the property, and it changed hands several times until it was acquired by the Sempervirens Fund for development as a park (ibid.).

The land sale netted the Hannas ample funds to donate generously to chosen beneficiaries. In 1975 they created an endowed chair of philosophy at Hamline University, their alma mater, and gave an equal amount to Hamline's general fund (Hamline University 1975,1). The gifts honored Professor Gregory D. Walcott, who had been "the most significant intellectual influence in shaping their life styles and careers" (ibid.). The Hannas originally planned a similar gift to Stanford's School of Education, but by the time of the land sale, they thought that they had not been treated fairly by the school and the Stanford University administration.

CONFLICTS WITH STANFORD

The Hannas' conflict with the university administration centered around use of the Hanna-Honeycomb House after the Hannas donated it to Stanford in the 1970s. In order to understand the depth of bitterness generated by the dispute, the Hannas' attachment to their home must first be understood.

Since their early courtship, the Hannas had shared a desire to build their own home. Both grew up in parsonages, their families never able to make significant alterations to suit their lifestyles (Hanna and Hanna 1963, 57). However, moving every few years afforded them the opportunity to experience living in a variety of homes with both good and bad characteristics. Throughout the first few years of their marriage, the Hannas collected architectural ideas. Then, in 1930, they came across newspaper reports of Frank Lloyd Wright's Kahn Lectures at Princeton University. Intrigued, they secured a copy of Wright's *Modern Architecture* (1931) and read it again and again. Wright's ideas resonated with the Hannas, and they decided that "there could be no other architect for us" (Hanna n.d., 1). Indeed, Wright's declaration that "I don't build a house without predicting the end of the present social order" resonated with the mood of Hanna and his colleagues at Columbia in those years. The Hannas were so taken with Wright's articulation of principles that they wrote him what amounted to a fan letter (Hanna and Hanna 1963, 58). To their delight, Wright replied with an invitation to visit him at Taliesin, in Spring Green, Wisconsin. Whether or not Wright expected his offer to be accepted, the Hannas included a trip to Taliesin in their regular visit to their families in Minnesota the following summer. Wright received the Hannas warmly and the young couple spent the day touring Taliesin, observing the interaction between Wright and his apprentices and listening to Wright describe his philosophy of architecture. As they departed, the Hannas somewhat impetuously asked Wright if he would design their house someday. He answered affirmatively (ibid.).

The Hannas were fond of telling people that upon receiving the offer of employment from Stanford, "We were overjoyed. We made two phone calls: one to Stanford accepting the appointment, and one to Mr. [Frank Lloyd] Wright asking him to think about a house for us in California" (Hanna and Hanna 1981, 17). Few events in Paul Hanna's life better illustrate his entrepreneurial abilities and determination than the design and construction of their home on the Stanford campus. Unfortunately, the Hanna-Honeycomb House became a cause of conflict between the Hannas and Stanford University.

The idea of a junior faculty member contracting with the world's most famous architect to design his private residence was audacious. The plan was alternately referred to as "Hanna's Folly" (Hanna n.d., 4) and "A dream castle come true" (*Stanford Daily* 14 February 1938). The Hannas' first challenge would be finding an appropriate site for the house. They hoped to lease a site from Stanford University in a previously undeveloped tract known as Frenchman Hills, which the *Stanford Daily* called "Stanford's most romantic spot" (ibid.). Wright enthusiastically approved the site, but Almon Roth, the university's comptroller, informed Hanna that Stanford planned to keep that tract as open space for all time.

Hanna employed his formidable political skills to address the problem. Grayson Kefauver also wanted to lease a building site in Frenchman Hiills, so he and Hanna devised a strategy to weaken the administration's resistance. Each week, one of the men met with Roth and the other met with President Ray Lyman Wilbur. Each made a particular case for leasing them the sites. The next week they switched, and each met with the other official. After several weeks of these exchanges, Wilbur decided to grant the requests of the two men. Hanna attributed this change of policy to his and Kefauver's persistence, but the prospect of a Frank Lloyd Wright house being built on university land must have helped sway President Wilbur.

The building site was leased for twenty years, renewable, at $100 per year. In a reflection of Hanna's trusting nature the deal was sealed with a handshake, as was the Hannas' agreement with Wright, and work was begun before a formal lease was executed (Hanna 1976, 2). In later years, Hanna's son John, an attorney, chided his father for this naive style of doing business (John Hanna 1998).

Wright's design, which became the basis of the final structure, arrived in California in January of 1936. The Hannas were "speechless, curious, electrified—in that order" (Hanna n.d., 3). The house was to be built in hexagonal modules, like a redwood-and-glass honeycomb laid flat. Wright explained, "I am convinced that a cross section of a honeycomb has more fertility and flexibility where human movement is concerned, than the square. The obtuse angle (120 degrees) is more suited to 'to-and-fro' than the right angle" (Wright 1938). The Hanna design was Wright's first use of the obtuse angle as an organizing principle for a residence (Hanna n.d., 3). The house was designed to be built in stages as the Hanna family grew and their needs changed. They added to it in phases in the ensuing decades.

Much of the correspondence between the Hannas and Wright during the design and construction of their home revealed anxious, impatient clients and a seasoned master who often had to allay their fears as he educated them. For example, in a letter dated October 15, 1936, the Hannas self-consciously wrote, "Children never had as difficult a time waiting for Santa Claus as we are" (Hanna and Hanna 1981, 29). Looking back, the Hannas characterized their language as "sharp, even abrasive," and their attitude as one of "intolerance and arrogance" (ibid., 50). They frequently pressured Wright to come and inspect the work personally. A letter dated August 15, 1937, stated, "WE and YOU will be better pleased if you come out *now* [emphases theirs]" (ibid., 68). Wright was in ill health during much of this time, and the Hannas' constant, sometimes peevish, entreaties must have grown tiresome.

Sources of the Hannas' anxiety varied. Much of it arose from the contracting arrangement they struck with Wright. The innovative design contained features never before seen on the West Coast. Because the Hannas knew as much about the philosophy behind the design as anyone, they chose to act as their own general contractors. In one of Paul Hanna's few admissions of failure, shortly after the start of construction in January, 1937, he hired an assistant, Harold P. Turner, to help oversee the work (ibid., 42). Apparently, even the supremely energetic Hanna could not adequately balance the roles of teacher, author, consultant, husband, father, and construction foreman.

Even with the addition of Turner, the project still encountered numerous setbacks and unanticipated problems. The structure was built primarily of wood, but the local carpenters were so accustomed to building with right angles that they found the obtuse angles in the plan confusing. The few who managed to adapt to the new design—and to Wright's and Hanna's exacting standards—proved themselves to be true master craftsmen. Still, mistakes were made because of the long-distance relationship between designer and builders, and some were quite costly (Hanna and Hanna 1981, 41).

Another source of anxiety for the Hannas was opposition and nay-saying from the local community. Some objected to their building on that pristine corner of Stanford land. Others complained about the unorthodox structure itself. President Wilbur later related to the Hannas that two senior faculty members visited him one day. They told Wilbur that he had a "madman" on his faculty. When pressed, they explained, "Dr. Wilbur, he's a new young faculty member building an atrocious house over on Frenchman's Hill; only a madman would consider putting up such an outrageous structure.

It's our recommendation that you get rid of him before tenure comes up" (ibid., 64). To his credit, Wilbur defended the Hannas. Wright attempted to reassure his clients in the face of this criticism by underscoring the long-term importance of what they were doing. On January 27, 1937, he wrote,

> It is no matter of taste but, if it were, good taste is all on the side of more human proportions for articles of human use. Habit is a hard horse to beat, as you know. But you and Jean are yet young, I believe. And the children will grow up with the new sense of things. They will start a little ahead of their parents, therefore, who grew up in the old order and have to turn now and look at it in the face for what it is worth. This is the new reality, Paul. Your house is a factor in it of no mean import if you stand up to it (ibid., 51).

More serious concerns were raised by Comptroller Roth. Among his duties was to approve all building on Stanford lands. He favored the predominant Spanish ranch-style architecture of the campus buildings, and the Hannas feared that he would find the Wright design too different and would not approve the final plans. For their important meeting with Roth, the Hannas prevailed on Wright to come to Stanford. After a meditative stroll among the fine old buildings of the inner campus, Hanna and Wright arrived at the comptroller's office.

> Mr. Wright, in his most charming manner, said, "Mr. Roth, I cannot tell you what an inspiration it is to stroll through the beautiful inner and outer quads of this campus. No university architecture can compare with what Richardson's associates gave you. It is truly a magnificent architecture." He paused, then continued, "But, Mr. Roth, I would like to take the person who has been responsible in the last decades and hang him from your tallest tree."
>
> Paul watched in horror as Mr. Roth changed his expression from pleasure to anger. Paul, as shocked as Mr. Roth, decided that approval of the plans had suddenly died.

But Paul glanced at Mr. Wright and was confused to note that his eyes were sparkling with humor. Then Mr. Wright said, "Mr. Roth, I will tell you what to do. You give me the commission, and I will restore this campus just as Richardson would have approved."

With this Mr. Wright burst into a joyful laugh. Mr. Roth saw the humor of Mr. Wright's approach and joined in the laughter. He thrust his hand toward Mr. Wright and said, "Mr. Wright, if Hanna wants you to design his house, I will approve your plans without even looking at them."

Thus began a friendship between our architect and Stanford's comptroller, and thus was set in motion our Honeycomb project (Hanna and Hanna 1981, 39).

In the fall of 1936, the Hannas spent a Sunday afternoon on their hillside lot, staking out the floor plan. They encountered Bailey Willis, a renowned geologist on the Stanford faculty, who stopped while on his Sunday walk. He asked them what they were doing. The Hannas proudly showed him their plans, to which he responded, "You can't build here; a minor earthquake fault runs right through this hill" (Hanna n.d., 4). When given this news by the worried Hannas, Wright cabled them simply, "I built the Imperial Hotel" (ibid.). Wright had indeed designed the Imperial Hotel in earthquake-prone Tokyo. It withstood all challenges but Allied bombing in World War II. Dr. Willis followed up his warning with a helpful letter of advice on how to build an earthquake-resistant house. His concerns proved to be justified in October of 1989, when the Hanna House suffered extensive damage in a major earthquake. After extensive renovation the house is once again open to the public as a museum and conference center.

The modular design of the house alleviated some of the immediate financial burden, but still the project grew immensely expensive. In their initial planning discussions, the Hannas had told Wright that $15,000 was the upper limit of what they could afford, but they quickly realized that figure was only the beginning of their costs. In a letter dated January 2, 1937, Wright attempted to educate them on the reality of building from a new concept on a sloping lot. He wrote, "This can't come down from heaven as things are . . . . So I think it is only just to say at this juncture that you should brace yourself against a minimum of $23,500 and a maximum of $25,000" (Hanna and Hanna 1981, 41). Cost overruns were frequent, and Paul Hanna received advances on future textbook royalties from Scott-Foresman and Company in order to finance them (John Hanna 1998).

Final expenditures topped $37,000, and Wright had to reassure his nervous clients. He wrote, "The only consolation I can offer you for being in debt, like me, is that it is a spur to action and that unlike most home owners you have something worthwhile to show for the 'indebtedness'" (Hanna and Hanna 1981, 70). Wright could not have been more correct. Their home mortgage weighed heavily on Paul Hanna, and it certainly spurred his publishing activities. It is likely that it turned him from strictly academic writing toward more remunerative textbook production. Over the years, expensive additions and renovations to the house kept him producing textbooks. The Hannas finally paid off the last note on their house and its many renovations in 1964, twenty-seven years after it was constructed (Hanna n.d., 5).

For all the concern their Wright house caused them, the Hannas deeply loved their home. It became a focal point in the young family's life. One of the original design principles established with Wright in 1935 was to create the structure to provide as seamless a transition as possible between indoors and outdoors. The result was expanses of glass and redwood facing rolling hills. Numerous doorways led to wide patio terraces bringing the outdoors inside the home.

The Hanna children were especially fond of these features (John Hanna 1998). Their bedrooms were small, but the furniture was efficiently built in and each room had direct access to the outside.

The overall effect was one of wide-open space. The children roamed the oak-covered hills and helped their parents cultivate a wide variety of fruits and berries on their nearly two-acre tract. They even kept goats for a time to provide milk for Robert, the youngest son, who was allergic to cow's milk. Objections from nearby neighbors ended this experiment in family farming (ibid.).

The Hannas were exceedingly proud of their home, and they realized the responsibility of owning such a unique architectural masterpiece. They hosted Stanford architecture classes and seminars on an annual basis and often opened their home to visitors from other colleges and universities (Hanna and Hanna 1981, 92–93). Individuals often arrived on their doorstep to request a tour, and the Hannas usually accommodated them. The Hannas' oldest son, John, recalled waking one day to find strangers peering through his bedroom window (John Hanna 1998). As this sort of inconsiderate intrusion increasingly interfered with the family's daily activities, the Hannas developed a system for showing the home by appointment only.

The house also was the site of various university events. Paul Hanna's students remember frequent gatherings there, including Sunday morning brunches for his graduate students at which he cooked flapjacks (Douglass 1998b). Paul and Jean Hanna devised ways to set up buffet tables on the wide terraces to accommodate more than a hundred people for outdoor barbecues (Hanna and Hanna 1963, 93). The Hanna-Honeycomb House also became the natural place to lodge visiting dignitaries and to host faculty receptions. Many of the later renovations to the house were performed to accommodate these activities, and Stanford University financed some of them (Hanna and Hanna 1981, 113).

In 1960, the American Institute of Architects named the Hanna-Honeycomb House one of the seventeen Wright structures that should be preserved as "an example of his architectural contribution to American culture" (Hanna n.d., 12). The house is also included in the Register of the National Trust for Historic Preservation (ibid.). The Hannas kept careful records of their fifty-eight-year association with Wright, and those priceless documents are housed today at Stanford. They also donated the house itself and many of its valuable furnishings to Stanford University in a series of gifts culminating in 1975. Sadly, controversy developed over the proper use of the home.

The story of the Hanna-Honeycomb House is important in the overall story of Hanna's career at Stanford for a number of reasons. First, it illustrates his dual qualities of supreme self-confidence and boundless energy. The project was much better suited to someone at the height of his career than to a thirty-five year-old associate professor still rising in the academic world. It made a negative impression on some of his senior colleagues at Stanford. Nevertheless, either because he did not care about that aspect of faculty relations or because he ignored it, Hanna chose to add supervision of the home's construction to his already busy schedule of teaching and writing.

The house also required the utmost of Hanna's political and entrepreneurial skills. He searched out materials for its construction, and recruited and trained craftsmen in innovative construction techniques to execute Wright's design (Hanna and Hanna 1981, 46). At the same time, he had to negotiate with Stanford administrators and assure them that his home would complement the older architecture on campus. Despite setbacks, he carried those tasks through to completion.

Perhaps most significant in gaining an understanding of Paul Hanna, the story of his devotion to his home illustrates his sense of priorities. Hanna risked collegial relationships and academic prestige so that he and his family could live surrounded by his own sense of beauty. He sacrificed other potential projects to produce the books that paid for the house, in large part because he valued quality of life over career. Quality of life formed the basis for Hanna's

decision to stay at Stanford rather than returning to the more prestigious Teachers College.

As early as 1959, the Hannas began to consider options for the
final disposition of the structure (Hanna and Hanna 1963, 105). It
stood on leased Stanford land, and university rules prohibited anyone but members of the Stanford community from residing on university property. This provision made selling the house difficult and
deeding it to family members impossible (Hanna and Hanna 1981,
121). The Hannas decided to give the house to the university for
use as a museum or conference center, but Stanford rejected those
uses as disruptive to the existing neighborhood and too hard on the
house itself (ibid.). The issue remained dormant until 1966, when
the Hannas conceived the establishment of an endowment to bring
a visiting scholar to campus, donating the house for use as his
residence while there. Their idea was this: "Annually, Stanford
could invite a man or woman of world distinction to be its guest in
residence. Such scholar, leader, or creative genius would live on
campus, sharing ideas and inspiration with faculty and students,
offering seminars or lectures as desired and appropriate" (ibid.,
125).

The Stanford administration approved the idea, although it
insisted that the visitor be an academic person. The house was
deeded to Stanford in portions: twenty percent was given in 1966,
another twenty-five percent in 1969, and an additional twenty-five
percent in 1971 (ibid.). After their 1971 gift, the Hannas were
informed that although they could state their wishes as to how their
house would be used by Stanford, their gift was unconditional. Their
concern was that the house ultimately could be put to a use radically
different from what they had envisioned. Upon relating this concern
to the Stanford administration, they received assurances that the
house would indeed be used as part of the visiting scholar program
(Hanna and Hanna 1981, 126).

In 1973, Stanford President Richard Lyman announced the

appointment of a board of governors to supervise maintenance of the home, manage the project's endowment, and suggest candidates for visiting scholar (ibid.). The Hannas served as nonvoting members. The board decided that two separate endowments were necessary, one to preserve and maintain the house, and another to fund the visiting scholar program. Stanford University embarked on a major capital fund drive in 1973, but no money was raised for either the house or the visiting scholar endowment. The Hannas and other members of the board questioned the university's commitment to the program and volunteered to raise the funds themselves (ibid., 128).

The Hannas planned to raise $500,000 to support the structure's maintenance and then raise an additional $1 million to endow the visiting professorship. To this end, they flew to Tokyo in 1975 to meet with old friends and admirers of Frank Lloyd Wright, and with officers of the Nissan Motor Corporation. Those officials later visited the Hannas at Stanford, but no commitment of funds was forthcoming.

In October of 1975, the Hannas deeded their last interest in the house to the university and moved to faculty apartments on campus. That same month, Stanford announced that since no money had been raised for the visiting scholar program, the Hanna House temporarily would be used to house the university provost. The Hannas thought that this was a sensible arrangement until funds could be raised (ibid., 132). Unfortunately, alterations were made to the house without consulting the board of governors. In fact, the board was never convened after 1974.

In 1976, Nissan Motors announced that it would fully fund the $500,000 endowment for the house, but that it could not help with the endowment for the visiting scholar. The Hannas and others spent the following year negotiating with other Japanese auto makers to help with the project. The responses were encouraging until a competing fund drive to establish a chair in Japanese studies at

Stanford approached the same companies. That appeal stalled the
Hannas' efforts (Hanna and Hanna 1981, 136).

In the years that followed, the Hanna House was used continually as a residence for Stanford officials, first the new athletic
director and then another provost. The Hannas were heartsick at
the turn of events, and Paul Hanna spent sleepless nights in his
despair (A. Hanna 1999). He could see his dream for its ultimate
use slipping away. John Hanna suggested that he fight Stanford in
court, but he refused, claiming that it would be too disruptive to
the community of which he had been so long a part (John Hanna
1998).

The conflicts with Stanford over the use of their house caused
the Hannas to reconsider their plans to endow a chair at the university, and other conflicts played a part, as well. By the time Paul
Hanna retired in 1967, Stanford had become one of the leading
schools of education in the nation. Hanna knew that he had played
a large part in building that reputation during his thirty years of
service. Still an active scholar at home and abroad, he requested
that the School of Education provide him with an office and with
clerical help to continue his work (Douglass 1998b). The university
had no policy to provide offices to retirees, and the dean refused his
request. Hanna was stung by what he felt was the ingratitude of the
institution. After all, Hanna's fund-raising and contract administration on behalf of the university had brought in more than $16
million. The Hannas own gifts added nearly another $2 million
(Hanna 1982a).

Of more serious concern than office space was the administration's choice for his successor at SIDEC. After his retirement, a
succession of social scientists became directors of SIDEC, and the
emphasis of the center slowly shifted from education to social science research (Foster 1998b). Under Hanna's leadership, SIDEC
admissions preferred students with some background in education,
but that preference slowly faded away after his retirement. Don

Foster recalled meeting post-1967 SIDEC graduates who took pride in the fact that "they matriculated without ever having to take an education course" (ibid.). In addition to the shift in emphasis, some of the directors who followed Hanna held political views that conflicted with Hanna's concepts of democratic education (Douglass 1998b).

Shortly after Hanna's retirement, H. Thomas James, dean of the School of Education, requested that Hanna help prepare a grant extension request for SIDEC. James recognized the cachet Hanna's name had in Washington, and wanted to make use of it. Hanna replied somewhat bitterly

> As you have so clearly communicated by word and action, you believe your philosophy and mine with respect to the roles of SIDEC, its program focus, and its management, are somewhat at variance. I would not presume to try to interfere with your efforts to shape SIDEC's future. For me to continue to represent SUSE [Stanford University School of Education] in the coming negotiations would only mislead the donor as to your expectations and could be a major deterrent to moving the research in the direction you desire (Hanna 1968c).

For one who had been such an influential figure at Stanford for such a long period of time, taking a back seat in important decisions—especially in decisions about a program he had founded—was humiliating. In his reply to Dean James, Hanna referred to himself in the third person as he occasionally did when coming to grips with unpleasant realities. He wrote

> Over the coming years, I hope to be able to continue to assist the University in fund-raising. But one principle I am sure we all agree upon: Hanna is no longer in a policy-making position in the Stanford community. Therefore, Hanna will concentrate his efforts to help fund what his colleagues in decision-making positions wish implemented. This is the nature of the ballgame as I clearly

read the record of action of the past few months—I understand, accept, and shall try to play the game loyally according to these rules (ibid.).

By early 1971, SIDEC was experiencing confusion as to its identity and mission. Frank J. Moore served as acting director for a time, in 1971, and was convinced that this confusion would "be the end of an effective and meaningful program, capable of attracting the financial support required to sustain it" (Moore 1973). Within a few years, SIDEC's financial instability was so acute that it jeopardized the retention of key faculty in the areas of Southeast Asian and Latin American regional studies and in economics. SIDEC Director Hans Weiler recommended that "if no budget provisions for this component can be made, the degree programs in International Development Education be [sic] terminated" (Weiler 1973). SIDEC eventually closed its doors. Moore termed it "a great pity, to have so promising a program fold for so patently wrong reason at so obviously the wrong time" (Moore 1973).

These factors weighed in Hanna's decisions about how to donate his money to Stanford. Instead of creating a chair in the School of Education, he decided to give funds to create the Hanna Collection within the Hoover Institution (Gross 1998). Hanna's goal was to create a collection of materials that could be used for important research into the relationships between education and economic, social, and political development in the twentieth century. Hoover provided him office space and secretarial help to develop the collection (A. Hanna 1999).

When the dean of the School of Education, Arthur Coladarci, learned of Hanna's gift to the Hoover Institution, he requested a lunch meeting with Hanna. He told Hanna that he could not believe that his donation went to the Hoover instead of to the School of Education, and asked why he had redirected the money. Hanna answered that the school's refusal of office space and staff, and its handling of SIDEC, had made the decision for him (Gross 1998).

Clearly a man as involved and energetic as Paul Hanna would not suddenly step away from his professional life upon retirement. He continued to work on so many projects in publishing, consulting, philanthropy, and other areas that he needed an official base. The Hoover Institution offered him this home, funded through his own gifts.

HANNA'S LAST YEARS

The major scholarly activity of Paul Hanna's final years centered on the Hanna Collection at the Hoover Institution. From his early career in academia, Hanna had been interested in the ways in which government could use education to achieve national goals. His post-war experiences in international education only deepened his interest. With a substantial endowment, the Hannas created within the Hoover Institution the Paul and Jean Hanna Archival Collection on the Role of Education in the Twentieth Century. Paul Hanna stated their goal in a column for Stanford's *Campus Report* newsletter:

> There a can be no doubt that education has figured importantly in laying the groundwork for revolution and wars, in the creation and maintenance of peace, and in nation-building . . . . Yet curiously this kind of instrumental use of education has remained almost unexplored ground in the world of scholarship. An enormous amount of data exists throughout the world in private and public hands. The Hoover Institution will be the first to systematize as much of it as possible to facilitate research and publication (Hanna 1977, 2).

Hanna spent the final phase of his life working as a senior research fellow at the Hoover Institution. He solicited papers from organizations and individuals to add to the collection and oversaw publications resulting from the collection's use.

Some have assumed that Hanna's affinity for the Hoover Insti-

tution reflected his own political conservatism (Tanner 1998). Over
the years, he had indeed grown more conservative, "but not in the
vernacular that Hoover represents . . . . He was concerned with
what was best for education no matter which side it came from" (A.
Hanna 1999). More likely, he recognized in the Hoover a comfort-
able, prestigious post from which to develop the Hanna Collection.

Hanna provided the driving force for the collection from its
inception until his death. He began his work by surveying the existing holdings in the Hoover Institution Library to identify those
having to do with education. From that base, he developed a list of
individuals and institutions to contact about depositing records in
the Hanna Collection. Many of these people were his old friends
and colleagues. He estimated that the time from his initial request
for an individual's papers until their arrival at Hoover averaged six
years. During that time, he maintained regular communication with
potential donors, and he personally catalogued many of the dona-
tions when they arrived (ibid.).

The Hanna Collection grew rapidly under Hanna's leadership.
By the time of his death it included more than 750 separate archives,
and it is now the largest collection of its kind in the world (Hoover
Institution n.d.). Among its holdings are documents from organi-
zations such as the American Council on Education, the American
Educational Research Association, the Asia Foundation, and the
Atlantic Council, and from individuals such as R. Freeman Butts,
Otis Caldwell, William G. Carr, and several former U.S. commis-
sioners of education.

The Hoover Institution has published some of the results of
scholarly research in the collection as the Education and Society
series of booklets. Hanna was enthusiastic about these publications.
Of them he said, "We're beginning to turn out basic books that
ought to tell us nationally and internationally what we have to pay
attention to and what are the differences in objectives and methodologies of systems of education that result in the acceptance of

totalitarian, repressive governments as against the democratic ones" (von Kreisler-Bomben 1984, 47). Paul Hanna's final publication, *Assuring Quality for the Social Studies in Our Schools* (1987), was published as part of the series.

On behalf of the Hanna Collection, the Hoover Institution also has supported scholars in residence and sponsored seminars such as the national Seminar on Civic Learning for Teachers. Through these activities and others, the collection serves as a major research tool for scholars interested in the instrumental uses of education in this century.

THE END

Paul and Jean Hanna moved out of their Honeycomb House and into the Pierce-Mitchell townhouse development for Stanford faculty in October of 1975. Hanna had spearheaded the development, but after forty years of living in Wright's architectural masterpiece he was not content. He complained about the shoddy workmanship of the development and insisted on renovating his unit to accommodate his and Jean's needs. Nevertheless, the Hannas lived happily, traveling occasionally, visiting with friends and family, going to their offices at the Hoover Institution, and crossing swords with the Stanford administration—until Jean injured herself in a fall in 1985.

Both Hannas had experienced minor health problems over the years, but Jean's last illness proved serious. She suffered a fall in the townhouse and underwent surgery to repair the damage to her knee, but she never fully recovered. She lost mobility and required more care than Paul could provide, so they moved to a retirement facility with nursing care. Her health continued to decline and she died in March, 1987.

Following Jean's death, Paul Hanna married Aurelia T. Klipper, who had been his assistant at the Hoover Institution since 1981.

Although they worked closely together on Hanna Collection projects, Paul's proposal of marriage took her quite by surprise. After receiving the Hanna children's blessing, the two were wed on December 26, 1987. Their brief life together was filled with travel. Following a honeymoon trip to Hawaii, they journeyed to Guatemala to visit Mayan ruins there. This trip was special to Paul Hanna, because Guatemala was the site of the wartime trip for CIAA that had launched his career in international education. They traveled with a Stanford-sponsored educational tour, and Aurelia Hanna recalled that one day her husband presented her with a stack of books to read in preparation for the trip. Paul Hanna was worried about his ability to keep up with the younger travelers, but he had no problems. On the heels of that success, the Hannas planned a trip to the South Pacific, but they never traveled together again.

One night in the early spring of 1988, Paul Hanna awoke without warning, in excruciating pain. Mrs. Hanna rushed him to the hospital, where they waited many hours for diagnosis with Paul suffering great pain. The final diagnosis was an embolism in the aorta and Hanna was taken into surgery. The surgeons corrected the problem, but the trauma of surgery was too much for his eighty-five-year-old body. Paul Hanna died on April 8, 1988.

CONCLUSION

Paul Hanna's years at Stanford University were years of building. Having turned his back on the East Coast educational establishment by refusing a chair at Teachers College, he threw himself into contributing to Stanford University and to the development of his own career. He enjoyed spectacular success in both efforts. He developed an unassailable national reputation through his textbook publishing and his consulting work. He employed the financial rewards of those successes to build a marvelous Frank Lloyd Wright–designed home. In that home, he and Jean built a family.

Their children and grandchildren continue to contribute to their communities. Hanna's tremendous energy and entrepreneurial skill helped the university through rocky economic times during the war years. His continued work on behalf of the university increased not only its wealth, but its reputation as a major research center in education and other fields. His expertise as a teacher produced generations of leaders in education, both in the United States and abroad, and helped spread the reputation of Stanford's School of Education worldwide. His interest in preparing children for their roles as citizens in democracies expanded beyond American schools through his international development education efforts, and it resulted in the creation of SIDEC, a major center for such work. His devotion to the Hanna Collection archives in his retirement years built a major research tool for scholars interested in the re-lationships of education to national development in the twentieth century. Perhaps his most enduring legacy, though, are the gener-ations of children whose worldviews he helped shape through his publications.

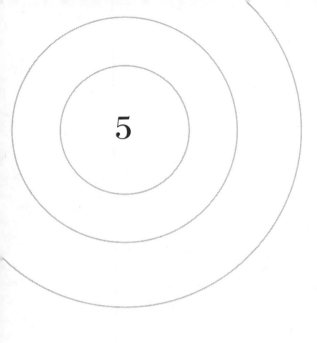

5

Paul Hanna's
Writing Career

During the course of his career, Paul Hanna wrote dozens of books and more than a hundred articles. These works include general social critiques, thoughtful pieces on the relationship between school and society and on curriculum development, calls for citizenship education through a community school model, reports of educational practices abroad, and some of the most innovative and influential social studies textbooks and curriculum materials of his day. He even wrote pieces on arithmetic instruction, the use of audiovisual curriculum aids, and—first with Jesse Newlon and later with his wife, Jean—spelling textbooks. His writing reflected the progression of his thought from social meliorism and social reconstruction to a more traditional *mandarin*-type view of social studies education, but the bulk of his work centered on the concepts of community and social change. From his earliest writing about community schools to his last publication—a reiteration of his proposal for a national commission for the development of a uniform school curriculum—Hanna insisted that the schools must provide children with a deep understanding of the social, economic, and political institutions around them, along with opportunities to improve those institutions.

Hanna's understanding of the importance of community developed out of his concern for the dilemma of modern man. From his extensive study of philosophy, the influence of his social reconstructionist colleagues at Teachers College, and his firsthand experience of the Depression, Hanna came to see that the rapid rate of technological progress since the industrial revolution was mankind's biggest challenge. In his pragmatic conception of social evolution, Hanna saw that the nature of human biological needs and the limitations imposed by the physical environment combined to give rise to problem-solving tools and techniques unique to individual cultures. The nature of these tools and techniques, Hanna believed, governed the institutional arrangements that people constructed to direct their use, and those institutional arrangements led to the formalization of values and ideology. Hanna claimed that this process "results in a philosophy that supports those social habits that have stood the acid test of usefulness" (Hanna 1939a, 2). He perceived that human institutions had not evolved quickly enough to adapt to changes in ways of life spurred by the new technologies of modern industrialism. The primary challenge of modern life, in his mind, was to develop "social institutions and arrangements that are a counterpart of our present degree of scientific control" (Hanna 1935a, 321).

One of Hanna's earliest statements of this analysis appeared in a speech that he gave to the New York Home Economics Association in March of 1932. He told the assembled teachers that the Great Depression was not just a temporary emergency, but a "fundamental change in society which offers an opportunity to commence an important reconstruction of society through the home and the family" (Hanna 1933, 386). The Depression fit into Hanna's theory of social evolution as an example of a maladaptive social and economic response to technological progress. To illustrate his point, Hanna listed several challenges confronting American civilization. He described the ravages of technological unemployment. "Our industrial civilization builds great factories and fills them with machines to do the work of many hands but offers no employment for these now idle hands" (ibid., 389). He decried the disintegration of home life and asked, "What will be the routine of the home of the future? Will the home simply be a place where relatives convene at intervals between attending school, club, business, or recreation; a place in which to change one's clothes, eat breakfast and dinner, and snatch a few hours of sleep?" (ibid.).

His critique was one that could be heard today, but his attribution of cause recalled an idyllic past. Disintegration of the home was encouraged, he thought, by the loss of its productive function in society: ". . . *buying* a living rather than *producing* a living is the characteristic of the modern home [emphases his]" (ibid., 390). A by-product of the modern dilemma, Hanna charged, was a declining aesthetic sense: "We have proved ourselves to be almost sterile artistically, unable to create a culture, an art, a music, a literature, a domestic architecture, a beautiful environment that is worthy of our people" (ibid., 388). Certainly his conversations with Frank Lloyd Wright about the potential of architecture to elevate the spirit impacted Hanna's critique.

One reason Hanna gave for the low state of American aesthetic culture was the American obsession with consumption and with the crass, functional art produced by advertising. He noted, for example, that for the typical consumer, "'High-powered' advertising plays upon his emotions—his fear, his pride, his self-esteem, his love for his family, et cetera. His ignorance frequently offers a tempting bait to the national advertiser" (Hanna 1933, 391). In a critique that might be heard on a modern talk show, he decried the increase in crime and divorce rates, the increase in nursery schools instead of the home as the locus of early childhood experience, the increase in women working outside the home, and the increased freedom of youth. These critiques formed the philosophical basis for much of Hanna's work in curriculum development.

Although his social critique resembles that of some present-day social conservatives, Hanna's proposed solutions were not conservative. He called on the home economists he addressed to help students reevaluate the role of technology in production:

> We cannot expect economic security so long as the machine is conceived as an instrument for the production of profits for private capital rather than as a tool functioning to release mankind from the drudgery of work . . . Selfish motives will undoubtedly have to be cast aside along with many outgrown social and economic theories. In their place we must substitute drives for general social welfare . . . Pupils must be indoctrinated with a determination to make the machine work for society, rather than to allow society to work for the machine (ibid., 393).

He insisted that "young consumers can be taught to be wise, slow to indoctrination by the wily advertiser, and capable of making a selection after due investigation of all factors involved." Above all, Hanna called on teachers to help students develop "a truer evaluation of what really makes happiness. Americans have been engrossed in a mad orgy of accumulating wealth, material goods, and services . . . In attaining this objective we have forgotten the joys of creating and the real purposes of consuming" (ibid., 395–396).

Hanna's call for the school to help children understand the impact of modern industrial economics on their lives became a recurrent theme in his work. In his view, the school was part of both the problem and the solution. As an institution in society, the school was partly responsible for failing to prepare students for the changing world. In particular, social science education in the past had been confined largely to history and to geography, subjects that Hanna saw as static, unable to offer solutions for the future by simply looking to the past. To replace them, he proposed a system of social education. He wrote, "The task of education is the challenge of our age—the task of designing social arrangements and values systems which will facilitate the basic human satisfactions under the conditions and possibilities of our new controls over nature" (Hanna 1939a, 14). Here Hanna outlined his pragmatic philosophy of curriculum making. Education, in his conception, is "the institutionalized and purposive intelligence of our culture." The schools serve as instruments of social critique through which democratic cultures like the United States "collectively examine our value system, our institutions, and our technics in the light of our needs and desires" (ibid.).

The second aspect of Hanna's call to the schools insisted that they provide children opportunities to use their newfound knowledge of social, economic, and political institutions to improve society. After adequate examination of their culture, the people "consciously design a culture toward which we desire to move," then "we construct 'learning' experiences for ourselves and our young which will make it possible to achieve the desired goals" (ibid.). This process is followed by more evaluation, criticism, and correction.

Obviously, Hanna was calling for a new vision of the school as an agent for social change. In this, he reflected the influence of the social meliorists and social reconstructionists at Teachers College and in the Progressive Education Association. He wrote,

> According to this concept of culture and education, the institutions of education are no longer responsible solely for passing on the accumulated social habits found satisfactory in the past. Education still has this task, but in addition a task far more significant—that of serving as a laboratory of culture in which the culture is examined for ways of continuously improving it, not to 'learn' the culture but to work with culture to better it—a challenge large enough for anyone (Hanna 1939a, 14).

Hanna felt that curriculum specialists must "create a climate of opinion friendly to new institutional arrangements and must encourage social, economic, political, and educational inventiveness to meet the demands of each new age" (ibid., 16). To meet this lofty goal, nothing less than "cultural reconstruction," Paul Hanna proposed a very different type of school (Hanna 1935a, 322).

THE SCHOOL IN ITS COMMUNITY

Paul Hanna's long and prolific writing career took him in a number of directions, but he always seemed to return to the theme of the school's role in its society. His writing on this theme reveals growth in his thought over time, but a few emphases remained constant. In a 1953 article entitled "The Community School Defined," Hanna listed the essential characteristics of the community school:

> Some kind and degree of school–community interaction is a characteristic of the programs. The role of education is seen to be more than intellectual training. The school is viewed as an agency for helping to give direction to community growth and improvement. Of necessity, the curriculum of the community school is flexible and changing in light of community demands. Education is a total community concern, enlisting the services of all citizens as they are needed and can contribute (Hanna and Naslund 1953, 51).

Hanna's writing about community and school relationships played off these themes throughout his career.

Hanna's structural vehicle for reaching the goal of teaching children to understand and take control of social change was the community school. This concept was not new. Robert A. Naslund, a student of Hanna's at Stanford who wrote his doctoral dissertation on the history of the community school concept, identified the roots of the community school in Europe. In the early nineteenth century, Phillip Emanuel von Fellenberg, a Swiss nobleman, developed schools on his estate at Hofwyl. Their purpose was the improvement of living through close association between the schools and the community. At about the same time, Denmark began to develop Folk High Schools as centers of community life and improvement.

Hanna referred to these schools in some of his own writing. Nineteenth-century American educators were aware of these developments overseas and many advocated similar experiments in the United States. Naslund particularly identified Henry Barnard, William T. Harris, and Colonel Francis W. Parker as planting the seeds of the community school in America. He wrote, "Each of these men saw education as having a vital role in social organization and development in the community and did much to change schools and their objectives in the light of these views" (Naslund 1953, 257).

Early in the century, Irving King had written that "The social nature of the modern man has not grown fast enough to keep up with his economic progress. The problem that confronts us today is that of extending and, if necessary, reconstructing the social ideas of a simpler social order, that they may dominate the modern world, with its greatly diversified activities and the hosts of problems that have grown out of these multiplied and enlarged interests" (1913, 18).

Although King and Hanna made similar diagnoses of the dilemma of modern man, their prescriptions differed drastically. King advocated a curriculum based on the "simpler social order" of the past. Hanna sometimes wrote wistfully of those past times, but he insisted that the schools must prepare children for the future. To that end, he suggested that "the content necessary to achieve this [social reconstruction] must be found largely in our contemporary world" (1935a, 322). The community school seemed to be a worthy vehicle for developing and delivering such a curriculum, and Hanna enthusiastically promoted the community school concept for decades both here and abroad.

The more immediate influences on Paul Hanna's conception of

the community school included the activity curriculum inherent in William H. Kilpatrick's Project Method and in John Dewey's concept of education as growth. Dewey especially guided Hanna on this point. In *The School and Society*, Dewey wrote, "When the school introduces and trains each child of society into membership within such a little community, saturating him with the spirit of service, and providing him with the instruments of effective self-direction, we shall have the deepest and best guarantee of a larger society which is worthy, lovely, and harmonious" (Dewey 1913, 44).

Integral to both Dewey's and Kilpatrick's conceptions of learning was student activity, and Hanna enthusiastically endorsed activity-based learning experiences over the older, more static instructional techniques. In a summary of ten years of curriculum experimentation at the Lincoln School, Hanna wrote, "Psychologists have given evidence that learning takes place best under conditions where the learner has active and meaningful experiences" (Hanna 1932c, 483). Not only were activity-based curricula better for the child, but Hanna thought that they were better for the teacher as well. He wrote that in the traditional curriculum, "Teaching was not a challenge for the teacher, for there was lacking the thrill of adventure with the unpredictable qualities of children and the stimulation of working with the released energy and interest of children under freedom" (Hanna 1936c, 271). In a 1939 article for *Childhood Education*, Hanna was exultant:

> The educational drought seems to be broken . . . . Through rich, varied, and direct contacts with life the modern child is given opportunities for growth which most of us lacked when we went to school . . . . Books become tools for extending and enriching ideas gained through significant first-hand experiences in social, physical, and natural sciences (Hanna 1939d, 339).

Hanna's most widely read work on the subject of community schools was *Youth Serves the Community*. This often-quoted book was a report of a survey of social service organizations and education administrative units on the local and state levels, both in the United States and abroad. The survey's purpose was to "collect descriptions of projects carried out by children and youth to improve some aspect of the community life" (Hanna 1936a, 34). Those projects that met criteria for "educational value to the individual and significant value to the community" (ibid., 35) were published in the volume. The criteria established give insight into Hanna's conception of what a worthwhile school–community endeavor is like.

In order for the individual educational criteria to be met, a project must give the youths who participate in it a sense of its social significance. Unless the project is truly helpful to the community in a way that participants can understand, it loses much of its educational value. Second, the youths must have a part in planning the project. Important democratic learnings are lost when children are deprived of the opportunity to identify and analyze a problem cooperatively, and to plan and carry out a program for alleviation of the problem. Third, the projects should be a reasonable match for the social and physical maturity of the children participating. Hanna believed that failure could be as effective a teacher as success, but only when success seemed to be a reasonably likely outcome. Fourth, the youths must accept responsibility for the success or failure of the project. A vital step in this type of learning is frank appraisal of the results of children's actions, both successes and failures. Fifth, there must be individual growth in those who participate in a project. Without growth, the project has failed in its educational mission and is simply exploitation of the youths' efforts (ibid.).

Hanna also established three criteria for the social significance of projects. First, projects must result in actual improvement of community life. Plans and proposals must be turned into action. Second, projects should concern something that is a responsibility of youth. In other words, adults should not call on youths to solve problems that are exclusive to the adult world, but children and adults may work together to improve their common lives. Third, projects should address underlying sources of social problems insofar as possible. Hanna thought that one-time charitable acts did little to alleviate long-term suffering, and might even develop an unhealthy class consciousness in children, an *us-and-them* mentality (Hanna 1936a, xiii). Projects that passed muster on both the social and educational criteria were described in the book under categories such as "Youth contributes to public safety," and "Youth contributes to civic beauty" (ibid.).

Youth Serves the Community expressed Hanna's ideas on the community school concept in other ways, as well. Unlike some of his colleagues, Hanna admired the work of the National Youth Administration (NYA) and the Civilian Conservation Corps (CCC) in enlisting young Americans to serve the nation, but he decried the lack of an integrated education program employing their work experiences to teach them important subject matter and life lessons. Hanna especially regretted that neither the NYA nor the CCC employed young people in one of his pet projects—surveys of community needs (ibid., 45). He wrote, "Youth was denied the educational experience of surveying the national community to discover the most immediately necessary, as well as the most desirable long-term tasks" (ibid.).

One reason Hanna insisted on using the schools for social service was that, aside from the educational considerations,

> The school is the one universal, well-equipped, and locally controlled institution in the community. The school, with its trained leadership and its physical equipment, could, with some addition to its staff and plant and with some reorganization of its program, conduct such a national project better than any existing group. Its local control makes impossible the dangers pointed out in the European [Fascist] youth movements (ibid., 46).

Primarily, though, Hanna saw the community school as a much more relevant educational vehicle than the traditional school. He wrote, "The school program must shift its emphasis from the classical and academic approach to an emphasis on the problems facing youth here and now. The typical curriculum of the traditional school has lacked vitality and meaning for children and youth. School tasks have been almost exclusively unrelated to the life of the community" (ibid.).

In a piece written in 1938 for the Ninth Yearbook of the National Council for the Social Studies, Hanna focused on the impetus the community school could provide to education for responsible citizenship. He began with an endorsement of activity-oriented curricula: "We know enough of the nature of learning to be able to evaluate certain teaching procedures as more productive of growth than others. We can say with confidence that we learn more adequately when we respond to the problems and demands of an actual experience than we do when we respond to the hypothetical problems of a described situation as set out in a textbook" (Hanna 1938a, 138).

In regard to citizenship education, Hanna claimed that "Probably the most significant learning in our democratic world is the consciousness of cooperative action as the process by which we continuously improve our lot" (ibid., 141). The pattern he advocated in the community school included children surveying their community's needs, planning strategies to meet those needs, and then carrying them out. This process gave students a deep sense of their role in society, and the positive changes that their actions could achieve. Social education became the core of the curriculum. "In this newer concept, the social studies teacher accepts the challenge that our culture may be improved by the process of analyzing the culture's shortcomings, projecting solutions, and taking the necessary action to translate plans into achievement" (ibid., 143).

Hanna applied these concepts of democratic involvement and community learning to curriculum development, as well as to instruction. In the late 1930s, he wrote several articles advocating increased teacher involvement in curriculum development. In a story reflected in editorial cartoons of the time, he reminded readers,

> You know what happened to the usual course of study, developed by the selected experts. A committee of trained specialists worked hard all summer preparing these bulletins. The proud principal stood at the opening faculty meeting with this pile of new courses of study on the corner of the desk. He praised the Central Committee for the great task of research, synthesis, and editing. And now he was ready to pass them out. The teacher, when she left that meeting, took this new bulletin under her arm to the classroom, and placed it on top of the desk (Hanna 1938b, 143).

Hanna went on to explain how, in the press of everyday classroom demands, the document winds up in the bottom of a desk drawer, where it is not rediscovered until the teacher cleans out her desk in June, "In the meantime it had not affected the classroom procedure, it had not improved the personality of the teacher who had it in her desk drawer" (ibid.).

As an alternative, Hanna advocated a program in which teacher growth was the focus of curriculum development. Drawing on his work in the Los Angeles and Santa Barbara schools as examples, he described a process in which teachers form voluntary study groups to increase their knowledge of their subjects and of society. They take field trips with experts to increase their subject knowledge through direct experience. They experiment with new instructional approaches in their classrooms, then share and refine their innovations. Hanna warned that old patterns of educational leadership were obsolete in this new model: "In this newer program the principal becomes a leader in teacher personality growth . . . . This leadership must come through recognized merit—recognized by his associates who accept his leadership because he gives them the opportunity for satisfying growth experiences" (ibid., 146).

In an article published in 1939, Hanna described a similar program instituted in the San Diego public schools. He claimed that "The San Diego Curriculum Development Program has grown out of an increasing awareness on the part of the entire professional staff of the necessity continuously to study the child and society in an effort to provide the best possible curricular experiences in our schools" (Hanna 1939c, 104).

However nobly spontaneous his description sounds, the program must have suffocated under the maze of committees and sub-committees established for review and cross-review of the curriculum ideas produced by teachers. An additional weakness was the lack of community input in the curriculum development process. Although Hanna asserted that "Continuously, while this program of curriculum development is going forward, the *Central Curriculum Council* will keep the public informed on developments and will invite lay participation [emphasis his]," there was no formal mechanism for public information, much less input, in the byzantine diagram of committees included in the article (ibid.).

Perhaps the most imaginative vision Hanna provided of the community school is found in the widely distributed John Dewey Society yearbook, *Democracy and the Curriculum: The Life and Program of the American School.* In a three-part chapter of that publication, Hanna presented his ideal program for the community school. He even renamed the school the "Institute for Individual and Community Development" to indicate the radically expanded program that he proposed for the school (Hanna 1939b, 381).

The first section of Hanna's chapter in the yearbook describes the total program of the institute, a cradle-to-grave system of social and educational services. The institute provides prenatal medical care and health education for expectant parents. After their child is born, they may return for consultations on child rearing: "Problems perplexing to the parents are analyzed in the School by parents and staff and suggested solutions worked out" (ibid., 384). Despite his earlier concern about the proliferation of nursery schools, Hanna's ideal school provides one. Parents may enroll their children at age two in order to encourage "the physical, emotional, intellectual, and social development of these early years" (ibid., 385).

Hanna envisioned a partnership between the home and the school in raising children: "Teachers and parents consult frequently and together agree upon ways of directing the growth of each child . . . Thus the School serves as a laboratory where each parent couple may take a child for clinical study and in addition the parents delegate to the School part of the actual daily care of the child in larger social groups of his own age" (ibid.).

When the child reached school age, he would enter an institution that had, besides typical school facilities, ". . . stations or branches in every enterprise in the community. Or to state it another way, every community organization and establishment has membership in the School, and they consider how the educative experience present in the organization or establishment can be made available to each child and youth in the community" (Hanna 1939b, 387–388).

This section may be Hanna's most fanciful. He envisioned every community institution viewing child education as a primary goal, and he expected everybody in the community to value education as highly as professional educators do. He even expected these institutions to incorporate children into their everyday operations: "Not only do industry, agriculture, transportation, communication, commerce, social and governmental agencies cooperate with the School in providing opportunities to *observe* life in the making, but wherever physically safe and not economically unsound provision is also made to have pupils become active *participants* in the processes [emphases his]" (ibid., 389).

Here, Hanna's vision reaches poetic heights:

> They [children] feel the throb of power machinery; they hear the din and rhythm of the factory; they smell the sting of gases and the odor of ozone; they see the vast movement of an assembly line as it adds piece to piece to make an automobile, or a book; they experience movement in modern transportation; they taste the

sweetness of raw sugar or the oily juice from the cotton-seed press; they feel, see, hear, taste, and smell life in the making (ibid.).

Perhaps most significantly, Hanna expected parents to surrender, at least partially, the responsibility for raising their own children. At this relatively early point in his career, Hanna advocated collectivism openly and forcefully. He also exhibited fewer reservations about indoctrination than he did in later years. As he grew older and observed the terrors of Nazi and Soviet statism and suffered the right-wing attacks connected with the *Building America* controversy, he became more circumspect in his advocacy of collectivism. Nevertheless, his advocacy of community schools overseas and a national curriculum commission at home demonstrated that, even later in life, he still held collectivist sentiments.

The educational services provided by Hanna's institute did not end at the conclusion of the traditional academic program. Career education was provided for professionals and tradesmen alike through "alternation of practical and theoretical experience" (ibid., 390). Hanna drew on his earlier experience with the Lincoln School to outline his vision for adult education:

> The School through its studios, laboratories, shops, libraries, and lecture halls offers the opportunity for continuous study and enrichment of personality . . . The community conceives of the School as a place where the guidance of a trained and stimulating staff is ready to assist the individual in carrying forward any personal or vocational interest or need he cares to pursue. No member of the community is too old or too young, too learned or too ignorant to use the facilities of the community School (Hanna 1939b, 391).

Parts two and three of Hanna's yearbook chapter provided examples of community–school cooperative projects and discussed curriculum issues. The examples were drawn from *Youth Serves the Community* to demonstrate how schools could conduct community surveys, develop beautification projects, construct housing, and improve agricultural methods. The curriculum section promised a framework for community schools, but it delivered only vague outlines that amounted to no more than brief descriptions of the sample projects. Hanna criticized the parochialism and lack of subject integration in the traditional curriculum, and he advocated a scope and sequence broad enough to provide common understandings nationwide, as well as attend to local concerns.

The outbreak of World War II provided a wealth of new activities for community schools. Total war required substantial contributions from all members of society, even children. Hanna served on the Commission on Resources and Education in the years before the war. A joint project of the National Education Association and the Progressive Education Association, the commission shared members with the government's National Resources Planning Board. Hanna's work on these two committees allowed him to see as clearly as anyone the need for schools to mobilize their students in the war effort. In a series of articles, he called on them to do just that in a community school-like setting.

In a 1941 piece for *Childhood Education*, Hanna warned that war was likely and that it might mean nutritional and medical shortages, interruptions of family life, physical danger from attacks and sabotage, and other kinds of suffering for children. He called on schools to prepare for these potentialities and to mobilize children: "The schools can be a means through which children can make a significant contribution to the defense program as are the schools in England where the children contribute messenger service, give first aid, supply vegetables and fruits for canning, and encourage similar activities appropriate to the ages of children" (Hanna 1941a, 102).

Hanna realized that some would resist using children in the war effort. He argued that "All of us recognize that the culture that creates an institution has a right to shape the work of that institution to emergency ends" (ibid.). To mitigate the unsettling effects of the war, Hanna called on schools to "continue to give children the basic understandings, attitudes and skills which will be essential for the rebuilding of America and the world when the crisis is over and today's children reach adulthood" (ibid., 102–103).

Hanna assigned to teachers the responsibility of looking out for their students' well-being during the national emergency. He called on them to toss off their traditional passivity and neutrality in the community and play the role of community activists in service to their students. "Once she [the teacher] is familiar with the community's inadequacies, she has a responsibility as a citizen to align herself with those community agencies which are working to improve the community" (ibid., 103). Hanna also warned teachers not to ignore parents in the educative process. He pointed out that teachers "often act as if we did not believe it is the parents and not the teachers who create and support the schools for the education of their children." He reminded teachers that their specialized knowledge of child growth and development obligated them to "inform them [parents] in much the same way that a good public health worker informs parents of the best thought and practice in health" (ibid., 104). These two points—the teacher as activist and parents as integral to the work of the school—recur frequently in Hanna's writing.

As a member of the National Resources Planning Board, Hanna helped draft Nine Freedoms as guidelines for postwar planning. In 1942, he wrote an article for *Frontiers of Democracy* about Freedom Number Nine, "The right to rest, recreation, and adventure; the opportunity to enjoy life and take part in an advancing civilization" (Hanna 1942a, 244). Hanna returned to several familiar social critiques in that piece. First, he decried the loss by workers of the "deep satisfaction in knowing that their labor made a difference in the lives of their neighbors" (ibid., 243). He attributed this loss to the fact that in modern industrial production, "for the worker the connection is lost between his repetitive task and the social usefulness of the finished product" (ibid.). He also criticized the rampant materialism of Americans: "The American people typically feel that they must purchase with money their satisfaction through commercial amusements or through the owning of objects" (ibid., 244).

As an alternative to these problems, Hanna called for opportunities for adults and youth to invest their leisure time "in substantial contributions to the general welfare of the community" (ibid.). As examples of such opportunities he described, predictably, community school surveys and cultural events. Strangely, he never mentioned the school as the locus of activity. In a foreshadowing of his future concerns, Hanna advocated young adults satisfying their sense of adventure through work in economic development projects overseas.

In 1942, Paul Hanna coauthored a section in the 1942 *National Resources Development Report* that amounted to a comprehensive plan to provide educational and social services for children through the schools. In his conception, the schools would be centers of organization for providing employment training and services, health and other social services, and recreation, as well as education for youths. However, Hanna intended that "Youth should serve as well as be served" (Hanna and Reeves 1942, 128). He argued that the healthy social development of children and youth requires that they have opportunities to be of use to others. Furthermore, he asserted that the daunting tasks of wartime mobilization and postwar reconstruction would demand their help. He believed that to accomplish America's wartime and postwar goals, "Young people should be admitted as junior partners" (ibid.).

Perhaps the most comprehensive writing Hanna did on the subject of community schools during World War II was an article that he wrote a month prior to the Japanese attack on Pearl Harbor. Hanna was convinced that war would come, and he entitled his article "The Classroom—A Defense Unit" (Hanna 1942b). It was published a few months after war was declared. In the article,

Hanna elaborated on the educational and community service possibilities to be found in the wartime curriculum. He suggested that science classes might study materials that have a strategic defense and military use, and then investigate ways to conserve, extend, and recycle them. Social studies classes might organize community discussion groups on war topics for which they could provide geographical and historical background information. Art classes might design posters and brochures to communicate information and maintain morale. His list went on, but he summarized it with the charge, "Imaginative and loyal teachers and administrators will organize their school work in such ways that America's children and youth may channel an appropriate amount of their energies to the jobs that must be done" (ibid., 376). Such school participation not only hastened the achievement of war goals, Hanna wrote, but also, "as a concomitant our children and youth will develop morale and an appreciation of the American way of life which we are defending" (ibid.).

After the war, Hanna shifted much of his attention to international education. He continued to develop his ideas on community schools in settings overseas, but his experience abroad also informed his writing on community and school relations domestically. In 1947, he led a committee of his graduate students in writing an article for the *Nineteenth Yearbook of the California Elementary School Principals Association* that outlined ways to use community resources in the school program.

Hanna's students advised teachers on techniques for using guest speakers in the classroom, doing service projects, leading field trips, and other activities. Hanna's influence is seen in their dictum that, "Democratic procedures in all human relationships involved should be accepted and practiced" (Hanna 1947b, 82). His stress on the importance of an activity-based curriculum is also echoed in their insistence that, "Facts live when they have been discovered first-hand by children themselves in answer to a real need" (ibid., 87).

Hanna's hand also was apparent in the 1948 publication *Education for All American Children*, a policy statement issued by the Educational Policies Commission of the National Education Association. As a member of the commission staff, Hanna contributed to the section entitled "The School and Its Community." Communication was essential to Hanna's conception of community, and in that chapter he emphasized the importance of communication as a component of community. Another section in the chapter, "The World in Our Time Is One Community," reflected Hanna's emerging internationalism.

The culmination of more than two decades of thinking and writing about community schools was Hanna's 1953 article in the fifty-second yearbook of the National Society for the Study of Education, *The Community School*. Coauthored with Robert A. Naslund, it revealed a deeper understanding of the concept of community and the school's role in it than some of Hanna's previous writing.

The authors began with a familiar critique of traditional classroom education.

> Traditionally, schools have been given the responsibility for developing men and women with sound and liberal education under the assumption that, if this were done, desirable and necessary social changes would inevitably occur through the effort of these individuals in their adult years. With some notable exceptions, schools have existed in a sphere more or less removed from contact with the real problems of community life (Hanna and Naslund 1953, 49–50).

They then described the variety of community school approaches by categorizing schools as those having a community-centered curriculum, a vocations-centered curriculum, a community center function, or a community service program. Hanna had formulated just such a classification system in *Youth Serves the Community*. In his definition, the surveyed schools took varied approaches, but they all shared a common vision of the importance of community–school interaction.

Many elements in the article reiterated Hanna's description of his ideal 'Institute for Individual and Community Development.' However, he was far more pragmatic in this article. For example, he recognized that the schools must be concerned with national unity within a context of local control, and he tried to balance these often conflicting goals. He also incorporated his growing sense of the multiple communities to which all people belong, writing that "The curriculum of the community school is oriented to the needs and problems of the communities of which it is a part as well as to the needs of individuals in those communities. Local problems will naturally receive the greatest attention, but the curriculum incorporates the needs of all communities and directs its efforts toward contributing to their solution" (ibid., 55).

Hanna had planted the seeds of a dilemma out of which he never really found his way. It was the tension between local control of schools and national educational goals. In later years, with his proposal for a national curriculum commission, he seemed to abandon at least one important mechanism of local control in favor of a more uniform curriculum for the schools. However, Hanna was always intrigued by the promise of collective action within the national community.

Hanna and Naslund went on to list criteria for implementing community school arrangements. Many of these were familiar, but some reflected change and growth in Hanna's thought. For instance, the criteria included, "all communities, from the local to the international, consciously use the school as an instrument to improve living," and "the curriculum of the community school is planned to meet the needs of all communities, from local to international" (ibid., 58). They made no attempt to reconcile communities that might have conflicting needs. In some ways, Hanna's later conception of the community school was just as visionary as his earlier one.

Although Paul Hanna's vision of the community school changed somewhat over time, it retained three elements that he thought were essential. First, the curriculum must be oriented toward activity rather than static, passive learning. Second, children have an obligation to serve their communities. Coincidentally, they learn best as they are serving. Third, all schools must seek to incorporate democratic practices in the interactions of all participants.

Hanna had a clear vision of a well-planned, democratically implemented future, and the community school as a vehicle to get there, but he never saw his ideal of the community school realized, nor anything very closely resembling it. One reason for this was timing. The momentum built up by the community school movement in the progressive era of the 1930s came to a halt with the outbreak of World War II. Educational historian Ronald W. Evans cited both political and social causes. He asserted that the 1930s decade was the high point for educational progressivism in its many forms, claiming that "After that time, it became clear that many educational reformers had exceeded the public's zone of toleration. A common perception developed across the land that radical educators centered at Teachers College were attempting to foist socialism on the nation through its schools" (Evans 1998, 8). In addition, Evans believed that World War II repudiated the notion in the public mind, much as World War I had done, that social improvement was possible. He wrote that "World War II brought the death of the progressive impulse and concomitant belief in redemption" (ibid.).

Social science educator Gary R. McKenzie also claimed that progressive education was overwhelmed by changing attitudes brought on by the war. The fascist nations had employed the schools to mold children's thinking to specific ideologies. Some progressive notions of community schooling, including Hanna's, used similar language to describe their programs, and the public would not have it. In addition, a perception grew that the increasingly technological world emerging from the war would require a more coherent, technical form of education. To many, this meant a return to traditional instructional methods. In the same vein, parents' aspirations for their children to attend college exploded in the postwar era, requiring a more strictly discipline-based curriculum than some progressives advocated. Finally, the constraints of wartime vocational training had forced many educational psychologists to reject genetic and behaviorist approaches in favor of the much more efficient, and measurable, cognitive theories of learning (McKenzie 1998).

Another culprit in the failure of Hanna's community school vision may have been the very modernization Hanna tried to counteract. One aspect of the modern world is the specialization of jobs in the community and the social fragmentation that results. The school is the institution designated to provide education. It is the specialist. Other institutions in the community are often uninterested in participating in the education of youth, or they believe that they are inadequate to do so. At best, education will be a secondary priority for them. This attitude counteracts a conception that is vital to the community school's success, namely, that education is the job of the whole community.

Paul Hanna was adept at reading trends, and the postwar trend was away from experimental, progressive approaches like the community school. Coupled with increased attention to his textbook production and international consulting, that trend induced Hanna to write less and less about community schools in the years after the war. Increasingly, he turned to new educational concerns.

ORIGINS OF HANNA'S
SOCIAL STUDIES TEXTBOOKS

The community school was only one of Hanna's modes for the preparation of children for responsible citizenship in a changing world. Early in his academic career, he became involved in the development and writing of textbooks for the schools. These books became a prime expression of his beliefs about citizenship development and social education. Hanna authored more than fifty social studies textbooks over a span of forty years. He also coauthored two series of spelling textbooks, first with Jesse Newlon, and then with Jean Hanna. All of the social studies books reflected Hanna's concern that children learn about the processes of social and economic evolution so that they might learn to control them, but the books can be seen in three distinct groupings. The first, and best known, were the several series of elementary social studies textbooks Hanna produced for Scott, Foresman and Company. These books came to be known as the Hanna Social Studies Series. In the process of writing them, Hanna developed his *expanding communities* curriculum design. The second group were not traditional textbooks, but monthly magazines known as the *Building America* series. The third was a series of three books written for students in the upper grades of elementary school and junior high school. These books specifically addressed the development of economic institutions.

Each of these textbooks and materials fit into Hanna's overall approach to social education. The Hanna Social Studies Series sought to inform young children about the nature and development of social, economic, and political institutions. *Building America* provided older students an opportunity to examine specific problems in American culture, in preparation for taking action to alleviate them. The three-book series on economics, released in 1943, blended information with mild critique in order to prepare students to address issues that had proved to be problematic in the decade of the 1930s. Together, these books provided the intellectual foundation for the social action Hanna called for in promoting community schools. Through them, Hanna promoted curriculum ideas and a model that became pervasive both in the United States and abroad.

By far the best known of Hanna's textbooks are the several series published by Scott, Foresman from the 1930s through the 1960s. These came to be called, collectively, the Hanna Series. In these books, Hanna developed and refined his *expanding communities* curriculum design as he sought to teach students the nature of their social, economic, and political worlds .

Hanna's books were designed to alleviate what he referred to as *cultural lag*:

> It is clear that much of this cultural frustration and confusion is the result of rapid advances in science and technology on the one hand, and on the other hand, the relatively slow adjustments in the laws and institutions and the adaptation of old values to new conditions. We speak of this imbalance as cultural lag . . . This cultural lag is now accepted by many leaders in public education as a major concern of the schools. The lessening of this lag or imbalance is listed as a major goal of education (Hanna 1946, 27).

Although Hanna clearly saw cultural lag as a problem, and looked to the schools to address it, the best curriculum design to effect a solution was not readily apparent. The approaches of the child-centered progressives, in which "the curriculum was that which the child wished to do . . . [and] could only be defined or described after the child had had the experience," were clearly insufficient (Hanna 1974). His work as a curriculum consultant in social studies for the Virginia State Education Department, begun in 1932, provided the seeds of an answer.

Hanna reported on his work with the Virginia Study in a 1934 issue of *Progressive Education*. In that article he declared two purposes for social studies in the schools: to help children in "experi-

encing a realistic understanding and appreciation of human relations," and to allow children to "participate in improving human
relations" (Hanna 1934, 129). During the Virginia Study, Hanna's
search for a pattern in children's interests that would prove an
adequate foundation on which to organize a curriculum was a failure. However, this failure forced him finally to abandon child interest and look for a more objective organizing principle.

The process led him to the central concept upon which all of his
textbooks were based. He hit upon twelve major social functions as
an integrating concept for social science instruction across the
grade levels in Virginia. These social functions were production,
distribution, consumption, conservation, transportation and communication, exploration and settlement, recreation, education, extension of freedom, esthetic expression, religious expression, and
individual integration. Through refinement they became the Nine
Basic Human Activities in his later works.

In order to provide a sequence for the curriculum content surrounding the basic human activities, Hanna and Hollis Caswell
adapted the *expanding environments* pattern then in wide use, in
which children learn concepts first in the context of familiar people,
places, and events, and then move to the less familiar by stages. Leo
W. LeRiche traced the origins of this pattern to curriculum concepts
of the German Herbartians, whose ideas were popularized in the
United States around the turn of the century primarily by Charles
McMurry (LeRiche 1987, 141–142). By 1930, a significant number
of school curriculum guides featured this pattern for sequencing
content (ibid., 148). LeRiche wrote that the expanding environments pattern grew out of the cultural epochs theory of child growth
and development, in which individual child development mimics
the cultural development of mankind through the ages. However,
Hanna and Caswell did not adopt the expanding environments
model for that reason.

Hanna chose his centers of study based on children's experience, not developmental stages. He saw that "Human relations range all the way from the personal relation of 'me' and my family, my school, my community, to the general relation of the exchange of culture between races and nations" (Hanna 1934, 129). Consequently, grades one and two investigated the expression of the twelve social functions in the home, the school, and the local community.

Thus far, the sequence is recognizable to anyone familiar with Hanna's design, but at this point the Virginia plan diverged from what finally became the pattern for his textbooks. The next few grade levels focused on the theme of pioneering. Grades three and four dealt with geographical pioneering, grades five and six with technological pioneering, and grade seven with social pioneering. At grade eight, the focus shifted again to the social world, grade nine focused on the American scene, grade ten on the western world, and grade eleven on the world as a whole. The twelve major social functions were woven throughout these themes. Hanna claimed that his innovation was an improvement over the traditional "chronology of political events in history, the spatial–expansion sequence of geography, or the logical–structural outline of civics," because it was more in tune with "the pupil and his interests, abilities, and needs" (ibid., 132). Hanna later developed the more elaborate expanding communities curriculum design that incorporated a complex pattern of concentric circles of community in which each child participated, but the genesis of that design was in the Virginia curriculum project.

Another theme in Hanna's social studies curriculum for the State of Virginia, later incorporated into his textbooks, was an *integrated* approach to the subject matter. Instead of presenting information classified into the discrete content areas of the traditional social sciences, Hanna organized the subject matter into the twelve major social functions. He felt that approach was more in line with the psychology of learning, but Hanna was neither a social scientist nor a child psychologist. His work in philosophy at Hamline University and his exposure to the work of Harold Rugg may have convinced him that integrating disparate fields of knowledge was desirable. His supreme self-confidence convinced him that he could accomplish the task. Hanna wrote, "Human relations are those unitary life experiences that the specialists have broken up and classified into such subject-matter fields as history, geography, civics, economics, sociology, political science, esthetics, ethics, anthropology, individual and social psychology" (ibid., 130). His design was structured to incorporate information from these fields in a way that would mimic questions that interest children, such as "What makes some people live so differently from us? How were our grandparents able to live without modern machinery?" (ibid.).

Of course, these were Hanna's own versions of children's questions. As Professor O. L. Davis has pointed out, "Curriculum does not integrate *for* individuals. Only individuals integrate; only individuals make their meanings . . . What another (e.g., the teacher) has integrated still must be *engaged* and—it is hoped—be *integrated* by pupils" (Davis 1997, 95–96). Although Hanna's textbooks sought to provide the "intellectually rich curriculum resources and situations" that Davis asserted students require for integration to occur, he certainly framed the world for them in his curriculum design.

For a period of time in the 1930s, Hanna devoted considerable energy to statewide curriculum revisions. In the summer of 1933 he worked on curriculum revision in Arkansas. In 1935, he became chairman of the Society for Curriculum Study's Committee on State-Wide Programs of Curriculum Revision. After moving to Stanford, he worked in a number of curriculum revision projects, including the California Committee on the Scope and Sequence of Major Learnings. From his experiences on this last committee, he wrote a series of articles for the *California Journal of Secondary Education* further refining his curriculum design.

Hanna's design for the California schools was a reiteration of his understanding of the socioeconomic evolution of man. In his conception, man's existence has been a constant struggle to satisfy material wants and needs. The struggle was relatively slow and unsuccessful until modern times, when man gave up superstition and magic in favor of science and reason. This new approach brought relative material prosperity, but the resulting technological change has outpaced the evolution of our social institutions. As a consequence, modern man is at an impasse. The improvements to life that should accompany his newfound control over nature are frustrated by outmoded social controls. The next period of human progress must come from social pioneering, which Hanna claimed "must consist of the cooperative efforts of all interdependent people to plan for the improvement of social and economic objectives deemed desirable and possible" (Hanna 1935b, 425).

Hanna's article went on to propose a curriculum for California's schools much like the one in Virginia. Other ideas familiar from the Virginia Study recurred as well. Prominent in the curriculum design were Hanna's major social functions, providing the scope of study. These had been reduced from twelve to ten, the only differences in the two lists being that production and consumption, separate items on the Virginia list, were now combined, and exploration and settlement were dropped completely. Hanna might have assumed that with physical, technological, and social pioneering as dominant themes, exploration and settlement might be redundant. Hanna again claimed that these functions "encompass all the significant problems confronted in the man-to-man relationship in all cultures existing in time and space" (ibid., 422).

Hanna also made another strong argument for subject matter integration. He claimed that his design covered the "large number of separate subjects formerly taught" (ibid., 421). He claimed that the traditional content area divisions were unnecessary, because "The studies in spiritual and aesthetic living, together with the social studies, constitute the sum total of the curriculum" (ibid.). Consequently, Hanna proposed his design as the core curriculum with "economic geography, economics, sociology, political science, United States history, or state history" relegated to the status of electives (ibid., 426).

Hanna again stressed the necessity of activity in the learning process. In describing the function of the California Committee, he gave the objectives of social studies in the schools as, "(1) to direct pupils in such experiences as will develop a realistic *understanding* [emphasis his] and appreciation of human relations; (2) to direct pupils to participate in improving human relations" (ibid., 421). Later in the article, he reiterated the point: "But *understanding* alone is not sufficient. Teachers of the social studies have the further obligation of providing students with experiences in *improving* human relations [emphases his]" (ibid., 422). In a companion piece written the following year, Hanna again proposed that his curriculum design was the solution to the "vexing problem" of "translating into classroom practice those major educational objectives for which as yet we have no demonstrated pattern of pupil experiences" (Hanna 1936b, 375). Hanna often made audacious claims in his writing, in part as a rhetorical tool to establish a polemic position, but also in part as an expression of his tremendous self-confidence.

Perhaps Hanna's most biting indictment of the traditional social studies curriculum came in a 1937 article published in *Childhood Education*. In it, he drew a distinction between *social studies*, "which brought to mind many weary hours of listless memorization of history dates, geographic place locations, and civic structures and virtues," and what he preferred to label *social education*, which was intended to "develop the child's ability actually to live more effectively and richly as a member of a social group" (Hanna 1937c, 74). Hanna's view was that the underlying purpose of teaching the social sciences was lost in efforts to convey the factual information. As evidence, he claimed that

With all our reciting of the facts that Columbus, an Italian, discovered America in 1492 and that the Pilgrims, from England,
landed at Plymouth in 1620 we go on hating foreigners as much
as if we hadn't learned the historic fact that most of us are originally from foreign shores. With all of our 'book learning' of the
structure of city and state government we still have corruption in
high places and indifference among our citizens. With all our
geographic fact teaching we face increasing national insecurity
because geography has not taught us to conserve our soil, forests,
and other natural resources. Nor have we much evidence that
through social studies we have aided in promoting happier family
relations, bettering juvenile social behavior, obtaining higher
standards of living, or generally in solving the vast number of
problems that plague our culture (ibid.).

Hanna's familiar solution was an activity-oriented curriculum that
would provide children "more experiences in which they can contribute to socially significant projects" (ibid., 77).

By the mid-1930s, however, Hanna was doing more than pro-
posing solutions in narrow-circulation journals. His consulting
work in local and state education agencies had afforded him the
opportunity to experiment with his scope and sequence ideas in
actual classroom practice. In some California school districts,
such as the Santa Barbara city schools, his *basic human activities*
had become the scope of the districtwide curriculum (Santa Barbara City Schools 1935). At the same time, Hanna was developing
textbooks with the Scott, Foresman and Company that would
make his model the dominant one in schools throughout the country.

In 1935, after considering offers from other publishers, Paul
Hanna entered into a contract with Scott, Foresman and Company
to produce the first two textbooks that would eventually become the
embodiment of his expanding communities curriculum design.
Harry Johnston of Scott, Foresman and William S. Gray, a renowned reading specialist, had developed the idea of a unified set

of curriculum materials built around a core of reading texts (Hanna 1974). Vocabulary, sentence structure, paragraph structure, and the like were first introduced in the reading books, then reinforced in series publications in science, social studies, and other subject areas. The program was called the Everyday Life Stories Series, and it relied heavily on stories as a means of conveying information. Hanna developed immense respect for Gray and his ideas while working on the project, remembering him as "one of the most gentle scholars that I have ever known" (Hanna 1974).

Hanna wrote *Peter's Family* in 1935 and *David's Friends at School* in 1936, initially as part of the Everyday Life Stories Series. Their purpose was to introduce children in first grade to similarities in the ways the basic human activities were carried out in the home and in the school. The teacher's edition for each book included a cumulative vocabulary list indexed to the pages on which the words appeared in the book, suggested activities for each section, and an index of social studies concepts showing where the application of each concept could be found in the book. Such aids for the teacher were typical features of curriculum materials in the 1930s, an era in which teachers often taught "from the textbook" (Cuban 1993, 71).

More books followed in quick succession. In 1937, *Susan's Neighbors at Work* was issued to "broaden the pupil's understanding of human relationships and increase his ability to participate constructively in the life of his home, his school, and his community" (Hanna, Anderson, and Gray 1937, 232). The book reflected Hanna's design, in that students were shown how the basic human activities introduced earlier in the series were carried out by workers in the community. The teacher's edition followed the pattern of the earlier books. Teachers were expected to use activities or discussion to introduce new material, then help students read through sections in the text and devise activities to extend learning or to answer questions that arose.

The third grade book in the series, *Centerville*, described the interactions of a town and its surrounding areas in performing the basic human activities. Students in the text were portrayed as active participants in the community, visiting businesses, contributing to community events, and the like. This portrayal must have exerted subtle pressure on teachers to copy that model in providing instructional activities for their own students. If subtlety was ineffective, the Chapter for Teachers at the back of the book admonished that, "Reading Centerville straight through without discussion or the exploring of many by-paths which are opened to view is not recommended" (Hanna, Anderson, and Gray 1938, 278). For the less imaginative teacher, the authors included a section entitled Special Study, listing ideas that the book only touches on that could be elaborated, and one entitled Things for Children to Do, with suggestions for productive activities. The To Do section reminded teachers that, "Doing things is necessary in the study of social ideas" (ibid., 280). The Chapter for Teachers also suggested that two questions frame the study of each reading section: "How is Centerville different from our community?" and "How is Centerville like our community?" Through careful investigation of these questions, the authors hoped that children would "learn that all people, by living together in communities of various kinds, obtain food, clothes, homes, entertainment, and all other necessities of American Life" (ibid., 279).

The fourth and fifth grade books in the series, *Without Machinery* and *Pioneering in Ten Communities*, expressed Hanna's grand curriculum design based on the state curriculum studies by focusing on technological, geographic, and social pioneering. The front material of *Without Machinery* acknowledged the contributions of academic specialists to the book's presentations. Two anthropologists, one orientalist, and one Egyptologist received thanks. This was the first book in Hanna's series to acknowledge the input of social scientists. It represented one of his contributions to the social studies—enlisting prominent social scientists in curriculum development for elementary schools. In later years, even more social scientists expressed a willingness to work in the curriculum development field when they perceived that Hanna had created a serious-minded program for instruction.

Possibly due to the influence of the social science professionals, *Without Machinery* opened with an academic discussion of the ideas and concepts explained in the book, instead of moving immediately into a story as the earlier books had. The book then developed, through stories, the overall concept that people in other parts of the world perform tasks similar to the ones Americans do, but without the help of the machinery that Americans use. It did this by profiling everyday life in villages around the world. In the Chapter for Teachers, Hanna expressed his concern that children understand the dilemma of modern man: "Reading about people who don't build machinery, who develop ways of living to fit the circumstances in which they find themselves, helps the child to understand the changes which the machine has brought in our own lives" (Hanna 1939, 272–273).

Hanna's books were hugely successful. Within a few years, they had sold nearly 1.5 million copies, second only to the Rugg series in social studies textbook sales (*Time* 1943, 25). Hanna benefited in several ways. First, his royalty of two percent of sales brought income when he most needed it to pay the huge expenses incurred in the construction of the Hanna-Honeycomb House. More significantly for his career, the textbooks spread his name far and wide. Textbook salesmen promoted Hanna as they sold the books. Hanna recalled that "The sales force at World Book, the sales force at Scott, Foresman, the sales force at Houghton Mifflin, the sales force at any number of agencies and professional educational organizations had gotten in the door by saying, 'we want to bring you a message from Paul Hanna'" (Hanna 1974).

He acknowledged that these sales techniques had boosted his career:

> By constantly hearing the name of Hanna people said, 'Well, let's take a look at him. Let's invite him in as a consultant; let's have him speak to our teachers, or we will invite him to write an article.' These things have a way of reinforcing each other. I know I would not be where I am today if it hadn't been that I had salesmen and consultants in commercial organizations who just daily rapped on doors and talked about, 'here is a product that Hanna has conceived' (Hanna 1974).

The textbooks were even printed overseas; a number of editions include copyrights in the Philippines. From the 1930s through the 1970s, Hanna promoted the Scott, Foresman textbooks whenever he spoke or wrote about his curriculum design, and whenever he promoted the books, he spread the influence of his design. This reflexive relationship became so important to the publisher that in 1938, Willis Scott of Scott, Foresman annotated a contract signed that year with the remark, "Dr. Hanna's name shall appear first on each book" (Scott 1938).

TEXTBOOKS AS TOOLS FOR SOCIAL CRITIQUE

The Hanna Series established Paul Hanna's reputation as an educational leader. It also introduced into thousands of classrooms his curriculum concept that children should investigate the basic human activities as they have been performed by people throughout human history. However, Hanna thought that social critique was just as essential to children's citizenship development as was the development of a fundamental knowledge of their social, economic, and political environments. This critique was a necessary first step in any community service project, or in any other work toward social improvement. Hanna's father and the currents of progressivism surrounding him in his youth and early adulthood influenced him in this belief. For example, education historian David Warren Saxe pointed out that as early as 1916 curriculum panels such as the Social Studies Committee of the Committee on the Reorganization of Secondary Education called for social criticism as an integral part of the school experience. Unfortunately, curriculum materials to support these efforts were not rapidly forthcoming and the movement languished for some years (Saxe 1991, 80). Paul Hanna hoped to correct the situation by providing attractive, high-quality supplemental texts to augment classroom discussions and projects in social improvement.

Teachers, however, are not known as pioneers of social change. In fact, this charge was brought against George Counts's stirring arguments for greater social activism on the part of schools by some of those who opposed his *Dare the School Build a New Social Order?* (1932). Many teachers conceived their role to be maintenance of the culture, passing it on to children intact rather than promoting change. In responding to Counts, Agnes de Lima wrote that teachers were "a class long trained to social docility" (de Lima 1932, 317). Moreover, compiling information for students on social problems that faced the nation was a daunting task for teachers, and Hanna understood the need for curriculum materials to help teachers accomplish it. In 1934, he approached his colleagues in the Society for Curriculum Study to enlist their support for the production of materials that could be used to aid classroom discussion of problems facing the country. The result was the *Building America* series of monthly magazines for the classroom.

Hanna presented his concept for Building *America* at the 1934 annual meeting of the Society for Curriculum Study. He hoped that thought-provoking pictorial materials would prompt school children to investigate and work to improve social conditions in the United States. An announcement in the Society's *Curriculum Journal* claimed that

> *Building America* tries to make American youth and adults more sensitive to the problems which must be faced if the nation is to realize its great possibilities. To promote a realistic understanding of the basic activities and problems of American life, economic, political, and social, *Building America* plans to select and present verified data; as objectively and impartially as possible; it plans to suggest the various sides of controversial issues, holding to no special solutions and leaving the reader free to formulate his own conclusions (Society for Curriculum Study 1935a, 3).

Some Society members worried that the project would be too controversial, but Hanna was not deterred. In an article written the following year for *Progressive Education*, he divided progressive educators into two groups: the romantics and the realists. Romantics, he wrote, "recognize and to some extent grant the major maladjustments in our age, but they would not deal directly with negative aspects of the environment. Children, they say, must be protected from the destructive influences of poverty, squalor, corruption, meanness, and fear (Hanna 1935a, 318).

Realists, on the other hand, "guide these children into facing this, our baffling world, and learn the techniques with which we can cross over the threshold into the promise of tomorrow" (ibid., 319). Hanna placed himself squarely in the realist camp and went on to brand the romantics as un-American. He wrote, "To ignore these tragic conditions in America is to perpetuate the charge that progressive education is essentially class education; and if class education is the dynamic of this movement, it is thoroughly un-American" (ibid., 320).

The inaugural issue of *Building America* was entitled "Housing." It was dedicated to "the national problem of providing good homes for everybody" (Society for Curriculum Study 1935a, 2). It was distributed with a promotional brochure that stated, "We believe *Building America* represents a unique type of curriculum material which will assist in making American youth and adults consciously intelligent about the problems of our time" (ibid.). The brochure claimed that the magazines would contribute to all social science courses, as well as "science, health, home economics, art, industrial arts, and other areas of the modern school curriculum" (ibid.). It explained the origin of the series as a response to the "persistent and widespread demand of educators for a new type of classroom material that will give students a working knowledge of social and economic forces and institutions" (ibid., 1). It touted the *problem method*, by which "Every issue of *Building America* is presented to the student as a problem to be solved. The facts and ideas presented in each number and the questions raised are all intended to challenge the student's thinking and help him to enter upon some constructive line of thought toward a solution to these problems (ibid.).

High standards of scholarship were also claimed: "The facts presented in the *Building America* series are the result of painstaking research into the most reliable sources available. In addition, these materials are carefully reviewed by a representative Editorial Board and by reputable authorities on the topics treated" (ibid.). Finally, the brochure called on "all friends of education" to promote the new publication (ibid., 2).

Following the issue on housing, *Building America* issues were published at the beginning of each month, October through May, from 1935 until 1948. The 1935–1936 volume included titles such as "Food," "Transportation," and "Health." Paul Hanna's direct influence as chairman of the editorial board was seen in topics such as "Men and Machines," "Communication," "Power," "Recreation," and "Youth Faces the World." Each issue included many photographs and enough text to inform students and stimulate discussion.

A teacher's guide accompanied each issue, and the guide to the housing issue is typical. In its introduction, the authors offered the following statement of purpose:

The progress of our democracy and the advancement of our American standard of living have been dependent upon the education of the mass of our people with regard to the major social and economic problems which they confronted. Today even more than in the past the school as an educational institution is obligated to help young people to understand and to cope with these problems which so vitally affect their welfare no less than the welfare of adults. If correctly presented, these crucial problems of life can grip the imagination of our youth and in turn stimulate them to work for a satisfactory solution (Society for Curriculum Study 1935b, 1).

The guide suggested that the housing issue might be used in the Problems of Democracy course then popular in schools, as well as for "adult discussion groups" (ibid.). It then proceeded to give some detail as to how the issue might be used in a variety of classes across the curriculum.

The longest section of the guide offered a wealth of ideas on age- and course-appropriate activities teachers might use to extend the classroom use of the housing issue. It reflected Hanna's concern for the importance of activities by arguing

One of the most important principles of psychology is that people *learn by doing* [emphasis theirs]. This principle applied to education means that the teacher should provide a wealth of activities in which students participate. These activities stimulate their interest in a problem, help them to acquire vital information, assist them in achieving habits of cooperative work, and finally bring them face to face with the world outside the school (ibid., 2).

Building America had wide appeal throughout the educational community. By its second year of publication, the Society for Curriculum Study was unable to accommodate the number of requests for subscriptions. The Society instructed Hanna to seek a publisher better equipped to handle the large volume of printing and distribution. In a qualitative measure of the series' popularity, Hanna collected testimonials from teachers and administrators across the country. A high school teacher from Philadelphia stated, "Building America seems to me decidedly teachable material . . . I hope the series goes on and on" (Hanna 1936?, 4). A junior high school teacher in Maine wrote, "I find it of great help in teaching Vocational Information." A superintendent in Minnesota commented, "This material challenges the imagination" (ibid., 6). One in Arkansas claimed, "This publication is very unique and we think it will serve to 'Build America'" (ibid.). An elementary school principal in Michigan wrote, "This looks like a real contribution to teaching. I hope to see it widely used in our system" (ibid.). One in New York City predicted, "Building America promises to be an excellent magazine for all grades from kindergarten up. Covering so many subjects it will assist in complete correlation. It solves the difficulty of securing suitable pictures and of course is highly educational as a visual aid" (ibid., 7).

A junior high school principal thought that the series was so "beautiful and suggestive" that it "ought to be on the New York City supply list for Junior High Schools." A curriculum director in Virginia wrote, "The material is a most valuable tool for teaching. It deals with vital problems in an interesting and understandable way for girls and boys. It seems to be a splendid contribution to education" (ibid.).

Unfortunately, *Building America* ran afoul of changing trends in education. The World War II and postwar eras saw a turn away from practices of educational progressivism such as social criticism and the problem method of instruction. The ultrapatriotic mood of the times caused some to look on social criticism with suspicion, and some politicians chose to further their careers by attacking such practices. This led, in 1947, to a California legislative investigation of the ideological foundations of *Building America* and its founders. The negative publicity generated by this investigation resulted in canceled subscriptions and the magazine's ultimate demise.

Although not as directly in the social critique mode of instruction as *Building America*, perhaps the clearest expression of what Paul Hanna wanted to communicate to schoolchildren about their culture was embodied in a three-volume series of textbooks published during World War II by Scott, Foresman and Company. These books, written for fifth, sixth, and seventh graders, were an extension of the Hanna Series textbooks for the lower grades. They focused particularly on economic concepts and also stressed such perennial Hanna concerns as the interdependence of all peoples.

The first book in the series, *This Useful World*, set the stage for the volumes that followed. Designed for fifth graders, it incorporated physical geography to describe the abundance of natural resources in various locations on the globe. Then, employing concepts from cultural geography, anthropology, and economics, it demonstrated how these resources are used in the production of goods.

The second book in the series, *Making the Goods We Need*, was written for sixth graders by Hanna and his Stanford colleagues I. James Quillen and Paul B. Sears. Its stated purpose was "To help the youngster of this age see how these things [modern technological advancements] have come to be, how they affect his life and that of his fellows, and how they may be used for human advancement" (Hanna, Quillen, and Sears 1943, 274). The textbook was a departure from Hanna's earlier ones in that it did not convey information in story form. Instead, it used history as the narrative structure and stressed elements of economic theory where applicable. The conclusion included an admonition that is typical Hanna:

> Man has used his hands and brain to invent machines which produce more and more goods. Now he must use his intelligence to invent ways of using the goods produced so that more and more people can get the things they need and want. Man must invent ways of helping people to live at peace with one another so that they will use modern machines, airplanes, for example, to improve life, not to destroy it. Man must invent ways of helping people use their spare time so that they can lead happy lives even though

their work may not be particularly interesting. These are some of
the great tasks of the future. They are tasks that mean work for
you and other young people who are now in school (ibid., 270).

The third book in the series, *Marketing the Things We Use*,
targeted seventh graders. Coauthored with Edward A. Krug, it presented the many facets of distribution and promotion, and also
invited students to engage in mild social critique. One of the stated
goals of the book was to encourage students to "hold to and act in
accordance with democratic values" (Hanna and Krug 1943, 305).
Chapter Ten, entitled Rules for Playing the Game, applied those
values to business. It described honest and dishonest practices in
retailing, producing, transporting, and storing goods. It explained
why fair play is important in maintaining a strong economy and
gave children tips on how to encourage honesty in business. Of
particular interest was a section on advertising practices. Hanna
felt that one reason for the attacks on Harold Rugg's textbooks was
the way in which they dealt with advertising in America. According
to Hanna, "Rugg wrote a chapter on advertising in which he stated
that advertising contributed little or nothing to goods and services
and was an unnecessary expense to the consumer" (Hanna 1973a).
Hanna, by contrast, merely characterized the excesses of advertising as inconsistent with *democratic values* and *fair play*. This de-
fused much potential criticism that might have been leveled against
him.

Student chapters in the three books concluded with exercises
and suggestions for extending student learning. The chapter on
advertising even recommended that students organize panel discussions on such topics as "the need for more protection for the
consumer," and "how advertising increases our wants" (Hanna and
Krug 1943, 294). Likewise, each book concluded with a Chapter for
Teachers that described the purposes of the textbook, provided
instruction in proper lesson planning, and offered suggestions for

learning activities. One section dealt with the desired behavioral outcomes of instruction. Another listed the generalizations to be found in each text chapter and explained how to make the best use of them. A final section suggested useful visual aids.

THE *EXPANDING COMMUNITIES* MODEL REFINED

In the years following his initial success with the Hanna Series, Paul Hanna continued to refine his curriculum model. In a 1942 address to the American Association of School Administrators, Hanna walked his audience through a fictional school employing his curriculum design. The first grade classes learned reading and number skills as they focused on the basic human activities carried out in the family, school, and neighborhood. Second grade classes investigated the local community. Hanna explained,

> We observe that these second graders are eagerly studying the workers in their community who protect them, provide them with food and clothing, transport people and goods, and the workers who help the community to have a good time. These children see that community life is made possible by a division of work and that only as each worker gives his best effort to carrying out his responsibility can the total community welfare be served (Hanna 1942c, 163).

Hanna's vision of the third and fourth grade classrooms reflected the scope and sequence established in his Scott, Foresman books, but he introduced something new for the upper grades. Instead of focusing on pioneering efforts in various spheres, the fifth and sixth grade children in his fictional school embarked on studies of *larger-than-national communities*. Seventh and eighth graders would study man's creation of social, political, and economic institutions in order to "facilitate their human associations" (ibid., 165). Hanna and Quillen developed a scheme for carrying the curriculum design through high school and even into the first two years of college. Their three-part textbook series on economic concepts, described above, was the first step in this series for older students, but administrative obstacles at Scott, Foresman kept their plan from reaching fruition (Hanna 1974).

In the 1940s, a revision of the Everyday Life Stories series reflected a refinement of Hanna's curriculum design. Hanna had come to see that technological advances create greater possibilities for communication, as well as for production. As communication increases, it enlarges communities. In a 1946 article for *Educational Leadership*, he outlined a new scope and sequence with a wider purpose. Its overall theme was "Helping children and youth develop understanding and behavior essential to survival and progress in our world community" (Hanna 1946, 30).

As reflected in the Scott, Foresman textbooks, Hanna's design became more tightly focused on the expanding communities pattern. A revised *Peter's Family* (1942) stressed how the basic human activities are played out in the home. *David's Friends at School* (1936) became *Hello, David* (1944), focusing on the school community. *Susan's Neighbors at Work* (1936) was replaced with *Someday Soon* (1948), presenting the concepts that the child's neighbors do helpful work in the community and that the child himself will do so *someday soon*. *Centerville* (1938) became *New Centerville* (1948), and *Without Machinery* (1935) was replaced by *Cross-Country* (1942).

The new books all conveyed information through stories as the earlier editions had, but *Cross-Country* was perhaps the most imaginative of the series. To present concepts of the basic human activities as practiced in a variety of communities throughout the United States, Hanna and his coauthor, geographer Clyde Kohn, followed a fictional family as they traveled by car from Los Angeles to Washington, D.C. This device allowed the introduction of sophisticated geographic information and skills. A floor map on which students could trace the family's progress accompanied the book. Hanna hoped that this beginning geography text would "arouse the interests and initiate the skills and attitudes which will enable a child to evaluate the geographical significance of what he does, reads, hears, sees, thinks, or otherwise experiences for the rest of his life" (Hanna and Kohn 1950, 153).

The revised books reflected a growing trend toward publishers' including *teacher aids* in textbooks. Less was left to the teacher's discretion. Each unit featured *work pages* that included activities for modeling attitudes, concepts, and values. Instruction and ideas on lesson planning were included for teachers, as well as a bibliography: Books for Teachers and Parents. Teachers were encouraged to extend lessons with activities, become familiar with their students' home lives, and incorporate parents in the learning process. Separate teacher's editions were published to accompany many of the revised books, a feature not found in Hanna's earlier series.

The version of Hanna's Scott, Foresman textbooks produced in the 1950s and 1960s, known as the Basic Social Studies Series, part of the larger Curriculum Foundation Series, reflected further refinements in his model as well as new trends in educational publishing. The series clearly mirrored Hanna's growing interest in international communities of people, with a progression of titles like *At Home* (1956); *At School* (1957); *In the Neighborhood* (1956); *In City, Town, and Country* (1959); *In All Our States* (1956); *In the Americas* (1956); and *Beyond the Americas* (1956). In a new iteration of his design, Hanna conceived of the sequence as a set of concentric circles to represent the expanding communities of people, instead of one axis on a grid. Each widening circle represented a larger community to which children belong. As children matured through the grade levels, they were exposed to these ever-widening communities. Here, at last, was the expanding communities model for which Hanna is best known. Through this model, Hanna finally achieved a design in which he combined both the historical concept of continuity and change over time and the geographical concept of continuity and change in space with material from the other social sciences to explain to children the evolution and nature of their social world.

The basic human activities continued to define the scope of the content as children made their way through the concentric spheres, but those activities also underwent refinement. They were reduced from ten in number to nine:

> 1. Protecting and conserving life, health, resources, and property.
> 2. Producing, distributing, and consuming food, clothing, shelter, and other consumer goods and services. 3. Creating and producing tools and technics. 4. Transporting people and goods. 5. Communicating ideas and feelings. 6. Providing education. 7. Providing recreation. 8. Organizing and governing. 9. Expressing esthetic and spiritual impulses (Hanna 1956a, 36).

Hanna sponsored a series of doctoral dissertations at Stanford University in the 1950s in order to identify generalizations from the social sciences that might be incorporated into this model.

The specific communities of people and the placement of their study in the schools also was more sharply defined in the new series. In kindergarten and first grade, students focused on the home, family, and school. In second grade, they studied the neighborhood, and in third grade, attention turned to the local community. Fourth graders studied the state and regions of states. Fifth grade students studied the nation and the inter-American community. Sixth graders focused on the United States and the Atlantic community, seventh graders studied the United States and the Pacific community, and eighth graders studied United States history. Hanna organized a second phase of doctoral dissertations to determine the proper placement of social science content in each of his concentric spheres, but that research was never completed.

The format of the Scott, Foresman books also was much refined for these 1950s editions. The books reflected an increasing concern

that children be instructed in high-level academic content as opposed to simply by creative methodologies. The texts, particularly
for the upper grades, eschewed the storytelling of the earlier editions, and they included more social scientists as coauthors. Hanna
expressed his view on the *content versus method* debate in a 1954
issue of the *NEA Journal*. He wrote,

> I cannot agree with those who say, 'we teach children; we do not
> teach subject matter.' Children learn *something* and we are defi-
> nitely concerned that this something be good subject matter. I
> cannot agree with some who say that *any* content is of equal value
> with *any other*, or that content generally must be subordinate to
> process. Both content *and* method—both the stuff of culture and
> the nature of childhood—are indispensable to a balanced curric-
> ulum [emphases his] (Hanna 1954, 273).

Certainly, this attitude of Hanna's toward content helped attract
social scientists to the work of producing social studies textbooks.

The books also reflected a growing trend toward *teacher-proof*
curriculum materials. Teacher aids composed two-thirds of the text
in some cases. *At Home* began with an essay to teachers entitled
"Between Two Worlds." The essay concerned child development
and children's adjustments to school in the early grades. It contained suggestions for classroom management practices, establishing teacher–student interactions, evaluation, and learning activities. A teacher's guide entitled Guidebook detailed teaching ideas
compiled from teachers throughout the United States, lists of helpful books, and audiovisual materials. The familiar vocabulary lists
were appended to the books, along with "thinking abilities, social
understandings, behavior traits" to be developed in each section.

A major emphasis in the Basic Social Studies books was citizenship education. Hanna had always been keen on that subject as a
purpose of social education, but he had not always been so blatant
about it in his texts. The Second World War and postwar tensions
in the world were having their effect. Hanna wrote, "We live in a

confused world arena in which poverty, disease, ignorance, fear, and greed combine to enslave peoples under the banners of communism and fascism. We cannot leave to chance the development of democratic understanding and behavior in our young" (Hanna 1954, 274).

Throughout the series, Hanna admonished teachers to make citizenship education a primary goal. For example, in *At Home* he wrote, "Children are not talked into citizenship. They learn it slowly by practicing it and by assuming its obligations and responsibilities as well as its privileges" (Hanna, Hoyt, and Gray 1956, 9). In *At School*, Hanna reminded teachers that "Learning responsible citizenship in the home and school communities is a continuing experience for children" (Hanna and Hoyt 1957, 5). The teacher's guide in *In City, Town, and Country*, the third grade text, concludes with a section entitled, Your Goal—Responsible Citizenship.

Paul Hanna was a prolific writer, in part due to his tremendous energy. *Time* magazine called him "one of the most rapid-moving parts of the Stanford School of Education machine" (15 November, 1943). Harold Drummond, who served as Hanna's secretary for a time in the late 1940s, described his writing routine: "During that time I typed everything he wrote (usually the first draft on a Saturday, keeping up with his handwriting a page at a time, so that he could start proofreading and revising as soon as he had finished) . . . we started again Sunday morning—and tried to get finished before we were both exhausted" (Drummond 1997).

Only working at such a rapid pace enabled Hanna to teach, write, and travel extensively. Those activities, in turn, spread his influence while enriching him and his publisher. A consolidated contract dated 1966 paid Hanna royalties for 49 different Scott, Foresman titles. This contract was a statement of both Hanna's financial success and his great influence over educational content and practice.

Despite its popularity, Hanna's curriculum design drew opposition. Some complained that Hanna's interdisciplinary approach to the social sciences minimized the significant contributions and perspectives of the individual social science disciplines. In their book *Teaching Social Studies Skills*, June Chapin and Richard Gross wrote, "the interdisciplinary approach refuted the usefulness of the unique, separate social science structure" (Chapin and Gross 1973, 133). Others objected to the *step-by-step* nature of Hanna's concentric circles design, asserting that it did not allow students to revisit topics. Clements, Fielder, and Tabachnick claimed that "The Expanding Communities design, for example, seems to move in a direct line from the communities composed of family and neighborhood outward to the communities composed of nations. Linear schemes characteristically do not repeat or return to particular topics" (Clements, Fielder, and Tabachnick 1966, 144). Ord added that "this particular approach is too age–grade oriented. For example, the family has value as a focus of study for more than the first years a child is in school" (Ord 1972, 41). Hollis Caswell leveled a critique against Hanna's expanding communities when he wrote that Hanna's design for the Virginia curriculum placed too much emphasis on learning the content of social life, "and too little on the individual appreciative and creative phases" (Caswell 1935, 184). Hanna responded that his design was not intended to eliminate individual interest. He wrote, "curriculum design must *not* be interpreted as an excuse for returning to a traditional curriculum . . . We must be eternally vigilant to foster the unique and creative potential of each personality, for in this diversity of human resources lies the secret power of a democratic community to keep on growing" (Hanna 1954, 274).

Others also thought Hanna's design was too restrictive. Some argued that defining scope in terms of the basic human activities discouraged the use of current issues and problems in the classroom (Ord 1972, 41). Hanna had developed *Building America* to meet this need, but it was not a part of his Scott, Foresman textbooks. Some complained that there was too much repetition in the themes presented in the early grades (ibid., 42).

Professor Malcolm Douglass, a former Hanna doctoral advisee, and the National Council for History Education criticized Hanna's integrated approach as not academically rigorous enough. Hanna responded by emphasizing that he did not advocate creating a curriculum based solely on child interest. He contended that his design was *not* based on principles that, "1. The curriculum be limited to a child's interest in his immediate community; 2. The central theme or continuing core of the curriculum be a study of the local community; 3. We debunk reading or burn our books, nor depend primarily for our instructional material on community resources; 4. The curriculum be confined to the 'here and now'" (Hanna 1942c, 163).

The impact of such a critique is seen in Hanna's broadening of the course study in the upper grades and in the pains he took to enlist social scientists to ensure that his content reflected current thought in their fields. This was especially true of the last series he worked on for Scott, Foresman—*Investigating Man's World* (1970). The story of that series is told later in this chapter.

Some have claimed that Hanna's analysis of the dilemma of modern man is so deeply philosophical, and his classroom approach to it required such a broad understanding of the social sciences, that effective application of his ideas was beyond most teachers. In his 1935 text, *Curriculum Development*, Hollis Caswell discussed the Virginia Study at length. He sharply criticized the Virginia scope and sequence for holding unrealistic expectations of teachers. "Many teachers, as now trained," he wrote, "do not have adequate background in the content subjects to deal with many aspects of centers of interest included in an outline such as the one in the Virginia course of study" (Caswell 1935, 184). Hanna was concerned about adequate teacher education as well, and that may account for the steady growth of teacher aid materials and instructional essays included in his series.

Perhaps the most effective critiques of Hanna's work deal with the concentric circles model for curriculum design. The concerns raised by longtime social studies educator Richard Gross typified this point of view. He contended that although it seems logical to introduce information to students within a familiar context such as the home and family, when Hanna first proposed it there was no psychological support for such an approach. He added that in an age of instantaneous electronic communications, Hanna's slow progression through the communities of man was unnecessary. Through exposure to modern communications media, many children have information on foreign lands even before they enter school (Gross 1998). This critique was echoed by Rooze and Foerster, who wrote that "Such a pattern ignored the impact of mass media to which children are exposed and which vastly increased their experiential base" (Rooze and Foerster 1972, 33). Hanna never answered these concerns, but he might have insisted that however flawed the design, at the time of its development it effectively addressed the need for children to be presented with adequate information on the nature of their world so that they could participate as intelligent citizens to improve it.

THE INTERNATIONAL COMMUNITY

By the outbreak of World War II, Paul Hanna had begun to draw on foreign school systems, both to inform his understanding of the American school experience and to export his educational ideas. His experiences working with school systems overseas had important impacts on his curriculum thought from the postwar era until the end of his life. First, his concept of community expanded to incorporate regions of nations, hemispheres, and finally the entire globe. At the same time his concept of citizenship expanded to include citizenship functions and styles more appropriate to developing nations without a strong democratic tradition. Oddly, as his view of citizenship became more inclusive his political ideology narrowed considerably. From his observations of fascist ideology in World War II and communinism in the postwar years, Hanna affirmed his commitment to liberal democratic values. He also gained from these observations a keener understanding of the use of schools to promote social, economic, and political ideologies.

His earliest writing on the subject of education overseas resulted from his travels in Latin America at the behest of the Coordinator for Inter-American Affairs. In an address to the 1941 annual meeting of the National Education Association, Hanna called on the United States and its educational organizations to help nations in that region improve their educational systems. He also pointed to comparisons between the traditional education in those countries which did not seem to serve their needs for modernization, and the traditional secondary curriculum in the United States, which did not serve the "needs of community or national life" (Hanna 1941b, 125). He called for an entirely new curriculum that would be "directly related to improving the health, sanity, safety, housing, civic beauty, recreation, family relations, and economic income of every American community. Further, we must see that our economy is so organized that each young person has a chance and a challenge to engage in useful work" (ibid.).

The following year, Hanna wrote an article for *School and Society*, a journal edited by William C. Bagley, which sounded themes he repeated throughout the rest of his career. The wartime stance of the Americas helped him to see the necessity of international cooperation and the part education could play in promoting it—not just in terms of providing information, but also in modifying children's attitudes. He called for "modification of the curriculum of schools in the United States to help our citizens understand the nature of hemispheric cooperation" (Hanna 1942d, 458). He called attention to the connections between education and economic growth abroad, and security at home: "By assisting the common man to attain a better standard of living, and by assisting the scholars and the political leaders to prepare themselves for their life work we, in the long run, will be contributing immeasurably to our own security and welfare" (ibid., 462). Education abroad, in support of American national security, became a major focus of Hanna's work in the postwar world.

As much as any educator at the time, Hanna foresaw that the interdependence of the postwar world would be the key to keeping the peace. He proposed new emphases in education to prepare for a new world. In a 1942 article for *Childhood Education*, he warned that achieving the goals of the Atlantic Charter would require "world-wide institutions of government, courts, economic authorities, and education." He wrote that such world cooperation meant that "we shall never return to many of the ways of life that we have known before" (Hanna 1942e, 3). To prepare for the new world order, Hanna proposed that schools "universally teach more accurate and more inclusive concepts of the unity of our planet" in order to counteract the "anarchistic nationalism" previously taught (ibid., 4). He assigned to schools the unique responsibility of preparing students with both the knowledge and the attitudes to "take the leadership at the peace conferences throughout the century in establishing a world community organization" (ibid., 3).

At the same time, Hanna was increasingly cognizant of the reflexive relationship between schools and society. At the annual meeting of the National Education Association (NEA) in 1942, he warned his audience that

> Education will inevitably be shaped by the pattern of the postwar world. If we follow the course of imperialism, we shall educate our youth to their role as citizens of a ruling nation. If an international organization is established, then education will emphasize world citizenship. If we move back to a position of isolation

and the other nations go their competing ways, we had better
prepare our children to be ready for the next world war (Hanna
1942f, 77).

Although thoroughly an internationalist, Hanna was not open to
education from just any ideological viewpoint. He claimed that
"Education is essential for the survival and improvement of democracy—but not *any* education. *Only the education appropriate for
free men* will suffice [emphasis his]" (ibid. 76).

In a visionary article written in 1950, Hanna predicted the
sources and nature of change in the second half of the twentieth
century. He foresaw ever-increasing interdependence among the
earth's peoples—socially, economically, and politically. To allay the
fears of Americans about this development, Hanna pointed to the
analogy of the historic shift in political loyalties in the United States,
from state governments to the national government. This assertion
likely was no comfort to some readers, particularly those in the
South, where sentiments for states' rights over federal power remained strong.

During the postwar decade, Hanna's experiences working with
school systems abroad and the attacks he had suffered in the *Building America* controversy pushed him ever further into the role of an
educational cold warrior. He expected that "The clash between
ideologies is likely to increase in intensity" (Hanna 1950, 11).
Hanna was not a cold warrior in the mold of McCarthy and other
politicians who saw anticommunism as a means of political gain.
He was more in the pattern of Dean Acheson and other diplomats
who saw democratic governments as guarantors of a peaceful and
prosperous world. For that reason, Hanna called on democratic
nations to employ educational tools for the creation of "a democratic
one-world government." He also contended that the United States
must remain vigilant at home to protect against the kinds of attacks
he had suffered in the *Building America* controversy. He wrote, "It
makes more important than ever the necessity of keeping our dem-

ocratic values, our institutions, and our reliance on faith and reason free from totalitarian ends with their reliance on fear and dogma" (ibid.).

Hanna then repeated his familiar prescription for the kind of preparation that all children need from the schools—data and experiences appropriate for international leadership, understandings and skills necessary to mold technology to human needs, and relevant community involvement for all young people. To this formula, though, he added some new elements. He stated more forcefully than ever that "the schools must sharpen their work of developing a clear understanding of and allegiance to our democratic values." For the first time he indicated a theme that he would revisit at the end of the decade: "Our schools must find a satisfactory solution to the problem of central versus decentralized authority and control" (ibid., 12). Hanna also insisted that education is not the exclusive domain of the professional educator. "It is unrealistic, if not arrogant, to assume that educational leaders alone, or even primarily, possess the *word* which they must give to laymen" (ibid., 13) He called on educational leaders to facilitate the participation of community resources in the schools.

Paul Hanna directed tremendous energy in the 1950s toward working through American and international aid agencies to improve education in developing countries. Early on, his most intensive work was in the Philippines, where he acted as a consultant to various projects for most of the decade. United States agencies funded some of those missions with the intent of using education to stem the tide of communism in the third world, and that thrust influenced Hanna's writing. In a cold war paean to the efforts of leaders in the Philippines, Hanna asked, "What makes a people so clearheaded about the precious bill of rights guaranteeing personal freedom from dictators? What gives a people the courage to fight the ruthless forces of communism?" (Hanna 1956b, 601). He attributed the stand against communism in part to "President Magsaysay who has dramatically crushed communism in his nation with a judicious use of force and by correcting many of the economic and social shortages in which communism breeds." Ultimately, though, he attributed the democratic spirit in the Philippines to the schools (ibid.).

In the Philippines, as nowhere else, Hanna was able to test his ideal of the community school. Although critics have attributed mixed results to Hanna's work there, he would have none of it. He claimed that, "of all the activity on behalf of the up-grading of the human resources, none is more exciting or productive than the community-school movement in this new Republic . . . Under modern school leaders the *barrio* school in the Philippines is becoming the center, the learning force in *barrio* health, economic productivity, social organization, and democratic living [emphasis his]" (ibid., 609).

Most important, Hanna asserted, "There is a clear cause-and-effect relationship between the community school success story and the dramatic defeat of communism in the Philippines" (ibid., 610). He wrote that other nations in the region looked to those schools in the Philippines as models for their own countries. Subsequent political events throughout Southeast Asia, as well as in the Philippines itself, cast some doubt on Hanna's claim that either the people or their leaders had internalized the concept of *democratic living*, as he understood the term.

In another 1956 article, Hanna surveyed the educational situation throughout East Asia. All over the region he observed educational systems that were insufficient to help nations become "strong, democratic states, participating as equals in the modern, fast-moving, technological world" (Hanna and High 1956, 431). In a critique of the educational vestiges of colonialism that Hanna would repeat in later surveys of school systems throughout the world, he found that "Almost invariably, the curriculum is formal, bookish, rigidly copied from foreign models of some years ago, and unrelated to the environment of the pupils." He complained that much of what the children learned in school was irrelevant to their lives because the elementary curriculum was usually driven by the secondary curriculum, which was determined by college entrance requirements, even though only a very few students ever went to college. The instructional emphasis was almost always "rote memorization and concert recitation" (ibid.). In one of the few bright spots he found in the region,

> Elementary, secondary, and college teachers were instructed to integrate theory with practice in their teaching, to conduct field trips to farms and manufacturing establishments, to deal with actual problems of economic development in their classwork, and to have pupils undertake practical activities such as agricultural projects on the schoolgrounds and part-time work in the mines, in industrial plants, and on farms (Hanna and High 1956, 429).

Unfortunately for the educational cold warrior, these promising schools were in the People's Republic of China!

Hanna recommended that the leaders and their people in the region "think through the things they desire from their education program, and work out a curriculum which will achieve their objectives . . . Such a curriculum should be drawn from indigenous roots, and should serve to perpetuate those aspects of the cultural heritage which the people wish to pass on to their children" (ibid., 431). Inevitably, he advocated the community school model as it was practiced in the Philippines.

In a nod to the dominance of western ways of thought and practice in the process of industrial modernization, he also suggested that the school should "introduce to the rising generation the fundamentals of science, modern practices of health, sanitation, and agriculture, an understanding of the developing economy and technology, and an ability to cope with change. It should emphasize the democratic processes, and should create an awareness of the wider national and world communities" (Hanna and High 1956, 431).

No written work of Hanna's illustrates more pointedly than this one the difficulty his friends and critics alike have had in categorizing his political ideology. On one hand, he developed strong anticommunist sentiments through his experiences overseas. On the other hand, he forcefully criticized western colonialism and consistently favored collectivist solutions to social and educational dilemmas. He moved in the power circles of big business, but he favored small, local community schools as the locus of economic development. Perhaps, in matters of education for economic development overseas, Hanna must be classified as a Jeffersonian democrat. He was certainly not the first Brahmin to claim populist sentiments.

In the 1950s, Hanna seemed to ignore the wrenching difficulties in developing countries when "indigenous roots" and "the cultural heritage which the people wish to pass on to their children" came into conflict with the dominant western patterns of thought and practice in technology, science, economics, and government. He did not comment on the potential for tension between modern and traditional worldviews.

Years later, Hanna seemed to recognize the dilemma that conflicting worldviews posed for the creation of the world community he so vigorously promoted. In a 1973 editorial, he pointed out that modern technology has made it possible for disputes that would have remained local or regional in the past to become international and worldwide today. He warned that "The problem of conflicting values WILL be solved eventually in one way or another [emphasis his]" (Hanna 1973b, 1). Describing several possible solutions, he suggested that global warfare could continue to decimate mankind, or that a single power could rise to impose its "particular and narrow ethnocentric value system on the entire human family" (ibid.).

Hanna dismissed both of those solutions as unacceptable. As alternatives, he proposed two "promising, although admittedly idealistic" approaches.

In his first proposal, some international group of scholars, working presumably through the United Nations, would identify "through research the core values that are found universally in all viable cultures." Then, the nations of the world would "use every teaching and learning technique to inculcate humans with these identified universal values" (ibid.). These nations would,

> having achieved a global community in which a majority understands and is committed to a set of eternal verities, give encouragement to the preservation and creation of pluralistic sub-values that make up the unique life styles of each different group. Within an essentially harmonious global community, living by the standards of commonly held first-level values, tolerance for and even an appreciation of diversity within second-level values could follow (Hanna 1973b, 1).

Implicit in Hanna's proposal was his belief that all value systems are merely cultural tools. He naively assumed that most people on earth share this modern, western view, but even a cursory look at traditional cultures shows that few believe that "eternal verities" are arrived at by either scientific research or democratic consensus. Few take their belief systems so lightly that they would be willing to modify or reject them by majority rule.

Hanna's second, more modest, proposal was more plausible. A panel of scholars could identify, through research, "those commonly held values that make possible in our time significant multinational communities of men." The findings could then be used to suggest ways to encourage more multinational combinations. He concluded with a warning that "one global approach or another must be tried before history records 'too little and too late'" (ibid.).

THE LAST SOCIAL STUDIES TEXTBOOKS

Hanna's work in international education and social science education came together most forcefully in his last Scott, Foresman textbook series, known as *Investigating Man's World*. This series was not merely a revision of his past textbooks. It grew out of research that Hanna supervised at Stanford in the 1950s to search for social science generalizations useful in improving the social studies curriculum. Still, it incorporated some features of the earlier books.

The search for social science generalizations was not new. In the 1920s, Neil Billings—in conjunction with Harold Rugg's social studies pamphlets—identified 888 generalizations, categorized in seventy-nine divisions, that were useful for social education (Smith, Stanley, and Shores 1957, 259–260). Billings developed his list by surveying the writings of *frontier thinkers* in the social sciences. Rugg used some of these generalizations as overarching themes in his social studies textbooks, including concepts (similar to Hanna's) such as technological progress forcing ever-greater human inter-dependence.

Hanna revived Billings' technique in 1954 when he employed Malcolm Douglass, a graduate student at Stanford, to do a similar survey for *World Book Encyclopedia,* for which Hanna served as social science editor. Douglass and his wife, Enid, surveyed the writings of leading contemporary authorities in the social sciences. They identified 550 major topics and 5500 subtopics, which they painstakingly referenced and cross-referenced on 3×5 index cards (Douglass 1998b). Hanna used their findings to survey *World Book Encyclopedia* for the currency of its articles on social science subjects (Hanna 1974).

This work led to Douglass's dissertation, a description of generalizations from geography that could be used in social studies curriculum development. Hanna was excited by the commercial possibilities: "He sensed this was something that would be very useful to him" (Douglass 1998b). In Douglass's opinion, his work accomplished two things for Hanna. First, it provided a means to unite the expanding communities model with the effort to define and use social science generalizations in the school curriculum.

Second, by doing so, it provided a basis in academic research for the expanding communities model Hanna had used in his textbooks for so long. In a 1957 article, Hanna cited Douglass's work on the identification and use of social science generalizations as "the most comprehensive and scholarly report based on the assumption that the educator must draw on specialists in selecting curriculum content" (Hanna 1957a, 43).

Hanna used Douglass's work as a model in other ways, as well. He pondered the value of such research in a 1952 article entitled, "Needed Research on Textbooks." In it, he cited some generalizations Douglass had identified from geography. He suggested that children be encouraged to observe those generalizations in their immediate environment and then extend that knowledge to other places and other times. He concluded by claiming that "The same research approach might be made to any subject matter" (Hanna 1952b, 299).

Hanna also planned two series of dissertations to be completed by Stanford graduate students. The first employed Douglass's research design to identify generalizations along the lines of Hanna's basic human activities in various social science fields. Hanna and Richard Gross coordinated the completion of ten dissertations in this series. Nine of them corresponded to Hanna's basic human activities, and one focused on the creation of "tools, technics, and social arrangements" (Stanford University n.d.). The second series, which was never completed, was intended to place these generalizations in the appropriate spheres of Hanna's expanding communities model. Although these dissertations did not draw directly from Douglass's dissertation, much of Douglass's work was later incorporated into a 1966 textbook for teachers (Hanna et al. 1966). His dissertation is cited no fewer than six times in that book.

Although Hanna's plans for two separate series of dissertations was never fully realized, the work in social science generalizations was incorporated into his final textbook series, *Investigating Man's*

World. Work began on the series in 1966 and it was introduced in 1970. Although it retained some of the features of Hanna's expanding communities model, it was a radical departure from his earlier Scott, Foresman textbooks.

The most significant difference between Hanna's earlier social studies textbooks and *Investigating Man's World* was that each unit in the new textbooks was keyed to the formal divisions of the social sciences. Although first graders still studied family life in units such as Earth, Wants, and Rules, a promotional brochure for *Investigating Man's World* assured textbook buyers that those titles referred to "physical geography," "economics," and "political science," respectively (Scott, Foresman 1969, 10). In editions for the upper grades, the units were named for the social science subject areas directly. Fourth graders, for example, studied the state and region through units such as Anthropology, Sociology, and History. The brochure explained that the series "departs from the traditional pattern of combining a smattering of many disciplines in one unit. Instead, each unit leads the children to investigate one discipline at a time" (ibid., 2). In less than fifty years, the curriculum innovation of integrated social science instruction, which Hanna advocated so strongly, had become the "traditional pattern" in elementary social studies curriculum.

Another difference between *Investigating Man's World* and Hanna's earlier textbooks was the degree to which Hanna's sense of internationalism suffused the new books. Examples in all the books were drawn from foreign countries. First graders studied family life in Mexico, second graders studied a local community in France, and third graders compared cities in Africa and Japan. Throughout the text, the role of national boundaries was minimized.

With *Investigating Man's World*, Hanna continued the trend of employing experts in social science fields for the production of textbooks. Each volume listed an impressive array of social scientists as consultants. Consequently, the trend toward simple, expository prose to replace the imaginative stories of his earlier books continued as well. Each book also included a large number of in-text activities, continuing the trend of less reliance on the creativity of the classroom teacher.

The contract for these books, signed on the eve of Hanna's retirement from Stanford, reflected his declining influence, even with his primary publisher. It referred to Hanna merely as "Consultant," and assigned him no proprietary interest in the program. A note in Hanna's hand next to one such reference read, *"NO!"* In an agitated notation at the bottom and on the back of the page, Hanna wrote,

> Not for a moment would I be legal and insist that S.F.C. [Scott, Foresman and Company] (1) live up to the 1946 contract which specifically states that this program shall be known as the *HANNA SOCIAL STUDIES PROGRAM*, or (2) call the 1970 edition the *Hanna Program*. What I am asking is that any agreement I sign make absolutely clear that Hanna has a *property* in the design of this 1970 program which is of value and must be protected by Hanna as *his* property. I am *not* a consultant to be employed or dismissed at will by Publisher [emphases his] (Scott, Foresman 1966).

Instead, Hanna proposed that he be termed "Author or Chief Program Designer or some term that adequately recognizes HANNA as 'owner' of the design of the program [emphases his]." In the final version of the contract, Hanna was referred to simply as *Hanna*. He took on *supervisory duties* for a royalty of one and one-half percent of sales (ibid.).

A COMMON CURRICULUM TO BUILD COMMUNITY

As Hanna's textbook writing career progressed, his books included increasing amounts of instructions and aids for teachers, as well as in-text exercises, making the classroom teacher's unique viewpoint on the subject matter increasingly irrelevant. That content reflected the rising trend toward *teacher-proof* curriculum materials, but it also reflected Hanna's own growing concern that American children should be taught a common curriculum. As early as 1946, he called for large-scale curriculum planning to provide "learning experiences adequate to develop understanding of and loyalty to the larger community" (Hanna 1946, 29). He felt that a task "of so great importance calls for an overall framework which will be the product of the combined judgment of the leaders in our culture" (ibid., 29–30). In a 1958 article published in *The Nation's Schools*, Hanna declared that "During the last 25 years we have witnessed a splintering of the curriculum in American public schools as each school district has insisted on curricular independence" (Hanna 1958a, 43). As a result, he warned, "There is no truly American curricular design of significant content and suitable learning experiences on which the nation can rely for creating the universal understanding of and loyalty to the values, laws and institutions essential to perpetuate and improve the way of life of a free society" (ibid.). A solution, Hanna claimed, would be the creation of a national curriculum center.

In his conception, the center would develop in several stages. First, a conference would be held to determine if his proposal had merit, whether a workable process could be created by which to proceed, and who would be likely candidates for participation in the second phase of the project. The second phase would see a team of thirty fellows produce a series of papers addressing various aspects of the national curriculum problem. Fifteen of these fellows would be chosen for their expertise in major subject matter fields, ten would be specialists in curriculum theory, and five would be laymen. Their papers would be published widely and would invite responses from the education community. The third step would be the appointment of a new commission of thirty, with some overlap from the first group, to consider the education community's responses to the first set of papers and further refine the national curriculum idea. Hanna predicted that these three phases would take two years to accomplish, and he hoped that they would lay the foundation for "a permanent, nonfederal National Curriculum Center or several such Centers whose goal would be the continuous examination of the exploding frontiers of human thought and achievement and to identify generalizations that must be incorporated into the national curriculum design" (ibid., 44).

Hanna's proposal generated considerable comment. The editors of *The Nation's Schools*, for example, agreed with Hanna that such a concerted curriculum effort was needed, but raised questions as to who would select the commission fellows, the sources of funding, and the extent to which professional jealousies might hinder the work. They invited readers to comment on the proposal and published many of the comments in subsequent issues.

Many readers expressed support. Several felt that the plan was a worthy counterattack against some of the educational conservatives of the time. One supporter thought Hanna's idea was "more in harmony with our democratic tradition than any I have seen" (Ragan 1958).

Most respondents who opposed Hanna's idea expressed concern about the centralization of curriculum control. W. W. Charters questioned the appropriateness of placing power to define the purpose of public education in the hands of a few experts (Hanna 1987, 38). David D. Henry, president of the University of Illinois, warned that citizenship education is a local task beyond the scope of simple subject matter content decisions. Political scientist V. O. Key Jr. feared that the Center would become a vehicle for political indoctrination. He preferred that resources be poured into improving the subject matter knowledge of teachers. C. C. Trillingham, superintendent of the Los Angeles public schools, expressed concern that teachers were not included in the planning process. He reminded readers that regardless of what experts say or do, change in the schools does not happen without enlisting teachers in the effort (ibid.).

Perhaps the most stinging criticism came from Hanna's old friend and colleague, Hollis Caswell. Then president of Teachers College, Caswell made an annual report to the school's trustees. In his report for 1961, Caswell critiqued Hanna's proposal on several points. First, he claimed that the arguments that a unified curriculum was necessary because the current one was splintered, or because of the increased mobility of Americans, were not new. Harold Rugg and William C. Bagley had made similar observations in the past. Next, he pointed to the centralized control of schools as a tool of fascism: "We had seen in both of these countries [Germany and Japan] how the national governments used the schools as a direct means of serving their inhuman, tyrannous ends" (Caswell 1961). Caswell asserted that local control of the curriculum was one of the nation's "great democratic strengths" (ibid.). He argued that local education leaders have a better sense of what children should know to become citizens of the community. Caswell went on to warn that by consolidating curriculum decision making, a national commission would restrict innovation and experimentation; that a single national commission would be more subject to "capture" by special interest groups; and that a national commission would contribute to the general trend toward centralization and homogenization in American society. He thought that centralized curriculum planning should be opposed on principle. As an alternative, Caswell proposed the creation of a system of curriculum development laboratories at universities around the country, along with increased attention to sound curriculum development and instructional supervision in the school districts, and the establishment of national standards for teacher preparation.

Hanna's proposal surprised some who thought they knew him.

His long career had given both progressives and conservatives cause to claim him as their own. His promotion of the centralization of curriculum development was incongruous with the vision either group held of him, but attempts to fix Hanna too firmly in a doctrinaire political position have often failed.

None who had read him closely throughout his career should have been surprised at his proposal. His experiences and observations during the war years developed in him a deep distrust for centralized power, but he held an even deeper conviction that democratic control of social institutions required concerted effort based on the commonalities among people. In an echo of his analysis of the modern dilemma from early in his career, Hanna argued in a 1960 article on the national curriculum commission that

> Our social, economic, and political endeavors have lagged so far behind the material and physical achievements of our society that we are in a serious state of cultural imbalance. A necessary step toward recreating a dynamic balance for our nation lies in improvement of the school curriculum. For this reason, the creation of a nongovernmental national commission for curriculum research and development is proposed for nationwide discussion (Hanna 1960, 25).

In addition, his thirty years in curriculum development had seen trends change and fads come and go. Hanna felt that decentralized curriculum planning was too random and unstable to produce a curriculum that would serve national goals in any coherent way, and he had always appreciated orderliness and sound planning.

Hanna sought to implement the first phase of his proposal by organizing a conference to discuss the idea. Held January 24–27, 1959, the Conference on Policies and Strategy for Strengthening the Curriculum of the American Public School was attended by a small, elite group of educational leaders. Hanna and Ralph Tyler cochaired the event, and I. James Quillen, James B. Conant, and William Carr were among the participants (*Conference on Policies and Strategy for Strengthening the Curriculum of the American Public School* 1959). Although the conference did not lead to implementation of step two, the appointment of a curriculum commission, it did cause Hanna to modify his idea. In subsequent articles on the topic in the *NEA Journal* (1963), *Phi Delta Kappan* (1961a), and elsewhere, Hanna continually stressed the nongovernmental nature of his commission and the voluntary nature of schools' compliance with its findings.

In the end, Hanna's proposal went nowhere. That failure was due, in part, to his underestimation of the fierce independence of local and state school boards and of the strong allegiance Americans have to the concept of local control. Even more significantly, Hanna may have minimized the extent to which the United States already had a national curriculum. In a letter responding to Hanna's proposal, Thomas B. Livingston of Texas Technological College, now Texas Tech University, wrote, "I have a feeling that our publishing companies, through their textbooks and other media, probably contribute a great deal of commonality to the nation's school curricula" (Livingston 1958). To support his assertion, Livingston related this anecdote: "Once, while visiting a number of schools very rapidly in rather widely scattered school systems, I found certain of the primary grades doing identical things on identical dates. After some searching, I located the cause, the Scott, Foresman calendar, distributed to primary teachers, which contained little daily suggestions to the teacher!" (ibid.).

Hanna's proposal may have failed because it was redundant with what was already being accomplished through the publishers of curriculum materials. In fact, although he never articulated it, Hanna's idea may have resulted from his recognition of the dominance of textbook publishers in the curriculum-making process. He likely thought that a national curriculum from a commission staffed by scholars, whatever its flaws, was preferable to the trend-following, market-driven curriculum that issued from the textbook publishing industry. If he thought so, Hanna was acting somewhat disingenuously. He had grown rich and influential largely because of the role he played in establishing the publisher's role in curriculum formation. Or perhaps his unique vantage point helped him to see the pitfalls of allowing commercial forces too great a hand in school curriculum. In either case, Hanna thought that of all his contributions to education, the concept of a national curriculum commission was of such importance that he recounted his arguments and those of some of his critics in the last publication of his life, a compilation entitled *Assuring Quality for the Social Studies in Our Schools* (1987).

HANNA AND MATHEMATICS EDUCATION

Long before he wrote about the national purposes of education or published his analyses of the role schools could play in the social, economic, and political development of nations, Hanna wrote about mathematics education. His 1929 doctoral dissertation was a study of students' arithmetic problem-solving processes. As any enterprising graduate student might, he turned his findings into two solid articles, published in 1930 and 1931. More significantly, his findings reflected his educational thought even at the earliest stages of his career. Hanna found that students gained the most on post tests when they were allowed the freedom to choose their own strategies and when they were taught the underlying patterns of interrelationships—or generalizations—among numbers, rather than when they were simply asked to memorize formulas and taught to use them in narrow applications. Those findings were consonant with Hanna's belief that the newer, more progressive methods of education were superior to the traditional approaches then employed in the schools.

In later years, he used his dissertation research as a basis for advocating one of his more familiar themes. In an article written in 1935 and reprinted in 1958, Hanna showed how mathematics can be taught within the context of an activities program. He argued that learning difficulties arise in mathematics because skills are taught in isolation from real world applications. Hanna asserted that "Normal children find no particular *learning difficulty* in improving their roller-skating, or in mastering the rules and plays of a game of checkers, or in reading and following directions for assembling the parts of a model airplane" (Hanna and others 1935, 86). Likewise, mathematics should be taught in the context of activities and curriculum elements in which it is used. The authors went on to list a number of possibilities for such integration in the third and sixth grade curricula.

SPELLING INSTRUCTION

Another curriculum interest of Hanna's was spelling instruction. In a series of Houghton Mifflin textbooks cowritten with his wife, Jean, in the 1950s and 1960s, Hanna adapted his conception of generalizations as teaching tools from the social studies to language arts. He had first established himself as a textbook author in 1932, when he and Jesse Newlon, his mentor from the Lincoln School and Teachers College, collaborated on a spelling book for Houghton Mifflin (Newlon and Hanna 1933). The two authors split a five percent royalty on all sales at wholesale prices. According to one of Hanna's Stanford students, the later spellers were Jean's brainchild (Douglass 1998b).

The Hannas' Houghton Mifflin spellers were intended to span grades one through eight. The first, *Building Spelling Power*, was contracted in 1955. It was followed by *First Steps, A Speller for Beginners* (1963), *Power to Spell* (1966), and *Words in Your Language* (1967). Accompanying these were many practice books, and an instructor's text entitled *The Foundations of Spelling and Its Teaching* (1967). The basis for the Hannas' instructional approach was a study that identified the 3000 words most commonly used by young children and determined that, for the most part, these words followed predictable spelling rules, or generalizations.

Hanna claimed that he led the study, although it was first described in a doctoral dissertation by James T. Moore Jr. (Moore 1951). Hanna and Moore coauthored an article in which they advocated a commonsense instructional approach that emphasized the generalizations and only slowly introduced exceptions (Hanna and Moore 1953). Why Moore did not work on the spelling textbooks along with the Hannas is unclear, but the incident may have fueled the rumors among some of Hanna's students that he profited personally from their work.

Predictably, Hanna drew a contrast between his approach and the traditional methods of teaching spelling, which were based on memorization and repetition of more or less arbitrary lists of words. He asserted that "The only reason for learning to spell is the necessity for correctly transmitting our ideas on paper," so spelling rules and words should be taught as the children need them in their writing (ibid., 18) Hanna and Moore also suggested that spelling be taught across the curriculum, not solely in conjunction with reading, as was often done, because the process of symbolic decoding used in reading was the reverse of that used in writing. In reading, children move from symbol recognition, through the medium of speech, to meaning. In spelling, the sequence moves in the opposite direction—from meaning to speech to symbols.

Paul and Jean Hanna coauthored a series of articles that blended description of their spelling program with promotion of their books. In one, the Hannas decried the lack of application of neurology, endocrinology, physiology, cybernetics, and computer science to the pedagogy of spelling. They pointed out that "The complex neurological behavior of the spelling act is not understood at the moment," but described it as "essentially a matter of neuro-logical *input, imagery,* and *output* [emphases theirs]" (Hanna and Hanna 1959, 50). They proposed a "systematic program of developing oral-aural, visual, and haptical imagery . . . the one new, powerful spelling tool of *phonemic* analysis . . . [and] the current theories and practices of forming and using generalizations about the structure of the spelling of our language [emphasis theirs]" (ibid., 51).

In practice, their program would have teachers begin the school week with a presentation of new spelling words in context, along with a generalizable spelling rule, the "major phonemic principle illustrated by the word list" (ibid., 52). Any exceptions to the rule were pointed out and the students were given practice writing the words. On day two, students were quizzed over the words. Day three was dedicated to further study of the words missed on the previous day's quiz, more practice on the phonemic principle, and a review of words from past lists. On day four, students were led in an oral-aural analysis of the word list and application of the spelling rule using new words not on the list. They formed derivatives of words on the list and created an individualized vocabulary list from their reading and writing. The last day of the school week culminated in a spelling test using words from the current list, past lists, and the students' individual lists. Teachers still use many of these suggested practices in the classroom today.

THE *WORLD BOOK ENCYCLOPEDIA*

Throughout most of his career, Paul Hanna served as an editor for *World Book Encyclopedia.* On the heels of their collaboration in the Virginia Curriculum Study, Hollis Caswell brought his friends and colleagues Hanna and J. Paul Leonard onto a board of consultants he had organized to advise *World Book.* In Hanna's recollection, "I was his first appointment and chief buddy" (Hanna 1974). During their tenure, the encyclopedia grew from seven volumes to twenty-two. Hanna's contributions included encouraging a truly international view of the topics covered. In a 1961 letter to Bailey K. Howard, president of *World Book*'s parent company, Hanna suggested, "The emerging world community needs a totally new world encyclopedia which is written not from a nationalistic point of view . . . but treats all cultures and civilizations with equal space, simpatico, etc." (Hanna 1961b). Hanna also used his international travels to gain information of use to *World Book*. In 1962, he apparently gathered information during a conference in Italy, and Bailey K. Howard wrote to thank him in advance for "finding out as much as you possibly can from the gentlemen assembled about the need in their educational systems for an internationalized version of *World Book*" (Howard 1962). Hanna replied, "I will certainly keep my ears and eyes open to glean whatever information and advice I can" (Hanna 1962b).

Hanna also published his definitive concept of community in *World Book*. His article on the subject "has been referred to over and over by scholars as a framework for organizing one's observations or one's thoughts about the world" (Hanna 1974).

A *World Book* editorial board meeting was the site of a tragic rift in one of Hanna's oldest and dearest friendships. The seeds of the rift were sown when Hanna's consulting contract with *World Book* was renewed for a period that ran beyond Caswell's retirement from the board. Caswell responded by arranging for *World Book* to dismiss Hanna at the same time Caswell retired. Hanna later claimed that "Caswell became jealous of the amount of attention which *World Book* was giving me" (Hanna 1974).

The final conflict arose over an invitation to a meeting. Certain officials in the Field Enterprises Corporation, which published *World Book*, planned to supplement the work of their board of consultants with a board of international consultants. Donald McKellar, a Field Enterprises executive, wanted members of the domestic board to meet with their international counterparts to explain how the board worked. To that end, while the consultants were meeting in Chicago in June of 1964, Caswell invited the domestic board members to attend a meeting of the international board—excluding Hanna. As a result of missing this meeting Hanna missed an opportunity to serve on the international board as the American representative. Caswell later told Hanna that McKellar had rescinded the invitation. Hanna relayed this to Donald Ludgin, the editorial coordinator for *World Book*, and Ludgin told McKellar. McKellar was incensed, and he confronted Caswell in what Hanna termed "as tense and unpleasantly dramatic [a situation] as any I can recall, ever" (Hanna 1964b).

In a letter to McKellar, Caswell attributed the entire situation to a misunderstanding on either Hanna's or Ludgin's part. He repeated the theme in a conciliatory letter to Hanna, in which he wrote, "In so far as I am concerned I am not going to let the unfortunate incidents in Chicago this week affect our long friendship. I hope you feel the same way . . . It is just one of those unfortunate and unhappy incidents in life which comes along from time to time, either by accident as in this case, or upon occasion by design" (Caswell 1964).

However, the damage was done. Hanna was convinced that Caswell had lied to the advisory board. Ludgin concurred in Hanna's interpretation, writing that "As time goes on, I become more and more convinced that the problem arose with Cas . . . I feel certain that he decided for some reason not to have Americans present [at the meeting of the international consultants] on Wednesday" (Ludgin 1964).

The preceding account is admittedly only one side of the story. Hanna reluctantly told this story to Martin Gill in 1974, while the hard feelings were still fresh. He regretted that the two friends were estranged, lamenting that "Caswells and Hannas now exchange

Christmas cards only" (Hanna 1974). In later years, the two men were reconciled (A. Hanna 1999).

CONCLUSION

In Hanna's long writing career he reflected the views of at least three distinct lines of thought in the development of social studies education: social meliorism, social reconstruction, and mandarinism. His upbringing, suffused with the best impulses of the Social Gospel movement, along with his training in philosophy, determined that his earliest writing would be social critique along the lines of the social meliorists. In the Depression years, under the influence of mentors such as Harold Rugg, Jesse Newlon, and William Heard Kilpatrick at Teachers College, Hanna's social critique focused on economic dislocation and its remedies. This placed him in the camp of the social reconstructionists. He continued to write in that vein, often critical of traditional educational methodologies, for many years. World War II marked a change in Hanna's thought. The devastation that fascism had wrought on the world caused Hanna to be more circumspect in his discussions of education as a tool for social change. He continued to advocate employing the schools in efforts to improve society, but he was much more insistent that change must come about only within the context of liberal democratic values. In the last phase of his writing career, he seemed more at home among the mandarins—those scholars in the subject areas who advocated substantive instruction in the discrete disciplines to form a knowledge base for democratic action.

Throughout these permutations, however, he consistently advocated a social education for children adequate to their roles as citizens. Early in his career, he was more insistent that the schools be vehicles of social change than he was later. In fact, his national curriculum commission would have removed a great deal of flexibility in curriculum making from classroom teachers and placed it in the hands of *experts*, arguably an undemocratic process.

Hanna's grand plan for social education was embodied in his Scott, Foresman social studies textbooks. His *expanding communities* design articulated through these books became the "major organizing idea for the elementary social studies curriculum" in the United States and abroad (LeRiche 1987, 139). The recognition he gained from his textbook production provided him opportunities to promote other ideas, such as his national curriculum commission and his views on education for international development. Hanna preferred to write about the large ideas rather than the more technical aspects of curriculum. For instance, rather than discuss research on how children learn values, Hanna proposed a means to determine what values are universal across cultural lines. His focus was usually on social studies education's role in shaping society.

The wealth that accompanied Hanna's textbook production allowed him to continue to add to the Hanna-Honeycomb House and contribute to causes he deemed worthy. It also alerted him to the financial possibilities in textbook writing. When an opportunity to expand from social studies textbooks to spellers presented itself in the 1950s, he did not hesitate. Despite the fact that his only work in spelling instruction had been twenty years before, and that his expertise lay in other fields, Hanna saw a potentially profitable approach and exploited it. Throughout his career, that type of entrepreneurship raised questions among his colleagues and students (Douglass 1998b), but writing was not the only way in which Hanna indulged his entrepreneurial side. He was instrumental in the formation of several professional organizations in education, and he was influential in many others. Networking with colleagues around the world allowed Hanna to spread his ideas even further.

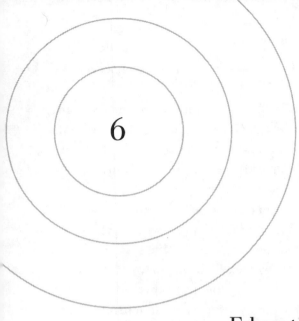

6

Paul Hanna's Involvement in Professional Education Organizations

Paul Hanna was a joiner. The list of organizations to which he belonged fills a significant portion of a single-spaced page of his final curriculum vitae. More important, he was a founding member of some of the most influential American education organizations of this century. Curiously, his role in these groups has been neglected by historians of education, quite likely because of the uneven pattern of his involvement in their programs through the years. Hanna's entrepreneurial personality prompted him to participate in the creation of an organization or a project, then to fade away as he pursued new challenges elsewhere. His restless energy and sense of ambition led him constantly to seek new forums for his ideas, both at home and abroad.

Hanna's arrival at Teachers College, Columbia University in 1924 placed him among an elite group of American educators. In the decades before midcentury, many of those who would dominate the curriculum field and its professional organizations for the next few decades passed through Teachers College as faculty members and as graduate students. Among these luminaries were Hilda

Taba, Florence Stratemeyer, Alice Miel, Hollis Caswell, William Van Til, Kenneth Benne, Frederick Redefer, and Paul Hanna. All of these individuals were more or less "progressive" in their outlook, and the networks that they formed provided momentum for the formation and reformation of several of the most important education organizations of this century.

Hanna's childhood provided the framework within which his conception of a liberal education developed. Much of the adult content of that conception, however, came from his work alongside figures such as Harold Rugg, Jesse Newlon, and others at Teachers College's Lincoln School and from his participation in teaching the 200F Foundations of Education course. Hanna also was impacted deeply by his involvement in what became known as the Kilpatrick Discussion Group. He continued to acknowledge his ideological kinship with members of the group throughout his life. For example, years afterward, he included himself with them as "very leftist in our thinking about what reforms had to be made in society. Then Roosevelt came along and we found in Roosevelt much that we could endorse . . ." (Hanna 1973a, 37).

The Kilpatrick Discussion Group profoundly affected Hanna's thought, as it did the development of education thought generally in the 1930s (Cremin, Shannon, and Townsend 1954, 144). In fact, lively debate has ensued as to which professional organizations and publications can trace their lineage to the Discussion Group (Tanner 1991, 15–20). The claims and counterclaims tend to be futile, because the organizational rosters and editorial boards of many professional organizations and publications seem to list the same social and educational reconstructionists again and again. The various organizations formed one great network for the reconstructionists.

Hanna's experience at Teachers College illustrates, in microcosm, how this network operated. The discussion group met on Sunday nights, and its members came together at other times again to plan and teach the innovative Education 200F course. Hanna, Rugg, and Newlon worked together at the Lincoln School and in other capacities. Others certainly met in similar collaborations. Hanna recalled that all of these venues of discussion were rich with intellectual ferment (Hanna 1974, 70). Similarly, the meetings of the Progressive Education Association, the National Education Association, the Society for Curriculum Study, the John Dewey Society, the Spring Conference on Education, and others crackled with ideas as the same individuals debated and refined their views on the school's role in society.

HANNA AND THE PHILOSOPHY OF THE
PROGRESSIVE EDUCATION ASSOCIATION

The Progressive Education Association (PEA) was founded in 1918 by administrators and teachers in experimental schools, most of them private institutions not affiliated with religious organizations. In her excellent history of the PEA, *Progressive Education from Arcady to Academe*, Patricia Graham characterized the association's first decade and a half as a time in which child-centered pedagogy dominated interest and discussion (Graham 1967). This emphasis reflected the concerns of the leaders of the private experimental schools who populated the organization's leadership. In 1924 the association launched its journal, *Progressive Education*, which quickly became one of the leading education publications of its day and helped the PEA attract national attention to its program and policies. By 1930, many popular publications had reported on the *new education* advocated by the Progressive Education Association (Graham 1967, 60).

Growing interest in progressive education was not an unmixed blessing for the association, however. University professors and public school administrators had long participated in the organization, but the PEA's growing popularity drew more prominent scholars to its ranks. Perhaps nothing better symbolized the association's rise in the esteem of academics than the acceptance of its honorary presidency by John Dewey in 1928, after declining the honor earlier in the decade (ibid., 41). The university professors, many from Teachers College, gradually assumed positions of leadership in the organization. After 1932, no school headmaster or headmistress ever again served as president of the Progressive Education Association.

The university professors brought a broader range of curriculum concerns to the association than had the private school leaders. Many, like Hanna and Rugg, were dismayed at what they considered the excesses of child-centered progressivism. As early as 1928, for example, John Dewey urged the PEA membership to pay more attention to the intellectual content of the school curriculum:

> An experimental school is under the temptation to improvise its subject-matter. It must take advantage of unexpected events and turn to account unexpected questions and interests. Yet if it permits improvisations to dictate its course, the result is a jerky, discontinuous movement which works against the possibility of making any important contribution to educational subject-matter. Incidents are momentary, but the use made of them should not be momentary or short-lived. They are to be brought within the scope of a developing whole of content and purpose, which is a whole because it has continuity and consecutiveness in its parts" (Dewey 1928, 201).

Dewey's statement was a repudiation of the fuzzy notion, widely held by members of the Association, that children's interests alone should shape the curriculum. His thinking about children's interests and the curriculum had undergone some change over the years. In 1897 he had written, "The true center of correlation on the school subjects is not science, nor literature, nor history nor geography, but the child's own social activities" (Dewey 1897, 78). However, he later opposed the schools' granting unlimited freedom for children to pursue their interests (Dewey 1930). Paul Hanna's thoughts on child interest and the curriculum followed a similar pattern of change.

Concern over the proper basis for curriculum making grew as the dimensions of the economic and social devastation wrought by the Great Depression became clear in the early 1930s. The social reconstructionists thought that neither a school curriculum based solely on child interest nor one based on the traditional subject areas alone was adequate to prepare American children and youth to understand and address the mounting problems facing the nation. Then, in 1932, George Counts electrified the annual PEA meeting in Baltimore with his speech, "Dare Progressive Education Be Progressive?" In this address and the book that followed, Counts called for progressive education to throw off its identification with the middle class. This alliance, he thought, had led to the progressive schools' educational philosophy of extreme individualism (Counts 1932, 9). After all, the American middle class was the great repository for the virtues of individual achievement and competitiveness. As the industrial middle class grew, so did the influence of its ideology. Schools that served this group had little choice but to transmit its values faithfully to the next generation. However, Counts saw that the social and economic challenges facing American society called for a different approach entirely—a collective, even socialistic, approach in which the school would expand its role as a community center and social welfare agency.

Counts's challenge exposed the ideological disunity of the PEA. After 1932, the association increasingly became a battleground between those who believed that education was most progressive when the curriculum was determined by children's interests alone and those who thought that schools had a responsibility to teach children objective truths that would help them improve society.

A special meeting of the PEA advisory board held at Vassar College later that spring of 1932 devoted an evening to discussing

a topic entitled The Responsibility of Education for Social Reconstruction. The result was a stinging indictment of the type of school
that had been a model for the PEA. The Board claimed that "The
progressive school in emphasizing the development of the individual has often failed to develop an adequate social outlook. It has
cultivated openmindedness, but students are not moved to social
action or fired by great beliefs or causes. Students are critical but
undecisive, interesting and well-poised as individuals, but self-cen-
tered" (Progressive Education Association Advisory Board 1932).

This critique reflected the concerns that Rugg and Hanna had
voiced earlier about the Lincoln School curriculum (Hanna 1973a).
It signaled an attempt by the social reconstructionists to shift the
emphasis of the association (Graham 1967, 67).

However, even social reconstructionists disagreed on the proper
role of schools in social change. George Counts pleaded that "Progressive Education . . . become less frightened than it is today at
the bogies of *imposition* and *indoctrination*" (Counts 1932, 9). He
argued that "all education contains a large element of imposition,"
and that, in light of the crisis of the Great Depression, the schools
must use any means to help build a new order (ibid.). Not all social
reconstructionists agreed with Counts. William Heard Kilpatrick
responded, for example, "If, then, we believe in democracy, we shall
avoid indoctrination . . . There is no other safe rule. Democracy, to
be itself, cannot indoctrinate even itself" (Kilpatrick 1939, 57). An
editorial in *The Nation* argued that indoctrination applies only if
final truth has been discovered. It stated, "So long as one believes
that knowledge grows and changes, one must believe that the
younger generation has a right to compare and question, and that
free inquiry, not indoctrination, is the ideal of education" (1935,
293).

By the late 1930s, the PEA had proven itself unable to resolve
the differences between its members who advocated child-centered
education and the social reconstructionists. The association peri-

odically adopted statements of philosophy, but none was more than a temporary accommodation of the differing views. When the fragile consensus that produced an official statement evaporated, another statement was developed. From its membership peak in 1938, the PEA steadily lost members until its dissolution in 1955, as progressive educators created new organizations to address their concerns.

Paul Hanna played a key role in the PEA's attempt to reach a philosophical consensus and, in the creation of new organizations, to more directly address members' concerns. In 1938, PEA president Carson Ryan appointed Hanna chairman of the Resolutions committee for the upcoming annual convention. Hanna was fully aware of the philosophical conflict at work in the association. He recalled, "We had two groups: one that wanted nothing to do with school responsibility to society, and the other that felt the school must not only be interested in the child but in society as well. This was a very profound bone of contention" (Hanna 1973a, 64). In Hanna's recollection, those who opposed a social role for the schools still had considerable influence in the association.

The resulting Resolutions committee report was delivered to the 1938 national conference in New York City. The document revealed Hanna's clear hand throughout. It began with a gentle acknowledgment of conflicts within the PEA, declaring that, ". . . the use of education as an instrument for the improvement of the culture has been debated vigorously by the membership" (Progressive Education Association 1938, 4). The report then spun its argument. It stated that, "In a culture where dynamic democratic values are accepted, educational method and content should contribute to the maintenance and improvement of these values" (ibid., 4–5). In other words, the schools had a duty to society as well as to the individual. The document then developed two themes common to those who saw education as a means for remaking American society. First, it announced the dawn of a new era: "Whether we like it or not, we are moving out of the age of economic individualism into an age of collective effort" (ibid., 6). The implication was that schools focusing solely on the needs of the individual were educating for the past. Second, it raised the specter of American democracy's erosion by an unreflective traditional curriculum on the one hand, and by an indulgent child-centered curriculum on the other:

> We, in our century, are witnessing the rapid spread of dictator-ships and the defeat of democratic institutions so widely adopted during the previous century. . . It is too much to hope that the United States will escape this struggle . . . The outcome will depend upon the . . . wisdom of educational leadership in sharply contrasting the opposed value systems and critically evaluating the alternative roads to security, freedom, and peace (ibid., 6–7).

The document then sought to harmonize the earlier thrust of the PEA with that of the social reconstructionists:

> Where once we gave our attention almost exclusively to child needs and better learning techniques, now we broaden our educational goals to include the relation of education to the culture. Education is considered an instrument to be used by the culture for the perpetuation and improvement of the value system of the culture. In our culture this means that education becomes the chief instrument for the maintenance and improvement of democratic values . . . (Progressive Education Association 1938, 11).

This statement revealed Hanna's innate social conservatism and distanced him from concepts of democracy such as Kilpatrick's. The document went on to add that the new emphasis did not mean abandoning principles associated with progressive education. It stated that the PEA's emphasis on education as a tool of cultural transmission, ". . . cannot be construed to mean that we place less stress on purposive learning of the child, creative experience, freedom, and the many other educational advances of the recent past; rather these advances are now seen as facilitating educational goals more vital in our culture" (ibid.).

Six specific resolutions followed the committee's argument. They included calls for the membership to support the newly formed Committee on Teacher Education of the American Council on Education, to take political action regarding adequate public support of the schools and social issues, and to oppose militarism. Certainly, these resolutions addressed broader issues than just child-centered education, but the first one was reserved for the conflict over social reconstructionism. Resolution number one called on the PEA to

> ... give increased attention, through its conferences, publications, and particularly through the existing Commissions and Committees, to the problem of projecting and experimenting with curriculums on elementary, secondary, and higher education levels which will develop the insights, attitudes, and skills demanded to conserve and expand democratic values in an age of science and technological invention (ibid., 12–13).

That resolution was hardly revolutionary. In fact, it simply reiterated activities in which the association was already engaged. Nevertheless, the presentation of the Hanna committee report created a firestorm of controversy. Hanna recalled that "the Progressive Education members who were present at this annual meeting were so turned on or off by the Resolutions Committee that we departed from the agenda and hardly touched most of the items on the agenda because all people wanted to talk about was this resolution, which we didn't think was startling" (Hanna 1973a, 85).

Hanna described the ensuing debate as "a very profound discussion, very searching, very philosophical" (ibid.). Nevertheless, the resolutions polarized the meeting. Opposed to the Committee's report were Frederick Redefer, Roma Gans, Laura Zirbes, and some of Hanna's former colleagues from Teachers College. Supporters included George Counts, John Childs, and Jesse Newlon, also from Teachers College. Later in life, Hanna even invoked John Dewey in support of his position, claiming that Dewey "was very much upset at the tendency of [the] Progressive Education Association to forget the second and equally important role of education, which was to preserve and improve society as well as to bring out the very best in each and every individual. To him they were the two sides of the same coin" (Hanna 1974, 128). Hanna understood the debate over the Resolutions committee report as the watershed division between those educational progressives in the PEA who believed that the association's focus should be the child and those who thought that it should be the schools' responsibility to change society.

The polarization of the PEA meeting following presentation of the Hanna committee's resolutions revealed a decade of subtle conflict between university members of the PEA and those associated with private schools. The tension between these two political camps prompted their adherents to interpret the results of the 1938 meeting differently. Hanna recalled that the social reconstructionists interpreted opposition from the child-centered progressive educators as an indication that they should begin to "put our energy someplace else" (Hanna 1973a, 86). PEA founder Stanwood Cobb, however, saw the debate as just one more indication that the professors from Teachers College "took it [the Association] away from us" (Graham 1967, 57). One critic even accused the members of the Resolutions committee of having "joined the Association because they . . . wished to profit by its research and exchange of ideas, rather than to commit themselves to specific movements or methods" (*Progressive Education* 1938, 418).

None need have doubted the motives behind Hanna's work on the Resolutions committee. The front matter in the committee's report is a clear, heartfelt statement of Hanna's view that schools should employ the pedagogical techniques of the child-centered progressives in the service of social reconstruction. Indeed, the report was called "One of the most carefully prepared presentations on a relationship that might exist between education and culture" (ibid., 422). Hanna's subsequent career displayed his concern that education for democratic citizenship should employ learning by doing, critical analysis, and creative teaching. Nevertheless, criticism of the document and its authors was particularly vicious. One critic intentionally misrepresented the report when he asked, "Is it consistent with such basic ideals of democracy as freedom of thought, freedom of speech, and freedom of continuance or change of institutions as the people themselves shall at any time decide, for a democratic form of government to teach its children to perpetuate our present-day society as other systems teach their children to perpetuate theirs? I think not" (ibid., 418).

In the end, the PEA convention reached no decision on the Hanna committee resolutions, and hope for harmony between the warring factions within the PEA evaporated. The delegates refused to endorse even the most innocuous of the Hanna committee's resolutions as merely representing the "general sense and mood of the members assembled this afternoon" (Cremin 1961, 266). Patricia Graham credited this "inability to achieve a philosophical synthesis of the warring elements" as indicative of the ideological disunity of the PEA at that time (Graham 1967, 158). As a result of that disunity, some members sought other vehicles for the expression of their views.

His experience at the 1938 PEA Convention convinced Paul Hanna that the conflict within the PEA was beyond resolution. He and other social reconstructionists "decided to drop our active participation in the PEA and some of us got together and decided that we would support several other organizations" (Hanna 1973a, 66). Hanna allowed his membership to lapse soon afterward.

PARTICIPATION IN THE SPRING CONFERENCE

A growing number of professional organizations offered their meetings as venues for discussion of the relationship between the school

and society. These organizations included the Spring Conference
in Education, the John Dewey Society, the Society for Curriculum
Study, and the Department of Supervisors and Instruction of the
National Education Association. Paul Hanna used each of these
organizations as a vehicle to express his views about the role of the
school in social education.

The Spring Conference was organized to promote informal con-
versation among a select group of education leaders on issues surrounding the role of education in society. It first met in St. Louis in
1935, but the membership eventually settled on Chicago as the
location for its annual weekend meetings. William Van Til recalled
that the conference's unique meetings included no set agenda and
no paper presentations by members. Instead, they typically opened
on a Saturday morning with a free-ranging discussion of whatever
education topics members cared to put forward. At lunch, an ad
hoc committee identified four major topics from the morning's discussions and appointed panels to frame each issue. In the afternoon,
topics one and two were presented with abundant discussion from
the membership. The following morning, the Conference discussed
topics three and four. Van Til later tried, with limited success, to
institute the same types of free discussion sessions at meetings of
the John Dewey Society and the Professors of Curriculum conference that preceded the annual Association for Supervision and Curriculum Development meetings (Van Til 1983, 191–192).

Henry Harap recalled that Paul Hanna was a founding member
of the Spring Conference (Harap n.d.). Hanna participated in the
meetings from 1936 to 1942, along with Harap, Harold Hand,
Hollis Caswell, Harold Rugg, Frederick Redefer, and others. The
leader of the meeting was designated "factotum," and although
many of his colleagues served in that capacity, Hanna never did.
His growing involvement with textbook production and other activities precluded his taking active leadership in the Spring Conference or other professional organizations.

THE BEGINNINGS OF THE JOHN DEWEY SOCIETY

A January 1934 letter from Henry Harap to Paul Hanna launched the John Dewey Society (Harap 1970, 157). Harap asked Hanna to persuade his colleague and mentor Jesse Newlon to call a conference of selected *educational liberals* in conjunction with the regular February meeting of the NEA Department of Supervisors and Instruction. Harap believed that Newlon's prominence would draw leaders in education to a meeting for the purpose of giving "those who are interested in social and economic reconstruction a chance to become acquainted and possibly to serve as the nucleus of a permanent organization" (ibid.). Hanna's recollection of the new organization's purpose mirrored Harap's:

> It became clear that we could never bring the two groups, that is School-and-Society and School-and-the-Child, together . . . Now this did not mean that we were giving up the other side of John Dewey's philosophy. It was an effort for the child but we knew if we were to talk about school and society, we would have to do it through another organization, another set of journals . . . . Most of us continued membership in the Progressive Education Association until we saw that it was a dying organization . . . and we created this new organ [the John Dewey Society] not to kill the Progressive Education Association, but to balance the record (Hanna 1974, 129–310).

If Hanna's recollection of the reasons for founding the organization are accurate, the choice to name it in honor of John Dewey, the philosophical father of American progressive education, was indeed an affront to the PEA.

Newlon responded favorably to Harap's request, and the two exchanged letters with lists of prospective invitees. Newlon was especially concerned that they include no "stuffed shirts . . . who give lip service to liberal or progressive ideas but follow the line of least resistance" (Newlon 1934). Paul Hanna was not included on either man's list, but George Counts, Harold Rugg, William Heard Kilpatrick, Newlon, and Harap all recall that Hanna attended the founding meetings, so it simply may have been understood that he was to be a part of the group (Johnson 1977, 70).

A group of 35 or 40 people attended a luncheon meeting at the Hollenden Hotel in Cleveland Ohio, on Sunday, February 25, 1934. In describing the group, Henry C. Johnson wrote, "All in all, the 'liberal' educational leadership of the mid-thirties was fairly tightly definable, and the Dewey Society's original rolls represented perhaps its most select cadre." In fact, the organizational meeting was labeled informally as The Newlon-Harap Luncheon of Liberals in Education (ibid.).

Henry Harap recalled the interchange of ideas at the meeting as "vigorous and exciting" (Harap 1970, 158). The meeting was such a success that a second session was held the following Tuesday so that all present could voice their opinions. Although Harap claimed that the membership was more national in scope than that of some competing organizations, his list of founding members shows that the majority of them came from the East and more than one-fourth from Teachers College alone (ibid., 162–163).

After a second meeting in New York City the following fall, Counts, Rugg, and Newlon issued another call for a conference in conjunction with the superintendents' annual February meeting. It was to include "the left wing in education—Rugg, Newlon, Counts, etc." for the purpose of launching the new organization (Kilpatrick 1935). Hanna, Newlon, and Kilpatrick planned the meeting, which was held in Atlantic City on February 24, 1935, to "launch a strong national society for the scientific study of school and society" (Harap 1970, 161). At a luncheon session, the members took steps to establish an organizational structure for the group. After lunch, the attendees discussed the prospects for publishing society members' research. Harap held publication as a primary purpose of the society from its inception, and the John Dewey Society yearbooks were the realization of his vision. That same afternoon, Hanna described to the members the *Building America* project that he had launched under the sponsorship of the Society for Curriculum Study.

Paul Hanna took no part in the society's yearbooks until its third one, published in 1939. Harold Rugg edited that volume, entitled *Democracy and the Curriculum: The Life and Program of the American School*. In a wonderful sequence of logic, Rugg's introduction to the volume stated the social view of education shared by many educational liberals. He wrote, "This book has been written in the conviction that government can be democratic only when it is based on the consent of the people—and consent is given only when the people understand. This conception makes government in a democratic society synonymous with education" (Rugg 1939, x).

Hanna's contribution was a chapter entitled, "The School: Looking Forward," and it placed him firmly in the liberal camp. His piece reflected the vision he held at the time of the school as a multipurpose social service agency supported by and supportive of government. Drawing on his earlier advocacy of the community school concept, he described the school of the future as "tax-supported and its services free to all citizens . . . the School serves as the community's instrument through which the conditions essential for a <u>more adequate life</u> are progressively achieved (emphasis his)" (ibid., 382). He had a broad range of services in mind: "Better community health, improved recreation facilities, adequate housing, more beautiful physical environment, more efficient industrial and agricultural practices to provide a higher economic standard of living—in fact, any and all problems of concern to the community as a whole are brought to the School for study and proposals are made for solutions" (ibid., 382–383).

In later years, Hanna's involvement with the John Dewey Society, as with many domestic education organizations of which he was a member, waned as he became more deeply involved in international education. For example, his only subsequent involvement with a John Dewey Society yearbook was his service on the editorial board of the society's 1953 publication, *The American Elementary School*. Still, in 1957 he was nominated for election to the executive board of the society. In response to society president Gordon Hull-fish's inquiry as to his interest in serving on the board if elected, Hanna replied, "My answer is 'yes.' I'm turning down almost everything that comes of this nature because of other commitments, but the John Dewey Society is an organization to which I believe one owes whatever talents he may possess" (Hanna 1957b). He was not elected, nor was he elected when nominated again in 1960.

THE SOCIETY FOR CURRICULUM STUDY

The Society for Curriculum Study (SCS) was another forum in which social reconstructionists promoted their views. Scientific curriculum development was a fairly new field, and two distinct groups saw a need to create professional organizations as forums for discussion of curriculum issues. Again, Henry Harap was instrumental in the founding of this group. He proposed to W. W. Charters that a select group of college instructors meet to form an organization. Originally named The National Society of Curriculum Workers, it began in 1929 as an "intimate group of forty-eight college instructors in the field of curriculum" (Noonan 1984, 16). At the same time, a group of curriculum directors in the public schools were meeting informally during the conventions of the Department of Superintendence of the National Education Association (Saylor 1986, 7). The two groups first met jointly at the 1930 Department of Superintendence gathering in Atlantic City, and they continued to meet until they formally merged to form The Society for Curriculum Study (SCS) in 1932. By 1939, the Society's membership had reached its peak of 807.

With the onset and deepening of the Great Depression, SCS meetings were increasingly focused on the school's role in developing solutions to the crisis. The theme of an early meeting was The Relation of the Curriculum to the Present Economic Crisis

(Society for Curriculum Study 1932, 1). Henry Harap recalled that
the leaders of SCS were "liberal in outlook . . . committed to finding
ways to improve the social order through education" (Noonan 1984,
17). They were serious about scientific approaches to curriculum
making and saw curriculum reform "as a way of contributing to
social and economic reconstruction" (ibid.). That emphasis appealed to Paul Hanna and, uncharacteristically, he took leadership
roles in both the society's publications and its annual meetings.

In 1932, the society launched *The Curriculum Journal* as its
official publication. This journal is a particularly useful resource
for the historian of education because its early volumes include an
annual summary of activities of the society's members. Throughout
its eleven-year run, it also included an annual bibliography of members' curriculum-oriented publications. Paul Hanna contributed an
article on new curriculum courses being offered at Teachers College
to the December 1932 issue. In the following years of that decade,
he contributed at least five articles to *The Curriculum Journal*, but
his involvement dropped off in the early 1940s. The annual index
showed no articles by Hanna from 1940 through the end of publication in 1943. This period coincided with Hanna's increasing involvement with Stanford University Services to secure wartime contracts from the federal government. His work with all professional
organizations declined during these years.

The journal's reports of the society's annual meetings reveal a
similar pattern of involvement by Hanna. At the February, 1933
meeting in Minneapolis, Hanna participated with Hollis Caswell
and others in a roundtable discussion of the topic, The Curriculum
and the Changing Economic Life. The next year, the society's annual meeting was held in Cleveland and Hanna served as the program chairman. He also reprised a presentation of curriculum materials for dealing with current social and economic problems that
he originally made to the 1932 meeting of the National Education
Association. On Saturday, February 24 of 1934, he proposed the
development of a magazine format curriculum aid for teachers' use

in presenting current events using *social problems* instructional techniques. The entire membership voted in favor of his proposal the next day, and on the following Tuesday Hanna was named chairman of a committee to pursue the project. This action launched the influential and controversial *Building America* series, and for the next decade much of Hanna's work with the society centered on this publication.

The following year, 1935, was a full one for Hanna and his work in the SCS. The annual meeting that year was held in Atlantic City, in conjunction with the John Dewey Society and the Department of Supervisors and Instruction of the NEA. The SCS membership elected Hanna to the SCS executive committee for a three-year term and he also became chair of a committee on statewide programs of curriculum revision. In addition, he was appointed to two committees that were important for the future of the SCS. One was the Constitution committee, charged with revising the society's founding charter, and the other was a committee to study the feasibility of affiliation with the NEA. At the 1935 meeting also, Hanna reported a successful beginning of the *Building America* series. He noted that nearly 18,000 sample copies of its inaugural issue on housing had been distributed, including the Educational Department of the Civilian Conservation Corps' (CCC) purchase of 7500 copies. At the meeting, Hanna also chaired the Saturday morning session and participated in a panel discussion at the Monday morning session.

In the following years, Hanna regularly appeared on the society's program to report on *Building America*'s progress. He often had other duties as well. In 1937, he presided over a session devoted to state curriculum programs at the annual meeting in New Orleans. At the 1938 meeting in Atlantic City, he was a discussant for a session on Problems of Scope and Sequence of the Curriculum in Relation to Psychology, Philosophy, and Social Life. Unfortunately, the subsequent issue of the *Curriculum Journal* contained no report of this session. He was also named, along with C. L. Cushman, Doak

Campbell, and others, to an exploratory committee on the Experimental Study of Basic Hypotheses in Curriculum Development. The program for the society's 1939 meeting, held in Cleveland, lists Hanna only as a reporter on programs of *Building America* at the Saturday luncheon. His limited appearance at this meeting remains surprising because the meeting that year was held jointly with the National Council on Childhood Education and the Department of Elementary School Principals of the NEA. Obligations to these organizations may have limited the time he could devote to SCS. In 1940, at St. Louis, Hanna served as a discussant for presentations about the issue, What Are the Essential Qualities of a Curriculum Workshop or Laboratory?

Hanna's wartime activities on behalf of Stanford University limited his involvement in the last meetings of the Society. For the years 1941 and 1942, Hanna was not listed on the programs of the annual meetings in any capacity, even though the 1942 meeting was held in San Francisco, close to Stanford. The final meeting of the Society for Curriculum Study as an independent entity was to be held in St. Louis in February, 1943. For this meeting, Hanna was scheduled to lead a discussion of presentations on the question, How to Meet Wartime Demands and Maintain Long-Term Values. Unfortunately, that meeting was never held due to wartime travel restrictions and the pending merger of SCS with the Department of Supervisors and Directors of Instruction to create the Association for Supervision and Curriculum Development.

Paul Hanna participated in the Society for Curriculum Study as extensively as he did in any other professional organization, but eventually his interest in it waned. Richard Noonan characterized the society as a fairly closed group of curriculum "technicians" who reduced the complex political problems facing Depression-era America and its schools to technical problems of curriculum. He claimed that this reduction was inherently undemocratic because it removed educational problems from the political sphere and placed them in the hands of *experts*. He argued that "The de-politicizing

of educational decision-making can be understood as a manifesta-
tion of the modern societal attack on democracy in the name of
efficiency, manageability, and *competence"* (Noonan 1984, 119). For
evidence, he pointed to the connections between the SCS and the
American Council on Education. He cast the two in a single mold
of promoting a scientifically developed curriculum designed to prepare children for industrial work (ibid., 83).

Possibly some members of the SCS saw such a social utilitarian
approach to the curriculum as desirable, and elements of it must
have appealed to Hanna's interest in orderly planning amidst the
chaos of the Great Depression. However, that vision surely would
have been too narrow to sustain his interest over a long period.
Instead, for Hanna and others of like mind, the society provided a
forum for their pursuit of deeper questions about the relation of the
schools to society. Hanna's declining interest in the society more
likely was due to his career moving in new directions than to any
philosophical disagreements with other members. The Society for
Curriculum Study was to be the last professional organization in
which Hanna became intimately involved for even as long as a
decade.

THE ASSOCIATION FOR SUPERVISION
AND CURRICULUM DEVELOPMENT

The Society for Curriculum Study announced its merger with the
National Education Association's Department of Supervisors and
Directors of Instruction in 1942, although planning for the merger
had been in the works for several years. The new association was
named the Department of Supervision and Curriculum Development and continued operations under the nominal umbrella of the
National Education Association (Saylor 1986, 10). Later, it became
the Association for Supervision and Curriculum Development
(ASCD), and almost thirty years later it severed its only fragile ties

to the National Education Association. According to William Van Til, the organization's early dedication to both discussion and action toward school improvement from the widest array of viewpoints and backgrounds appealed to university curriculum professors. He claimed that by the 1940s, existing professional organizations such as the NEA were too limited to address the broad range of concerns confronting American education. He wrote, "To us, the National Education Association seemed too much dominated by conservative school superintendents; the program of the separate subject matter organizations too specialized; the membership of the NEA department enrolling supervisors and directors of instruction too limited" (Van Til 1986, 1).

ASCD enrolled a significant membership from the West Coast, although individuals from the East and the Midwest clearly dominated the association. Influential members from the West Coast included Hilda Taba, I. James Quillen, J. Paul Leonard, and Helen Heffernan. Other Hanna friends and colleagues who found a home in ASCD included Hollis Caswell, Harold Hand, and Donald Cottrell. The association's attraction for some members was described by Hanna: ". . . we felt that we might create in the ASCD an organization that dealt with both society and the child" (Hanna 1973a, 87). However, Hanna recalled "a big fight because we wanted curriculum and society and some who were joining us who were members of the old *progressive ed* wanted to hold the old banner [of child-centered progressivism] high" (Hanna 1974, 130). Such a "fight" was not mentioned by either William Van Til or J. Galen Saylor in their recollections of the first meetings of the Association (Van Til 1986). Hanna may have referred to the differences he perceived between the new organization and the small, intimate Society for Curriculum Study, or the ideologically unified John Dewey Society. ASCD was much larger than either of those organizations, and it included many more school administrators who were interested in the everyday details of curriculum and instruction rather than in the broader social issues with which Hanna had been concerned (ibid., 14; Van Til 1983, 192).

Again, Hanna's involvement with ASCD was spotty, and more frequent in the early years than later. The association's official voice was *Educational Leadership*, a journal formed by the merger of the NEA Department of Supervisors and Directors of Instruction's *Educational Method* and the Society for Curriculum Study's *Curriculum Journal*. Hanna was a frequent contributor to *Educational Leadership* during the journal's first year of publication. Throughout 1942–1943, for example, he wrote a monthly feature entitled "The Changing World." Hanna used the column to share his views of how world events impacted American education. His articles demonstrated his growing interest in the world beyond America's shores, and even beyond strictly curriculum issues.

Although Hanna stopped writing his column after the first eight issues, other authors revived it later. Hanna also contributed one article, "Education for the Larger Community," to the October 1946 issue and another, "Whose One World?" in April of 1952. Hanna did not write again for *Educational Leadership*, although many of his colleagues, including Taba, Quillen, Caswell, Counts, Kilpatrick, Laura Zirbes, L. Thomas Hopkins, and his sister, Geneva Hanna, continued to contribute to the journal.

The 1940s marked a turning point in Hanna's career as his vision of education turned international. One consequence of this change was his declining involvement in domestic professional organizations. World War II marked an enormous increase in Stanford University's contracted research for the United States government, and it did not end with the conclusion of the war. In fact, Stanford became a center for many types of strategic studies in the ensuing years of the cold war. As Director of University Services during these seminal years, Hanna was consumed with Stanford business. During these years, he shifted his personal focus toward international education. He was often abroad during the ASCD annual meetings, and his work in Latin America, Europe, and East Asia consumed increasing amounts of his time and energy.

Hanna served on ASCD's Board of Directors from 1944 until 1948, but he held no leadership position after that time. Even his participation in the annual meetings declined after the mid-century point. For example, he attended the 1946 annual conference in St. Louis in connection with *Building America*, but he was not listed as a presenter or discussant on any of the panels, even ones with such Hannaesque topics as The Community's School, and International Understanding at Work in the Classroom. The same pattern prevailed the following year when ASCD met in Chicago. Hanna was listed in connection with *Building America* again, but not, for example, as a participant in sessions on What Should Children Know About our National Social and Economic Problems? and How can Schools Aid in the Development of More Effective International Understanding? He next appeared on the program for the 1950 Meeting in Denver as one of several individuals having special responsibilities in the study groups. Subsequent programs did not list him as a participant.

A deeper philosophical reason also may explain the decline of Hanna's involvement in ASCD. Patricia Graham attributed the demise of the PEA partly to its inability to "play it safe" during the years of most intense reaction to progressivism. She claimed that organizations like ASCD and the National Council for Accreditation of Teacher Education weathered the political storms of the 1940s and 1950s by shifting focus from the controversial issues of the social role of schools to more technical matters of curriculum and supervision. She wrote, "After 1945, . . . many of the leaders of these groups were more concerned with practical curricular problems than with educational theories . . . Criticisms of capitalism had become distinctly less popular" (Graham 1967, 105). Daniel Tanner echoed her:

Those organizations that survived had changed with the times. They admitted into their number people who did not wholly subscribe to their doctrines, and they took on practical service activities. The Association for Supervision and Curriculum Development is a good example . . . . Now a field service organization, it has a huge membership, but its early commitment toward progressive doctrine has disappeared (Tanner 1991, x).

William Van Til disagreed. He thought that social education was very much a concern for ASCD. He wrote, "In the more than 40 years that followed my first experiences in the organization, ASCD has continued to demonstrate social concern and commitment to better education in its activities" (Van Til 1986, 2). However, he held a different view than Hanna on what "social concern and commitment" meant. Hanna called for social critique and activism through his advocacy of community schools and his work with *Building America*. On the other hand, ASCD's social concern apparently was expressed through such technical elements as "[recognition of] the interdependence of curricular sources derived from social, psychological, and philosophical foundations. ASCD has a long history of support for a balanced curriculum and effective leadership practices" (ibid.).

Hanna's personal interpretation was that "the ASCD became the replacement for the Progressive Education Association. But the same thing happened to the ASCD that happened to the Progressive Education Association—the child-centered group took over!" (Hanna 1973a, 87). He was concerned that the association came to focus too much on the technical details of curriculum at the expense of larger issues of the school and society. Helen Heffernan thought that the opposite had happened. She believed that the society-centered SCS had taken over the Department of Supervisors and Directors of Instruction (Noonan 1984, 20).

Hanna's belief in the correctness of his own judgment sometimes foreclosed the consideration of alternative views, however. In the early 1960s he expressed his dismay over ASCD's perceived drift in a letter to his sister. Geneva Hanna had just been elected to the Association's Board of Directors, and he was writing to congratulate her. Hanna wrote, "You know how much we are counting on you to put some life and direction into this organization" (Hanna 1961c). By that time, of course, Paul Hanna had only a distant perspective on the association and its work because he had not been an active participant for a decade.

Hanna's withdrawal from involvement in ASCD set the stage for a minor, yet poignant, event in his later life. In a letter dated December 20, 1977, written in response to Hanna's inquiry about his membership status, ASCD's Membership Coordinator, Clara M. Burleigh, replied, "I am unable to locate a membership for you. Life memberships are only given to those members who joined and were consecutive members for 20 years. I will be glad to enter a membership for you. Please check which membership you want and return the attached card. We will bill you later" (Burleigh 1977).

A note at the bottom, in Hanna's own hand, reads, "I took out life membership when Caswell, Cushman, I and others created ASCD many years ago. The present staff members have no file or recollection of this matter." He added bitterly, "I will not respond." Nevertheless, he later attended at least one ASCD annual conference that met in San Francisco.

THE NATIONAL EDUCATION ASSOCIATION

Although members of the National Education Association's Department of Superintendence merged with the National Society of Curriculum Workers to form the Society for Curriculum Study in the 1930s, the department continued as a separate entity, holding meetings and publishing yearbooks under its own label. The Department had long served as a venue for discussion of the relationship of education to society, with education leaders such as Newlon, Counts, Hopkins, Caswell, and Childs among its membership.

Paul Hanna joined the department when he first went to West Winfield, New York, to become superintendent of schools in 1926. By the early 1930s, the department's statements commonly addressed the school's role in society. A 1932 resolution called for the establishment of a committee to suggest such changes in the social studies curriculum ". . . in our junior and senior high schools as our present social and economic situation has made necessary and vital" (National Education Association 1932, 671).

The department's yearbooks reveal an inconsistent membership record for Hanna, although he participated in the organization's 1939 meeting at Cleveland. Hanna's record of membership in the Department of Superintendence mirrored his ambivalence toward its parent organization, the National Education Association. With a few exceptions, his involvement with the NEA was through associated organizations. One example was his chairmanship of the important NEA/PEA Joint Commission on Resources and Education in the prewar and early wartime periods. The thrust of the commission's work was to build an "educational program essential to an effective use of our human and physical resources" (Society for Curriculum Study 1940, 3). The commission proposed coordination among resource planning agencies to educate the general public, coordination among teacher education programs, and the publication of classroom materials on resource planning and use. In addition, the commission recommended holding conferences on resources and education. It received funding from the General Education Board to conduct two summer institutes and five regional workshops for teachers and others. The commission also recommended providing assistance to other agencies for educational purposes in the amount of $150,000 per year for five years. Although not all the commission's ambitious plans came to fruition, its recommendations reflected the Depression-era concern for scientific planning in the use of resources for education. This remained a deep-seated concern for Paul Hanna throughout his life, and the NEA was the primary forum for his efforts in that regard.

Hanna's name did not appear in the membership rolls of the department for two decades after 1929. His absence seems odd, because so many of his mentors and colleagues were active leaders in the organization and contributors to its yearbooks. Hanna was also strangely absent as a contributor to key department yearbooks such as "Social Change and Education" and "Social Studies Curriculum." Ralph Tyler, Henry Harap, George Counts, Charles Beard, and others contributed pieces to these books, but not Hanna. Other yearbooks on topics of interest to Hanna included "Improvement of Education for Democracy" and "Youth Education Today," but neither book included a Hanna chapter. Admittedly, these books were published during the mid-1930s when the Hannas were adjusting to their new life in California and building their new home. In addition, the influence of progressives in the yearbooks declined after the 1930s. Still, Hanna wrote nearly two dozen articles for other publications between 1929 and 1949.

When Paul Hanna's name reappeared on the department's membership rolls in 1949, he was listed as a life member. From that time on, he was more active in the organization. In fact, one of his Our Changing World articles for *Educational Leadership* enthusiastically promoted the NEA as a unified voice for teachers.

Hanna served on the Commission on Educating for American Citizenship that organized the department's thirty-second yearbook. He was a major contributor to the book, drawing examples of school–community interactions from his *Youth Serves the Community*. He also drew on his expanding communities curriculum design to articulate a scheme of citizenship education in a section of the yearbook entitled "The Seven Circles of Civic Responsibility." In a chapter in the yearbook entitled "Practicing Citizenship,"

Hanna lists "basic human cooperative activities," much like the basic human activities in his curriculum model.

In 1962, Hanna challenged the NEA membership at its annual convention to consider the establishment of a national commission for curriculum research and development. He called on the membership to expand the nascent Project on Instruction into a full-blown National Curriculum and Instruction Center. In his conception, the center would become a leading force in curriculum research, development, and proliferation. It would exert influence on teacher preparation programs in the colleges, as well as on local and state education administrations, in order to unify and standardize curriculum and instructional practices throughout the United States. The membership was unmoved, however, and little more than discussion came of Hanna's proposal.

Hanna became disillusioned with the NEA in later years. The association's support of collective bargaining rights for teachers set it on "a course of action that was to change the character of the Association in respects then unenvisioned" (West 1980, 45). A resolution passed at the 1961 meeting of the NEA's Representative assembly embroiled the organization's leadership and membership in discussions of union representation, dispute resolution, and strikes. Curriculum took a back seat. That vote was a radical departure from the past, when the NEA had served as a forum for debate on items of more immediate import to the classroom, and many were alienated by it. Hanna recalled,

> Since 1927, as a young member of the NEA, I had been inspired and educated by attending the annual and regional conventions of the organization. I read the journals and brochures, and still recall today the preponderance of excellent addresses and articles on curriculum and instruction. In the 1960s, the content of the publication and conventions changed. NEA swung its focus from curriculum and instruction to a union's concern about work conditions, tenure, and compensation for its members. While such

union goals are important, there remained little time and energy to pursue the original professional goals of the organization (Hanna 1987, 92).

The move toward union concerns marked a turning point in the balance of power in the organization. Previously, the association had been led chiefly by school administrators, but the decade of the 1960s saw the rise to power of classroom teachers within the NEA (West 1980, 242). The vote also revealed a change in Hanna's thought over time. His 1943 columns for *Educational Leadership* had included one extolling collective bargaining for teachers. By the 1960s, however, Hanna saw collective bargaining as a threat to the intellectual integrity of the organization. NEA records reveal no more involvement by Hanna after passage of the 1961 resolution.

THE NATIONAL COUNCIL FOR
THE SOCIAL STUDIES

Of all the organizations to which Paul Hanna might have devoted his energies, the National Council for the Social Studies (NCSS) appears to have been the most closely linked with his professional interests. However, his participation in its work and activities was marginal.

The NCSS began in 1921 as a department of the National Education Association, and its first yearbooks were published as part of the journal *Historical Outlook*. At that time, the organization held no independent national meeting (Thornton 1996, 4). Instead, members met in conjunction with the NEA meeting in July, with the American Historical Association in December, and with the Department of Supervisors and Instruction in February. The first independent NCSS yearbook was published in 1931, and its first independent national meeting was held in 1935 (ibid., 5). Hanna's involvement in other organizations sapped the resources he might have given to NCSS, and he never served in the council's leadership—although many of his associates did. His Stanford colleagues I. James Quillen and Richard Gross, for example, served as NCSS presidents—Quillen in the early 1940s and Gross in the mid-1960s.

Hanna had minimal involvement in NCSS publications as well, contributing to only two NCSS yearbooks. He wrote a chapter entitled "Social Education through Cooperative Community Service" for the 1938 yearbook and (with John R. Lee) a chapter on "Generalizations in the Social Studies" for the 1962 Yearbook. That relative silence seems odd. Hanna colleagues such as Quillen, Harap, Taba, Heffernan, Clyde Kohn, Harold Drummond, Fannie Shaftel, and others were regular contributors to volumes with titles that denoted topics of interest to Hanna such as *The Social Studies in the Elementary School, Education for Democratic Citizenship, International Dimensions in the Social Studies*, and *Social Studies Curriculum Development: Prospects and Problems*.

Hanna never revealed any reasons for his lack of participation in NCSS. He may have thought that his social studies textbooks were contribution enough to the field. Most likely, however, Hanna agreed with William Van Til that "the programs of the separate subject matter organizations [were] too specialized" (Van Til 1986, 1). Throughout his career, the bulk of Hanna's writing for professional journals focused on larger questions of schools and society rather than on the narrower issues of curriculum and instruction. His professional activity early in his career centered on organizations such as the Progressive Education Association, the John Dewey Society, and the Society for Curriculum Study, in which the members investigated ways that the schools could help mold the social, economic, and political institutions around them. Later in his career, he simply invested his energies in international organizations to address similar issues overseas.

CONCLUSION

Paul Hanna's decision to move to the West Coast in 1936 and to stay there for the remainder of his career impacted his place in the history of education. At Stanford, his career moved in different directions than it might have had he stayed in the East. As new interests dominated his activities his involvement in professional organizations declined. Consequently, some historians of education have overlooked his important role in many of the professional organizations to which social reconstructionists adhered in the 1930s.

Hanna's entrepreneurial personality also played a role in his estrangement from core professional organizations. An entrepreneur is a visionary, investing his energies in the creation of a thing and marshaling the resources to bring it to fruition. Once the enterprise is established, a different set of skills is required to keep it running. Established enterprises require effective managers—people who can attend to the thousand niggling details over a prolonged period of time. Rarely do real entrepreneurial and managerial gifts reside in the same individual, and Paul Hanna was more an entrepreneur than a manager. His development of the extremely successful Hanna textbook series for Scott, Foresman and Company took more and more time as the volumes increased and he became more involved in their promotion. Also, his work with Stanford University Services kept him involved in the administrative and financial aspects of university life, especially during World War II.

If Hanna's involvement in professional organizations fell off after the war, it coincided with the decline of progressive thought in education generally. The 1930s were the high point for the social reconstructionists. The aftermath of the world war reigned in both curricular experimentation and optimism about its social impact. War was followed by reaction, and progressives of all descriptions came under attack. The fifteen years after V-J Day saw anticommunist hysteria in education and elsewhere, along with a *back to basics* thrust in curriculum development. Social and educational reconstructionists found themselves increasingly on the defensive.

At the same time, the world literally opened up to Paul Hanna. He first became involved in international education issues in the period immediately preceding the war. His work for the Coordinator of Inter-American Affairs developed his appetite for international travel and study, and in the years after the war his energies increasingly centered on education as a tool for economic and political development overseas. As a result, Hanna's involvement in domestic education organizations declined. Some historians unfamiliar with his early career misread that phase of his career as an attempt to export Americanism in support of United States cold war–era foreign policy. Actually, he simply extended his efforts to instill democratic habits of mind through education to schools overseas. Through those activities, he became integrally involved with UNESCO and other UN-related organizations, the Asia Society, and the East-West Center looking west from California, and the Atlantic Council and other international organizations looking to the east.

Although those international enterprises affected his participation in conventional professional organizations, they did not deter his interest in educating children for democracy. In fact, they provided new forums for him to test and implement his ideas. In the final analysis, this explanation for Hanna's exclusion from the pantheon of key educational theorists of this century may prove the most compelling. Hanna was more than just a theorist—he was a practical innovator who sought to implement his ideas. Lawrence Cremin explained the failure of the radical reconstructionists significantly to impact policy by claiming that, "The brilliant polemicists of *The Social Frontier* were simply finessed by less imaginative men with more specific pedagogical nostrums to purvey" (Cremin 1961, 231). Whether less imaginative than other social frontiersmen or not, Hanna put a premium on practical results. He never wrote as much about the theoretical basis of his curriculum models as some of the other educational progressives did about theirs, but he influenced generations here and abroad with his ideas. First through *Building America* and then through the Hanna Social Studies Series and his consulting work with foreign school systems, Hanna spread his ideas far beyond the reaches of the eastern–midwestern alliance of progressive education and progressive educators' small-circulation journals. Chapter Seven describes the expansion of Hanna's interests to include education overseas.

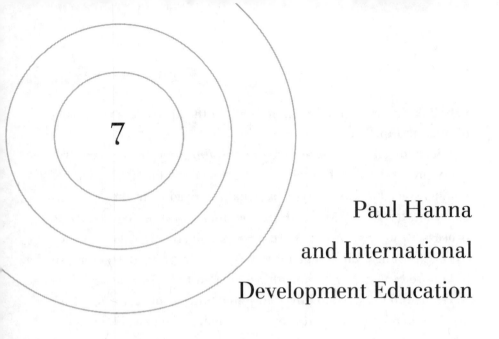

Paul Hanna
and International
Development Education

The years after World War II marked a change of venue more than a change of direction for Paul Hanna's career. His fundamental goals remained constant, whereas his theater of operations expanded. In the postwar era he became less involved in domestic education concerns and organizations and more involved in education for economic, social, and political development overseas. Hanna's approach to development education was far-reaching. It encompassed the development in students of habits and attitudes of democratic participation on a national and international basis, as well as the specific skills needed to create modern economies and social systems. Many reasons account for that expansion of his interests.

First, Hanna realized the potential for development education during and immediately after the war. Devising ways in which Stanford University could contribute to the war effort encouraged him to view education as an agent of the state. He recognized that study of the school's role in political, social, and economic development held great potential both in terms of its immediate application on behalf of American foreign policy and, in the abstract, as a subject of scholarship.

Second, Hanna's experience in the *Building America* controversy prompted him to seek new ways to implement his ideas of democratic education, ways somewhat removed from the ideological litmus tests of the McCarthy era. Hanna's loyalties to democratic processes and institutions were never seriously attacked, but they were questioned. He deemed it unwise to answer his detractors, so he ignored them, but he must have bristled to know that his ideas were misunderstood. Moreover, he noted the real and grievous damage inflicted by similar attacks on national colleagues like George Counts, men whom he considered just as patriotic as himself (Hanna 1974, 72). He likely turned to overseas work as one means by which to avoid the minefield of domestic American politics.

Third, moving into international education studies logically extended Hanna's interest in democratic education and supported his notion of the expanding communities model for a scope and sequence in social studies. In a sense, his concentric circles had to encompass "international communities of men" in order to be comprehensive. Just as the expanding communities model grew out of Hanna's concern to prepare students for life in a democratic society, so his work in international development education clearly aimed to spread American-style democracy across the globe. Hanna anticipated that the postwar world would be one in which the United States would play a greater role in international leadership than ever before.

Hanna was also a proponent of constitutional democracy. His summary of decades of study in forces of political and social change was that, "Everybody knows what the goals are. The goals are to improve the democratic open pluralistic society, and to do it by constitutional or accepted methods" (ibid.).

BEGINNINGS

Hanna's interest in the world beyond the United States dates at least to his days at Hamline University. Hamline had a number of international students in residence, and Hanna befriended Dison Po, a Chinese student. Po's English diction was poor, and Jean Shuman, Hanna's future wife, tutored him. The three became fast friends, and the Hannas later visited Po when he was governor of Taiwan (Hanna 1974). Hanna recalled no particular experiences at Teachers College that sparked his interest in international affairs, but living in cosmopolitan New York City certainly stimulated his interest in the larger world.

The integration of Paul Hanna's interest in education with his interest in the wider world came at the beginning of World War II. At a dinner party in 1940, Robert G. Caldwell first recruited him to serve as an observer for the Coordinator for Inter-American Affairs (CIAA). The coordinator's office technically was part of the Council on National Defense, but because of the inroads that the Axis nations had made in Central and South America, President Roosevelt brought the agency under his own direct control. As its head, he appointed an ambitious young New Yorker, Nelson Rockefeller. One of Rockefeller's first acts was to dispatch fact-finding missions, including Hanna's, to South America in 1940–1941 (Reich 1996, 186).

Hanna took a sabbatical leave from Stanford for the 1940–1941 school term and planned a trip to locations in Central and South America. In early October, Hanna, his wife Jean, and their children, John and Emily, set out for the highlands of Bolivia. They traveled to coastal Peru and coastal and central Ecuador, visiting small villages and archaeological sites. Their three-month journey ended with stops in Panama and Guatemala. Hanna followed this trip with a three-week visit to Guatemala in late 1941 and early 1942 (John Hanna 1998).

Hanna's trips to Central and South America resulted in a report to the educational section of the Office of the Coordinator for Inter-American Affairs. In it, Hanna revealed a sensitivity to the ravages of European colonialism affecting those nations he had visited. He remarked about the tremendous natural resources of the region and the innate intelligence of the people, but pointed to the underutilization of both. He found that the exploitation of natural resources was largely in the hands of foreign firms: "Wherever the natural resources are being developed, one is likely to find foreign capital and management in control. The people of these Republics themselves are generally not aware that the resources exist, nor would they be able to develop them if they had definite knowledge of their worth" (Hanna 1942?, 2).

Hanna believed that education was the key to economic development in the region. Using Peru as his example, he listed significant problems, pointing out that only a small portion of the population received a formal education. Even that small group was "exposed to a curriculum that would not be considered by modern educators to contain even the minimum essentials needed by these people individually or as a social group. The curriculum for the most part is patterned after European models of the nineteenth century." He decried the lack of locally produced curriculum materials, observing that "The textbooks generally are direct translations from German, Spanish, French and English texts . . ." (ibid., 3). They seldom mentioned problems of local or national concern or significance.

Hanna noted little tradition of professional teaching or scholarship in those countries. He observed, "The teachers are poorly trained, and education as a profession hardly exists. The teachers, particularly on the secondary and collegiate levels, earn their living in some other trade or profession and teach merely as an avocation" (ibid.). Likewise, native scholars contributed little in areas of research. Hanna noted, "Wherever I went I inquired concerning the status of research. I found little of it. Where I did find it, research was usually being conducted, or at least directed, by research workers from foreign countries" (ibid.). From these observations, Hanna concluded that progress in the region would have to await "the coming of universal education and native scientific workers" (ibid., 4).

Hanna then focused on how the United States could assist the republics of Central and South America in their development. He suggested a two-pronged approach. First, the United States must win the sympathies of the intelligentsia in the target nations. Here, Hanna displayed an understanding of the social structure of Latin American nations. He advocated working with these people instead of the economic and social elites, because "they are far more active in public affairs than in the United States, and their influence spreads through these countries like the mycelium of a mushroom; the journalists, engineers, medicos, poets, writers, et cetera, at least in much of the continent, touch the people far more generally than in the United States" (Hanna 1942?, 5).

Moreover, the educational opportunities in the United States already appealed to South American intellectuals. Hanna noted that "many of the most learned groups consistently look to the United States for the most advanced and best thought" (ibid.). He warned that while the United States had done little to cultivate these relationships, "the totalitarian European nations have been importing Latin Americans to study in their universities, student pilots to learn flying and fighting in their air corps, and so forth" (ibid., 5–6).

The second prong of Hanna's approach was to extend free public education to the masses. From the masses, he argued, "we may expect the great civil, educational, social, scientific and artistic leaders to emerge" (ibid., 6). He went on to argue that education for democratic citizenship must be an indispensable part of national curriculum goals.

Hanna's report further outlined a number of projects to help realize U.S. goals in the region. He thought that the United States should assist the Latin American republics in matters of teacher education, curriculum development, organization of teachers' associations, and development of curriculum materials and professional education libraries (Hanna 1942?, 10–23). Much of this work could be financed by private foundations in the United States. He also proposed exchange programs for students, scholars, artists, and athletic teams to promote mutual understanding (ibid., 32). He recommended that the United States aid the libraries of these nations, and even provide literature for them, including the *one hundred best books*, and special editions of *Building America* (ibid., 44–46). He concluded by recommending that the United States provide social and economic planning assistance in the region (ibid., 50).

None of Hanna's recommendations were new ideas, and some programs had already been launched to accomplish them. Still, by adding his support to them, Hanna helped shift the emphasis of U.S. programs in Latin America toward education. His report provided the CIAA with an informed analysis by which to consider how education might further the long-range goals of American foreign policy in the region. The missions to Latin America provided Hanna with his first opportunity to study the effects of education on the development of political ideologies and economic attitudes in specific settings outside the United States. On the basis of that work, Hanna consulted with the U.S. military in 1947 on the educational aspects of building a new Central American canal through Nicaragua.

HANNA AND POSTWAR GERMANY

In the years immediately following the war, Paul Hanna had an opportunity to export American educational ideals to Germany. The Supreme Headquarters of the Allied Expeditionary Force (SHAEF) faced the monumental task of reconstruction in Germany. One of the most daunting challenges was the development of a school system freed from Nazi influences. SHAEF's Education and Religious Affairs (ERA) section was assigned this task (Tent 1982, 16). ERA began by eliminating teachers and school officials with known Nazi sympathies from German schools, and by purging textbooks of the same bias (ibid., 52). Officials hoped that enough books from the pre-Nazi Weimar era might be located to serve the schools on an emergency basis. These books were scarce, and those that were available proved to be too nationalistic and bellicose for the American school reformers' purposes. Nonetheless, emergency copies were published by SHAEF with a disclaimer concerning their content (ibid., 111).

With that immediate need addressed, the War Department turned to a more deliberative study of the educational issues involved in the rehabilitation of Germany. The result was the first U.S. Education Mission to Germany, composed of education scholars and officials, religious educators, and a Textile Workers' Union official (ibid., 115). The team, led by George Zook of the American Council on Education, spent more than a month in the summer of 1946 studying the state of German education in the U.S. zone of occupation. The result, sometimes called the Zook Report, was a thoughtful presentation of what ought to be done in German schools and society to inculcate the habits of democratic living. It eloquently described the need to teach democracy and to teach democratically:

> The school emerges as the common center of mutuality, where
> ideally all children meet as fellow-children before any have been

narrowed by class or creedal bias. But even to approach this ideal
we must have not merely the essentially negative safeguards of
creed, race, and class toleration, but have also exemplified in the
school the positive *method* of living which a democratic citizenship
enshrines and climaxes. The goal of democracy is the democratic
man (*Report of the U.S. Education Mission to Germany* 1946, 14).

A well-marked copy of the 1946 *Report of the U.S. Education
Mission to Germany* in the Hanna Collection reveals that Hanna
closely studied the work of those pioneers in the study of German
reeducation. Many passages sound like Hanna's own writing from
the 1920s and 1930s. The conclusion to one section entitled "The
Development of Democracy" describes the school's pivotal role in
preparing democratic citizens:

> This is the way in which democracy as a form of government finds
> its spirit through a way of life. The school is central to this enter-
> prise. Its influence can slowly create a family in which mutuality
> rather than dominance help the child to equanimity as the inner
> fruit of formal equality . . . the school can fill the hand that feeds
> it, until sound minds in a sound society may yet justify the negative
> pains of purification and fulfill the positive faith America had and
> has in the potencies of democratization (*Report*, 16).

In the margin beside these words, Hanna wrote "excellent."

On the heels of the first education mission, the Education and
Religious Affairs section organized tours of the U.S. Zone by visiting
experts. Hanna was one of these U.S. visitors. He served on a team
of educational leaders in Germany to advise the Office of Military
Government-U.S. (OMGUS) on educational matters (Klous 1946).
Among the matters on which the War Department sought Hanna's
advice were "(1) the training of teachers for teachers' colleges and
teacher education work; (2) the general curriculum pattern for practice teaching in the broadest sense; (3) the content of such courses
as child psychology; and (4) principles of education, social studies,
and comparative education" (ibid.).

Visitors typically attended orientation sessions in Washington, D.C., then flew to Berlin for more extensive briefings before taking up their field assignments (Tent 1982, 261). A souvenir menu from the Allied Control Authority dining salon revealed that Paul and Jean Hanna were in Berlin by March 22, 1947. They were in the largest group of the thirty-five American educational experts brought to the U.S. Zone that year, and their presence was not entirely appreciated. Some on the OMGUS staff were leery of visitors with little expertise in European education and no knowledge of the German language posing as specialists on the German school situation. Walter Bergman, the ERA chief in Bavaria, was a particularly outspoken critic. He complained that they stayed only a short while, taxed ERA resources, and attempted to "transplant the whole American scheme of education to Germany" (Bergman 1947). He reported that "A few of the experts, who had never traveled in Germany or seen German schools, seemed more interested in gathering information and experience than in trying to be of immediate service in Germany" (ibid.).

Bergman singled out Hanna as an example of his problems with the experts. He claimed that "Dr. Hanna, though a very able and well-known man, did almost nothing for Bavaria. He did not understand German nor the German educational system. His plan was considered to be a stereotyped 'scope and sequence' plan that did not face realistically the present German situation" (ibid.).

If the OMGUS staff did not find Hanna's input useful, others did. Once back in the United States, he wholeheartedly supported the reeducation work in Germany. In a report on his visit, he wrote,

> My observations in Germany lead me with the irristible [sic] logic to accept the burden of putting our efforts resolutely behind the United States Office of Military Government and our State Department. The task will require money, materials, and personnel. And above all, it will require persistance [sic] to stay at so arduous a task. But persist we must, until we can see the fruits of our labor

in free men living under governments deriving their power from the voluntary consent of the governed. Persist we must until we can see institutions, firmly rooted, that guarantee the Bill of Human Rights to all. To do less, will bring upon us World War III (Hanna 1947b).

Hanna did not support the efforts at educational reconstruction in the occupied countries with stirring words alone. He attended the Second National Conference on the Occupied Countries in 1950 as Stanford University's representative. That conference was a joint effort of the American Council on Education, the State Department, and the U.S. Army to evaluate the progress and prospects of education in the former Axis nations. More significantly, Hanna told students in later years that he worked on a team to evaluate both the framework and the ideology of German textbooks in the postwar period, and that he "spent considerable time in 1945, '46, and '47 in Germany" (Foster 1998b). Although scant evidence exists of any extensive work by Hanna on textbooks for the reeducation effort, social science instruction in postwar Germany and Japan alike reflected many of Hanna's ideas. The postwar German schools taught recent history and the social sciences, but also analyses of contemporary society, including classroom discussions of controversial subjects (Hayse 1997). Hanna advocated a similar approach through the *Building America* series.

Likewise, postwar education reforms in Japan reflected Hanna's influence, even if indirectly. In 1949, the Japanese Ministry of Education and Culture introduced new courses of study as part of a national education reform in Japan. Ronald Stone Anderson reported that "Probably the most controversial break with the past curriculum was the elimination of the separate courses in morals, geography, and history, and their replacement by an integrated course called social studies . . . It was to educate for effective citizenship" (Anderson 1959, 102). Although Hanna did not invent the concept of integrated social studies, by 1949 he was among its primary advocates, and his textbooks spread integrated studies far and wide.

The influence of Hanna's social studies textbooks was more clearly seen in the curriculum model devised to present social studies in the occupied countries. Elementary school teachers in Japan were to present "... units built around the immediate environment of the child—home, school, and community. At the lower secondary level the area of study was expanded to include the life of the Nation and foreign countries. Here the course—general social studies— was to utilize the problem approach and the problems were to be based on studies of the needs of young people in Japan" (ibid.). The social problems approach within an expanding communities framework was pure Hanna.

Paul Hanna was not one of the major players in the rehabilitation of the German or Japanese school systems in the postwar era. Nonetheless, his pervasive influence in curriculum development in the United States influenced those who did take a direct, long-term role in rebuilding the schools of the former Axis countries. In fact, the pacifism and internationalism that have developed in the Japanese and German people in the postwar era are a fulfillment of what Hanna hoped his curriculum designs might accomplish in the United States.

HANNA AND THE PHILIPPINES

Hanna's work in international development education took on a much broader scope in the Philippines. That island nation became the focus of some of his most intensive and sustained efforts, and he worked there off and on for twenty years. He began with an appointment in late 1948 as an elementary education and teacher education specialist with the United Nations Educational, Scientific, and Cultural Organization's (UNESCO) educational mission to the Philippines.

The government of the Philippines had requested UNESCO's help in surveying elementary, secondary, and adult education. The resulting mission became the "first of the educational missions which UNESCO is undertaking" (Bodet 1948). The UNESCO consultants' reports were to help the Congress of the Philippines in drafting a new, comprehensive education law for the nation.

Hanna spent much of the spring of 1949 in the Philippines working on the project. The four-member UNESCO team met in Manila on Valentine's Day to plan its work, then spent the next three and a half months meeting with educators and laymen throughout the country, visiting schools and colleges, and gathering information. The team visited nearly two hundred grade schools and more than sixty normal schools and colleges in twenty-seven of the fifty Philippine provinces. Each member of the team was responsible for a specific portion of the survey, and they worked with officials from the government of the Philippines to gather data. At the end of the mission, the team flew to Paris to write its report at the UNESCO House there. Paul and Jean Hanna took advantage of this move to visit Hong Kong, Canton, Bangkok, Calcutta, Delhi, Jaipur, Brussels, and London. The team worked in Paris for two months and issued its final report on July 28 (*Report of the Mission to the Philippines* 1950, 7–8).

The report decried the impact of colonialism on the Philippine education system. It claimed that during Spanish colonial rule, the schools were largely private institutions with access limited to the social elite. Even then, their primary educational emphasis was religious instruction and the instructional language was, of course, Spanish. United States rule brought a change in focus toward political education, with the aim of preparing Filipinos for democratic citizenship. The instructional language was English. The Japanese invasion meant yet another shift in focus—toward integrating Filipinos into Japan's East Asia Co-Prosperity Sphere—with Japanese as the language of instruction. Mission members found that "each of the governing countries used education as an instrument for the development of its own ideals and culture" (*Report* 1950, 14). The ever-changing goals of schooling and the frequently changing instructional languages took their toll on the Filipinos. The mission found that literacy in the provinces ranged from nineteen to eighty-one percent, with a national average of only fifty percent (ibid., 17).

The report cited deficiencies in school facilities and funding, in teacher education programs, and in the availability of curriculum materials. It made recommendations to correct those deficiencies. Among the recommendations, mission members called for a broader curriculum. Many Philippine schools, especially the private schools, offered only an academic curriculum. Although those academically oriented institutions were a small part of the elementary education system, fully half of all secondary students attended private schools in 1947 (ibid., 18). The report conceded that the traditional academic subjects were important, but cited the "need for instilling in the pupils greater appreciation of the best national traditions and ideals, for imbuing them with the basic understanding necessary for the conservation and development of the country's resources, for developing the special abilities of each child, and for preparing them [sic] to participate more effectively in group and community living in the modern world" (ibid., 18).

To effect this broader curriculum, Hanna—the elementary education consultant on the team—recommended reorganizing the elementary school curriculum around sequentially unifying topics. His model was familiar. He suggested that students in grade one study Home and Family Life; grade two, Living in Our Schools; grade three, Living in Our Town and Province; grade four, Philippines history; and grade five, the island nation's resources. Grade six was to study The Philippines in the Community of the Eastern Hemisphere; and grade seven, The Philippines in the Community of the Western Hemisphere and in the Emerging World Community.

Apparently, Hanna believed that his expanding communities model was applicable universally.

Hanna also influenced the report's recommendation that community schools be developed further. He envisioned students in such schools becoming "more useful members of society through continuous participation in the study of the needs of the community" (ibid., 36). Working cooperatively, students and community members would identify, study, and work to address the needs of their localities. The community schools could also serve as "a significant instrument through which other community agencies may co-ordinate their efforts to attack the main problems of the community" (ibid.). The schools could serve as community centers for social and cultural functions. Hanna envisioned the school as "the center of the spontaneous and joyous life of the people" (ibid., 37). Hanna believed this type of school was a most valuable instrument of education. Through working together on real-life projects that materially affected their lives, the children and adults in the community mastered skills and subjects more quickly and understood them more deeply than through other pedagogical methods. They learned the applicability of academic information, as well as the importance of active and effective participation in their communities. Hanna hoped that community schools in the Philippines would "act as one of the agencies through which the nation can co-ordinate the human energy necessary to satisfy the material and spiritual needs of the people" (ibid., 38).

Many of the report's recommendations were incorporated in a 1951 report of the Joint Congressional Committee on Education to the Congress of the Philippines. Of special interest was a section of the report entitled, "A School for the Community" (*Improving the Philippine Educational System* 1951, 89–95). The section repeated a number of Hanna's tenets for the community school, listed examples of community-centered activities in which schools might engage, and concluded with several legislative proposals. One called for the reorganization of the school schedule to provide more student time for community service activities (ibid., 92). Another would delegate to the schools "the responsibility for leadership in community improvement, involving literacy, worthwhile recreation, home beautification, community sanitation, and increased agricultural and industrial production, not only as an end in itself but also as a means for implementing more concretely instruction in the classroom . . ." (ibid., 94).

The UNESCO mission provided Hanna with the opportunity to apply his ideas of curriculum organization and citizenship education on a national scale. In addition, the experience he gained, the contacts he made, and the understanding he gleaned of international education consulting and international contracts prepared him well for future work in the Philippines and elsewhere.

Hanna's next work in the Philippines began in 1952, when he joined the Special Technical and Economic Mission to the Philippines sponsored by the Mutual Security Agency (MSA). He took a one-year leave of absence from Stanford to serve as the mission's director of education, a post he filled from March 1952 to June 1953. The educational component of the mission was to "be helpful to the Government and people of this Republic in developing the educational institutions and methods essential to achieve the national goals of economic and social development" (Hanna 1953, 1). Hanna targeted three aspects of Philippine education for reform: vocational education, elementary education, and higher education. His goals included improving basic vocational skills, raising the literacy rate, and developing the technical fields of study in the universities. He also intended to develop a "national curriculum-making laboratory in which modern teaching guides and pupil instructional materials will be created" (ibid., 2). That laboratory was a precursor to his proposal of a national curriculum commission in America.

One thrust in Philippine education at the time was the devel-

opment of curriculum to combat communist ideologies. That effort
was certainly a goal of MSA's involvement, and that fact was not
lost on Paul Hanna. In a letter to Hanna, J. Russell Andrus, the
acting education advisor to MSA, wrote, "May I add a personal word
to say how very happy I am that you have expressed a willingness
to accept this post and to play an important part in our battle for
men's minds in Southeast Asia" (Andrus 1952).

Others shared those goals. For example, Juan V. Borra, a Philippine congressman, wrote in a 1951 report on education,

> In the Philippines there are some agitators who exploit the igno-
> rance of the masses and sow seeds of communism and unrest.
> Democracy cannot wait to be challenged on the battlefield by
> communism. Democracy must win the hearts and minds of men.
> No investment can be used to [better] advantage than the schools
> . . . a new program of education should be formulated to teach
> democracy as a way of life (*Improving* 1951, 6).

In a speech to the College of Education at the University of the
Philippines, Hanna cited U.S. President Harry S. Truman's claim
that "If communism is to be combated successfully in our country,
our democratic regime must offer better opportunities—educational, social, and economic—for all our citizens" (Hanna 1952a,
13). Surely such an altruistic goal could be transplanted to Southeast Asia.

Hanna's philosophy of democratic education seems to have
hardened in response to the cold war environment and his own
growing conservatism. On the other hand, perhaps it was suited all
along to serve political ends, and that fact simply was emphasized
during the era of fear and intolerance. His views on the purposes of
social studies education were instructive:

> My work in the social studies, with the elementary schools, has
> been of the same strand—that is, I would much rather help young-
> sters look at all the alternatives, values, institutions, et cetera and
> come to their own conclusions on the evidence or on the ability to
> persuade better institutions and values, rather than to go out and

lead a revolution, lead a march, or what not. That is, it is the
evolutionary concept, not the revolutionary [emphasis his] concept in which I believe (Hanna 1974).

Hanna's thrust was not simply citizenship education or the
social sciences, but vocational education with the aim of economic,
social, and political development. In an April address to the Third
Biennial Conference of the Philippines Association of Christian
Schools and Colleges, he declared that, "The Schools and colleges
must foster a sound program in industrial arts and economic education. . . . Every school and college needs to lead every boy and girl
through a variety of useful work experiences calculated to teach
them the dignity of labor, the nature of materials and processes,
and the joy of accomplishment in creating useful goods and services" (Hanna 1952a, 12–13).

The view that Filipino workers were "indolent and in need of
heavy doses of vocational and character education" was common
among American colonial and business leaders from the earliest
days of American occupation (Foley 1984, 35). Early solutions to
that perceived problem were pure industrial/vocational education
programs. In light of the dominance of communism in the two
largest nations in Asia and its appeal among factions in the Philippines, Hanna took a more refined approach. Perpetuating a large
laboring class ruled by a small elite class encouraged the type of
class resentment that Marxism–Leninism exploited. Hanna believed that simple skills training contributed to that class division,
and his version of vocational education was more far-reaching than
training in basic agricultural or industrial skills alone. He wanted
to create a large middle class, educating the elite and the common
people alike in the value of labor (Hanna 1952a, 12). Fortunately,
the educational aspirations of Filipino parents for their children
also went beyond training designed merely to make them better day
laborers or tenant farmers.

To press his point, Hanna asked, "How can an architect possibly

design an efficient factory building unless he has actually worked
with his hands at machines? To know efficient arrangement of the
flow of materials from bench to machine to assembly line is to have
felt it in one's own muscles" (ibid.).

As an example, he described the apprenticeship of young architects under Frank Lloyd Wright:

> Most of them have already earned college degrees. But each and
> every one of them, from aristocratic or humble homes, alike, must
> work with his hands in the fields, in the barns, in the kitchen, in
> the laundry, in the shop, in the office, as a part of his training.
> Mr. Wright believes that an architect cannot plan a good house
> unless he has worked in the kitchen preparing food, canning,
> washing, et cetera (ibid.).

In line with the conclusions he reached on his 1949 mission,
Hanna viewed the development of community schools in the Philippines as an integral factor in his plans. He was especially concerned about the fact that education in the Philippines "has been
attuned to the development of the political man. Little attention has
been given to the extractive industries, the manufacturing industries and business" (*The Manila Chronicle*, 24 March 1952 [?]). His
extensive writing in the prewar years about work with the community school ideal and social reconstruction through the schools prepared him to help Filipino educators launch community schools.
Hanna envisioned the community school as a locale for fundamental
education, but also for identifying and solving community problems. He declared that "the community school serves two purposes,
the development of the individual and the development of the community" (Bernardino 1958, 24).

Hanna's focus on community schools fed a long-standing Philippine interest in the concept. Before the turn of the century the
Philippines' "greatest hero," Jose Rizal, had created a community
school at Dapitan on the island of Mindanao (ibid., 36). Rizal and
others among the Filipino elite shared with American progressive

educators the belief that individuals and society as a whole were improvable, if not perfectible, through increased educational opportunities. That emphasis on schooling as a means of social development led to the unfortunate result of educational overproduction. As educational opportunities increased, the number of available positions in industrial plants and in professional education programs did not keep pace with the increasingly educated work force. The problem became even worse when politicians discovered that school construction was a useful means of rewarding their supporters (Manalang 1977, 227).

Many Philippine public schools took on community school functions early in the twentieth century. American colonial governors hoped to turn the local schools into major rural service institutions. In 1914, government schools were officially given the charge to conduct "civico-educational lectures designed to bring the influence of the school to the community" (Bernardino 1958, 36). Interest in these lectures waned after a time, but they were revived in 1933 under the governorship of Theodore Roosevelt Jr. After World War II, the economic and social dislocation caused by the war and by Japanese occupation once again revived the idea of community schools. It was thought that the problems in Philippine education and society were of such broad scope that community schools were the most appropriate institutions to address them. No less a personage than Philippine President Manuel A. Roxas said, "The time is long past due when the schools should serve as a decisive force to reconstruct society" (Roxas, 58). In 1947, the public schools were charged, not simply with child education, but with "the fundamental education of out-of-school youth and adult[s] . . ." (*Improving* 1951, 43).

Paul Hanna's promotion of community schools contributed to the growth of the idea in the Philippines (ibid., 23). Philippine educators wrote books and monographs addressing the community school idea and national conferences on community schools were held (Manalang, 227). An oversight apparatus was created within the government's education bureaucracy, and a doctoral program in community school studies was launched at the University of the Philippines. Courses in the development of community schools were taught at the Philippine Normal College, and the Philippine government contracted with UNESCO to create a Community School Training Center. That center, "although it made little impact in the field" (Foley 1984, 46), attracted educators from around the world to its model sites and programs. Hanna proclaimed that the Philippine community school movement was an innovation that the "free world will hail as one of the more significant social innovations of this epoch" (Tupas and Bernardino 1955, iv).

Paul Hanna resigned as education director of the MSA Mission to the Philippines in the spring of 1953, but he remained active in Philippine education. The International Cooperation Administration, later the Agency for International Development (AID), prepared to contract with institutions in the United States to meet some of the perceived needs in the Philippines. As he had during the war years, Hanna saw an opportunity to help Stanford University while he helped the Philippines. In 1953, he negotiated the first in a series of contracts between Stanford and various entities in the Philippines. In a seven-year agreement, Stanford was to help the University of the Philippines develop its teaching and research in business administration, education, and engineering. Stanford provided specialists in business finance, management, and marketing; in secondary education, teacher education, and educational administration; and in all phases of engineering and its underlying sciences. Stanford also committed to help the Philippine university reorganize and recatalogue its library, as well as procure books and other teaching materials. Twenty faculty members from the University of the Philippines undertook advanced study at Stanford and other American institutions. Nine American specialists were sent to the Philippines, and Hanna served as contract coordinator. The value of the contract was $1 million provided by AID, with additional funding from the Philippine government (International Coopera-tion Agency 1957, 306).

A second contract between the Philippine Department of Edu-cation and Stanford University was signed in March of 1956, with Hanna serving again as contract coordinator. Under a four-year agreement, American specialists assisted the Philippine Depart-ment of Education in developing preparation programs for voca-tional education teachers. Stanford provided teams of instructors and teacher educators, in fields such as agronomy, crafts, farm mechanics, and animal husbandry, to five different vocational schools throughout the Philippines (ibid.).

Hanna employed vocational instructors from secondary schools to carry out much of the work. Those instructors conducted semi-nars and workshops for Filipino instructors and administrators, and they developed improved courses of study for the vocational schools. That second contract was worth more than $1 million to Stanford.

The contracts were extended into the 1960s, but not without some disruptions. In 1957, Edward Arnold, the deputy director of AID, abruptly suspended the Stanford contracts. Arnold had come across information that led him to believe Paul Hanna might be a security risk. It turned out that a newspaperman in Washington, D.C., shared the name of Paul Hanna, and his political views were somewhat leftist. This was not the first time the two men's identities had been confused. In fact, Hanna regularly had visas and security clearances held up by Federal Bureau of Investigation reports that confused him with the leftist writer. In the political atmosphere of the cold war even such chance associations raised suspicions. Paul Hanna of Stanford wrote a pointed memo to AID in which he pledged that "we on campus would do anything reasonable and honorable to help fight the cold war against communism even though we had to endure rearguard obstruction" (Hanna 1957c). The matter was quickly cleared up and the contracts reinstated.

Paul Hanna's association with the Philippines continued into the 1980s. He served as a consultant on numerous projects, traveled there to address various groups, and continued to educate Philippine students at Stanford. Ultimately, the island nation saw the most comprehensive application of his ideas on education for development. Hanna's centerpiece for that effort was the community school, and the model developed in the Philippines became a pattern for UNESCO's efforts to modernize former colonies worldwide (International Cooperation Agency 1962, 10).

Despite its popularity and proliferation, the community school did not accomplish for the Philippines all that Hanna had hoped. One of the first scholars to study Hanna's vocational education and community school work in the Philippines was Douglas Foley, then a Stanford Ph.D. student. Foley served in the Philippines as a Peace Corps volunteer in 1962–1963, and he mastered two native Philippine languages. There he met Robert Textor, an anthropologist teaching in the Stanford International Development Education Center (SIDEC), who persuaded Foley to enroll in the program. Foley was educated at SIDEC from 1965 to 1970 and returned to the Philippines to conduct his anthropological fieldwork (Foley 1997).

Foley noted that, despite a heritage of service to the community and strong supporters in various government agencies, the community school movement in the Philippines had declined from its heyday in the 1950s. He attributed that decline to a number of factors (Foley 1984, 35). First, the Philippine education system was highly centralized and bureaucratized. The inertia inherent in that form of organization makes curriculum innovation nearly impossible. By definition, community schools follow unique, idiosyncratic curricula largely developed on site, and the Philippines' central educational bureaucracy simply could not accommodate that type of institution. Prishla Manalang agreed with Foley that a central bureaucracy imposing its authority on community schools defies the local control inherent in the community school concept (Manalang 1977, 227).

A second reason for the decline in Philippine community schools was the inability of teacher education institutions in that country to graduate enough teachers to provide for the proliferation of the community school. The type of preparation required for teachers in community schools was radically different from more traditional pedagogical training. Community school teachers must develop skills in community organizing and coordination of services with other agencies, as well as in adult and child education. The traditional teacher education programs were not geared to produce the needed teachers, and the few specialized programs that did—including UNESCO's Training Center—could not produce enough teachers to staff more than a few pilot sites (Foley 1984, 35).

Third, the community school was a new concept in some areas. Introducing new forms of practice in traditional communities was not an easy task, and some communities simply rejected the idea.

Fourth, coordinating activities and services among different social service agencies proved difficult. As the Philippine government modernized, agencies to aid in rural development proliferated. It was the community school's duty to coordinate all available services, but that was not always possible. Sometimes the goals of the various agencies conflicted, making cooperation difficult. Sometimes, interpersonal animosities intervened. In the end, many agencies found it easier to operate independently of the community school (ibid.). Manalang added that community school teachers who were charged with the coordination of the various services in the school did not receive rewards in proportion to their efforts (Manalang, 227).

Fifth, historical trends intervened. The multiplication of domestic and foreign rural aid organizations supplanted the community school's role as the social service center in many areas. The demand of parents for an academic rather than a vocational education for their children altered the community school curriculum. That trend toward a more academically oriented curriculum was bolstered by the resurgence of content-centered curricula in the late 1950s. Foley claimed that "Learning the vocabulary of modern mathematics and the laboratory approaches of discovery science has replaced sanitary toilet campaigns and literacy classes" (Foley 1984, 48).

Finally, international aid organizations shifted the funding of their educational interventions from elementary to higher education. Much of the foreign funding for community school development simply dried up. All of these forces contributed to the decline of the community school movement in the Philippines by the mid-1950s. Only the promotional activities of Paul Hanna and other American educators kept it alive after that time (ibid., 46; Manalang, 227).

A deeper problem was the effect of creating a model for development along purely western lines in the Philippines and elsewhere. UNESCO used the community schools in that country as models for other developing nations, but they failed to exert the social, political, and economic influence in the Philippines that Hanna had hoped, as subsequent events have demonstrated (Foley 1997). The Philippines has consistently lagged behind many of its Asian neighbors in economic growth and prosperity. In addition, the nation has been plagued with political unrest and scandals that have betrayed Hanna's dream of building a democratic society there. In his later years, Hanna seemed to acknowledge that failure. In a 1968 press release describing the reasons for SIDEC's creation, Hanna wrote, "We were making horrendous mistakes . . . by exporting the content of education that had worked for 150 years in the U.S., but had not tried to tailor educational structure and content suited to the needs of the countries we were trying to help" (Hanna 1968a).

IN SOUTHEAST ASIA

Hanna's work in the Philippines positioned him to take leadership roles in a number of other Asian development projects. In fact, by the mid-1950s he was recognized as a leading expert in development education. R. Freeman Butts reported that he and Hanna saw themselves at the pinnacle of that field. He recalled, "We used to joke that Paul at Stanford was reeducating the new nations of Pacific East Asia and I at Teachers College was trying to do the same for Africa and South Asia. Between us, the world" (Butts 1999). Hanna worked with the Asia Society, the East–West Center, and the Asia Foundation, which cosponsored much of his work in the Philippines. In 1955, Hanna's prominence in the field earned him nomination to the directorship of UNESCO's Department of Education (Adiseshiah 1955). Hanna's vision for the Mekong River Project is perhaps most revealing of how he came to see the role of education in national and international development.

The United Nations' Economic Commission for Asia and the Far East (ECAFE) first proposed a hydroelectric and flood control project on the Mekong River in 1957. The UN's goal was the economic development of the region. Hanna saw development of the Lower Mekong River Basin, along the lines of the Tennessee Valley Authority, as essential to the peace and prosperity of Cambodia, Laos, South Vietnam, and Thailand. More than just an economic boon for the individual nations, he thought that the project could be a case study in international cooperation to support his contention that multinational communities were the next stage in sociopolitical development (Hanna 1969, 254). He was concerned that although much effort had been poured into the political and technical aspects of planning such a massive project, there was a "lack of focused attention on the need for investment in human resource development through education" (ibid.).

As in the Philippines, Hanna advocated more than simply developing skills and technical expertise. Instead, he was concerned with people's ways of thinking. He asked, "What will motivate the illiterate masses in these nations to believe that by creating a larger-than-national community they can improve their lot? What will motivate them to develop at one and the same time attitudes of cooperation and loyalty to their mother nation and a sense of membership in a larger community of the Lower Mekong?" (ibid.).

Further, Hanna warned that

the Lower Mekong project is not going to "come off"' unless the people are helped to see how such a multi-national and multipurpose attack on the Lower Mekong could improve their lives and unless these people are helped to learn the appropriate attitudes, concepts, and competencies that are the sine qua non for the construction of the infrastructure in the first place and for its effective use in economic and social affairs once the network of physical mechanisms are built and in operation (Hanna 1969, 254).

Hanna saw the schools as a natural venue for the development of those concepts and attitudes, but education officials in the area were not planning in that direction. He criticized ECAFE proposals for the project because they included no studies that would "explore the instrumental use of education—formal and informal—in facilitating the river-basin projects or in preparing the masses to take advantage of the expected better economic, social, and political conditions that would flow from the larger-than-national community of the Lower Mekong" (ibid., 256).

The regional organization of education officials—the Southeast Asian Ministers of Education Organization (SEAMEO)—was not involved, and Hanna thought that disengagement was an enormous oversight. He urged the organization to "move the primary-, secondary-, and adult-education establishments toward helping the common people understand the essential role that the long-range multipurpose Mekong River projects must play in their lives" (ibid., 255).

In a predictable recommendation, Hanna advocated a structure akin to the community school to help ECAFE meet some of its objectives. Beyond that suggestion, he used his position on the Stone

Foundation board to try to arouse awareness of, and to bring some coordination to, education efforts in the region. In March of 1971, Hanna spent two weeks touring the area and meeting with SEAMEO officials. He then prepared a recommendation that the Stone Foundation support the establishment of ties between SEAMEO and the Mekong River Development Committee of ECAFE. SEAMEO would take on the role of planning for human resource development in the region. The Stone Foundation's executive committee ultimately rejected Hanna's proposal, but they agreed to employ a fund-raising consultant to help SEAMEO raise support in the United States (Southeast Asian Ministers of Education Secretariat 1971, 66–67).

His recommendations for Mekong River development displayed the depth of Hanna's thought about international development education late in his career. He had moved far beyond the vocational and citizenship education thrusts of his early work in the Philippines. By 1971, he was able to insist that the schools develop in children and adults the attitudes, concepts, and skills needed for their successful exploitation of economic development opportunities in international partnerships.

OTHER INTERNATIONAL WORK

Paul Hanna's work in international development education reached its fullest fruition in Asia, but it was not limited to that continent. His role changed, but his thrust was consistently the use of education as a tool for national and international development. In 1966, Hanna served as chairman of the Binational Yugoslav–American Advisory Commission of the U.S. Department of Education's Board of Foreign Scholarship. The commission met in Belgrade from November 21 to December 2. Its report on scholarly cooperation between the two countries displayed Hanna's influence. The report concluded that contemporary economic and social developments place great emphasis on education and the central roles that the natural and social sciences and technology play in modern educational systems. It is to our mutual advantage to discover better strategies of utilizing education in applying the most recent advances in sciences, in view of their great potential, to the improvement of social and economic conditions (Hanna 1966).

Hanna's retirement from the Stanford faculty at the end of the 1966–1967 university term freed him to take even more extended trips than he had previously taken. For example, in the fall of 1967 he undertook a tour of four East African nations on behalf of the U.S. State Department's Bureau of Educational and Cultural Affairs. He spent October and November meeting with education officials in Kenya, Malawi, Lesotho, and Ethiopia. Again, the resulting report of his observations provided insights into Hanna's thought on international development education at that mature point in his career. Additionally, it revealed his view of his own role in promoting development education.

Hanna's report began with his observations of conditions in the nations he visited. He found that both the leaders and the people had "great expectations for national development and for modernization that supposedly follow greater investment through education in human resources" (Hanna 1967b, 1). Hanna's use of the modifier *supposedly* indicated a decline in the idealistic faith in education's efficacy for national development that he had displayed earlier in his career. A factor contributing to that decline may have been Hanna's observation in these nations of "little evidence of an understanding of the relevance of the content and of instructional methods of schooling to economic development and to social and political modernization" (ibid.). Just as in the Philippines in 1948, he found in Africa a curriculum and related materials that reflected European colonial roots. The content and instructional methods were traditional, geared more toward college entrance and professional study than to preparation of students for the economic and social conditions of East Africa in 1967. An external examination system selected only an elite few for advanced study, ensuring underemployment and disillusionment for the rest (ibid., 2).

In higher education, no effort was made to guide students into fields necessary for their nation's development, and educational overproduction resulted. Some professional development programs enrolled too many students whereas others were left with too many vacancies. To make matters worse, the sparsely manned professions were often those technical fields most vital to industrial modernization. Hanna believed that the imbalance of supply and demand in the professions and the lack of technically trained individuals "only increases the dangerous gap between exploding aspirations and lagging fulfillment," both within individuals and for society as a whole (ibid.).

Hanna laid part of the blame for the imbalance on educators. He wrote that "The relevance of the curriculum to national goals must be the basic consideration . . . curriculum is too important to be left to the schoolmasters" (ibid., 2–3). The traditional academic approaches of colonial times were insufficient for newly independent, developing nations. Schools should be more attuned to specific manpower needs and adjust their curricula accordingly. Such curricula must be developed with input from technicians and planners as well as pedagogues (Hanna 1967b, 4).

Once again, Hanna's concern transcended simple vocational training. Instead, he wanted to change people's attitudes. He observed in those countries a lack of attention to "instruction in the purposes and the mechanisms of the emerging multinational communities of men" (ibid.). In Southeast Asia, he had observed that modern economies require such an array of resources that nations must often form international combinations for their effective exploitation. Education systems designed to help nations modernize, especially small nations with limited resources, must attend to the concepts, attitudes, and skills of international cooperation. Of course, education systems patterned after those formerly imposed by colonial powers would not include that feature. Particularly in Africa, the colonial competition among European powers had been so fierce that cooperation across national lines was anathema, and cooperation in the exploitation of natural resources was the antithesis of European colonialism there. Hanna insisted that the content of the curriculum must change.

Instructional methods likewise received Hanna's criticism. The nations he visited in Africa depended primarily on rote memorization of text passages as a mode of instruction. That approach ignored what Hanna perceived as "the relationship between instructional methods, and modernization and development" (ibid., 3). Instead, Hanna advocated methods employing inquiry, discovery, and experimentation, the very methods he had found most intriguing as a boy and most effective as a young school superintendent. Only methods directed at higher-level thought processes would develop the problem-solving skills needed for economic modernization.

Hanna's interpretation of his mission in Africa revealed much about how he operated on international consulting trips. He took a much broader view of educational consulting and drew a much broader field of actors into his activities than did most consultants. He anticipated meeting with cabinet-level officials in ministries dealing with education, industry, and trade. In addition, he expected to consult with school and university authorities to help them revamp the curriculum and the instructional methods in their schools. Integral to Hanna's mission was his "work with leaders of the private sector who are investing in the growth of the economy and who have general and specific information that must be a part of the preparation of human resources in order to facilitate the development and modernization of the nation" (Hanna 1967b, 5).

Hanna understood as well as any educational leader of his time that the accumulation of capital fuels development in market economies, and that human capital is a vital resource. Ignoring that factor in developing curriculum for economic and social modernization was futile, but Hanna's conception of addressing private-sector concerns in the curriculum went beyond simplistic ideas of vocational education for industrial and agricultural workers. As he had in the United States during the Great Depression, he perceived the need for schools to help children understand market economics, technological development, international relations, and a myriad of other complex concepts in order to contribute to their nation's, and their region's, development.

Hanna evaluated the success of his African mission as "two hits, one walk, and one strikeout" (ibid., 6). He attributed those mixed results less to the national officials with whom he met, or to himself, than to the U.S. embassy staffs in East Africa. His estimation of successful and unsuccessful encounters in each nation related directly to the power and prestige of those with whom he met. He clearly believed that it was his mission to act as an advocate for international development education at the highest levels of government.

The two "hits" were in nations where the embassy personnel appreciated the value of Hanna's celebrity status and prepared accordingly. In both countries, meetings were arranged between Hanna and the heads of universities, cabinet ministers, and other high government officials. In both countries, the prestige of Hanna's activities was enhanced by the participation of the U.S. ambassador. Invitations to meetings often issued from the ambassador himself, and in both countries the meetings were held in settings such as the embassy building that were appropriate for high-level consultations. Hanna's report claimed that

> in these two nations, it is my evaluation that our seminars with the top policy makers resulted not only in better understanding of the crucial role a revised school and university curricula (content and method) might play in nation and multination building, but, equally important, resulted in the beginnings of formal mech-

anisms through which, hopefully, these policy makers will proceed
to assist the Ministry of Education and the university staffs in
infusing the curricula with those concepts, values, and skills essential to achieve the goals in economic, social, and political sec-
tors (ibid., 7).

In the nations Hanna rated as less than fully successful, the
embassy staffs did not make suitable preparations for a visitor of
his stature. In the "walk," embassy personnel did not want Hanna
to meet with government officials before the newly appointed ambassador had. As a result, no high-level meetings were arranged.
Instead, Hanna addressed the staff of the American school there,
and gave several lectures to student teachers at a university. He did
manage to meet with "a few leaders" near the end of his stay, but
he left feeling that he had made little "headway in helping the
leaders with the central problem of using education as a tool for
achieving the goals of the various ministries or of the private sector"
(ibid., 6).

In his "strikeout," the embassy staff scheduled Hanna only to
speak to secondary school students. He perceived "no comprehen-
sion on the part of the ambassador or his staff of the purpose of my
visit." Even after Hanna explained what he had done in other countries and what he hoped to accomplish there, the ambassador refused to arrange consultations. He told Hanna that "the officials
locally were already too much bothered with foreigners telling the
host government how to conduct its business" (ibid.). Clearly, some
diplomats may have failed to grasp all that Hanna had to offer. On
the other hand, they likely understood the local culture better than
Hanna. His style of top-down dissemination of his ideas had proven
ineffective in the Philippines, but he insisted on continuing it. Obviously, Hanna placed the highest value on his own advice and
wanted to share it with only the most powerful officials in the African
nations he visited.

In all, despite his inability to operate as he intended in all four nations, Hanna was pleased with the results of his African tour. He was especially gratified at the heightened awareness in the region of the need for international cooperation. His visit coincided fortuitously with planning meetings in Addis Ababa for the development of an East African Common Market. The news media in the region covered that event thoroughly, and as a result Hanna found "the university authorities and the ministries challenged by these questions [of the school's role in creating conditions conducive to international cooperation] and in each instance they expressed a determination to work for inclusion of curriculum content that would help prepare citizens to participate in the emerging larger-than-nations communities" (Hanna 1967b, 8).

The effects of Hanna's short visit and limited input on the subsequent development of the four nations are difficult to assess. Kenya has continued its growth as a pro-Western, modernizing economic powerhouse in the region. Ethiopia has tended to move in the opposite direction. Malawi and Lesotho have been handicapped by their small size. Lesotho, especially, has suffered from its position as a nation landlocked within the Republic of South Africa. For all the excitement it generated, the East African Common Market never came to fruition. Hanna's brief visit likely had little effect on any of those events.

Later in 1967, Hanna attended a high-level conference on international education issues held in Williamsburg, Virginia. His inclusion in that prestigious gathering indicates the high profile he had attained in international education circles. The meeting grew out of a speech by President Lyndon Johnson the previous year calling for a meeting of world leaders to address issues in education across national boundaries. That call was consistent with Hanna's internationalism. The International Conference on the World Crisis in Education was held October 5–9, 1967. One hundred and seventy educators and education officials attended, representing fifty-two nations. Hanna served as one of the United States' representatives.

The goals of the conference included "(a) to diagnose the nature, causes, and prospects of the world education crisis, and (b) to make recommendations on a strategy and specific measures for meeting the crisis by both national and international action" (Perkins 1967). The choice of the term *crisis* to describe education worldwide was an interesting one, and the word was subject to interpretation. Dr. James A. Perkins, president of Cornell University and the conference chairman, recognized this ambiguity. In a letter to Hanna, he explained, "Obviously, this crisis takes different forms in different countries and some are already more deeply involved in it than others. But its common characteristic anywhere, and the essence of the problem, is that educational systems have been unable to keep pace in the last decade with their rapidly changing environments" (ibid.). That observation paralleled Hanna's 1930s-era interpretation of the social dilemma of modern times in the United States and his observations in Latin America, Asia, and Africa.

Hanna used the conference as an opportunity to expand and reinforce his vast network of personal contacts. He served on the conference's working group studying Research to Improve Education, but much of his time was spent visiting with friends. He wrote personal notes to university and government officials who were attending the conference from a number of nations in Europe, the Americas, Asia, and Africa.

Hanna's lifelong attention to such social details contributed to the building and maintenance of his vast network of friends and acquaintances around the world. Late in his life, Hanna was chided for his habit of writing *thank you* notes in response to Christmas cards. He replied, "At my age, if I don't respond, they'll think I'm dead!" (A. Hanna 1999). Hanna's attention to social conventions benefited him and his friends. In 1958, Harold Rugg enlisted his former colleague's help in organizing a trip to the Far East. He wrote Hanna that his last trip to the region had been in 1937, and many of his contacts there had passed away (Rugg 1958). Hanna wrote several letters of introduction for him (Hanna 1974). In 1965 Hanna wrote letters of introduction for Congressman Richard Hanna, who was preparing for a fact-finding mission, to a number of important officials in the Philippines. Those contacts also bene-fited Hanna; colleagues from the Philippines and elsewhere sent their students and came themselves to study at Hanna's Stanford International Development Education Center.

THE STANFORD INTERNATIONAL DEVELOPMENT EDUCATION CENTER

Paul Hanna built his sphere of influence in international education as much through the creation of a center for development education on the Stanford campus as he did through his work overseas. The idea for a center for the formal preparation of educators in inter-national development education sprang from Hanna's work in Latin America, Europe, and Asia in the 1940s and 1950s. The scholarly activities of data gathering and interpretation he had observed in the more traditional programs of comparative education did not seem to meet the needs of nations looking to education to help them build their social, political, and economic institutions. The focus of Stanford's program under Hanna's leadership was the use of edu-cation as an agent of change. Students in the program were to become "scholar–doers" (Foley 1997). At Hanna's instigation, Stan-ford approved a doctoral degree program in overseas/comparative education in 1954.

In its first few years, the program catered mainly to foreign students, and many of them later became important government and university officials in their home countries. By 1960, students from the United States had begun to enter the program, and many went on to faculty positions at influential universities such as Ohio State, Pennsylvania State, and the University of Quebec. Others served in UNESCO, USAID, and other international and quasi-governmental organizations and foundations (Foster 1998b).

By 1965, the degree program was housed in a formal unit of the university called the Stanford International Development Education Center (SIDEC). As Hanna's understanding of *development education* deepened, SIDEC's mission broadened. From its early focus as a training ground for technicians in Western modes of development, it grew into an interdisciplinary program to "improve American educators' abilities in helping under-developed countries build their own educational systems that were truly a reflection of needs for development and modernization" (Hanna 1968b). Instead of imposing a western model of modernization, SIDEC's graduates helped nations "build their own educational systems" (ibid.). Also, as Hanna's focus grew from national development to include multinational arrangements, he perceived that he was "constantly struggling to get SIDEC turned around so that they don't just talk about education and nationhood, but education and multination-hood" (Hanna 1974).

The expansion of SIDEC's mission also changed the degree programs. By 1968, students were designing their own programs of study under the guidance of a three-member faculty committee. The diverse student body in that year included doctoral students from Asia, Africa, the Middle East, Europe, Latin America, and Australia, as well as the United States and Canada (Hanna 1968b).

During those years of change, SIDEC took on a more theoretical bent. Hanna's ideal of the "scholar–doer" remained the pattern for SIDEC students, but a subtle shift had begun. In order to establish and maintain its prestige among academic programs, SIDEC had to produce theoretical research and recruit outstanding scholars in the social sciences. Its promotional literature of the late 1960s revealed the shift. A 1967 brochure stated, for example, that SIDEC "seeks theoretical and practical insights by comparative analysis of developmental processes in countries at various levels of advancement" (*The Stanford International Development Center* 1967). Although national development was mentioned, the statement could have issued from any of the more traditional programs in comparative education. The preparation of students to advise on education reform overseas is not mentioned.

In a 1968 press release, the preparation of "scholar–doers" is described as a goal of SIDEC, but it is put on a par with the production of "research-based literature to aid in educational policy making the world over" (Hanna 1968b). In addition, the focus of SIDEC research was expanded overseas to include more developed nations, rather than only developing nations. The shift in emphasis attracted a new type of student who was less apt to work overseas with education systems and foreign governments and more attuned to scholarly research in the theoretical aspects of "the role of education in the processes of social-economic-political development" (*The Stanford International Development Center* 1967). The recruitment of faculty and students with academic interests other than education no doubt enriched SIDEC, but also changed its character. After Hanna's retirement, SIDEC became even more academically oriented than service oriented and that change was a source of conflict between Hanna and the Stanford administration (Foster 1998b). Ultimately, Hanna shifted the focus of his scholarly study of education's interactions with the larger society to the Hoover Institution.

Perhaps to compensate for the increasingly academic character of SIDEC, Hanna offered a radical proposal to the United States government in 1969. The previous year he had been appointed chairman of the Special Committee to Study Peace Corps/University Relations. The committee met first in Washington, D.C., in mid-November, then in Honolulu to study Peace Corps training programs at the University of Hawaii in mid-December, and then in Palo Alto the following January. The resulting committee report, issued in April of 1969, called for an expansion of the Peace Corps into an International Volunteer Development Corps composed of "volunteers from most free nations of the globe" (Stanford University News Service 1969). The report suggested that "multinational teams of volunteers would work in the rural and urban ghettos of every nation, in the development of world or regional ecological balance, in preservation of pure water or air, in eradicating illiteracy and ignorance, in lessening disease, in enhancing beauty . . ." (ibid.).

Such an organization might prepare the force of bright young people dedicated to modernization in underdeveloped countries that Hanna had hoped would issue from SIDEC. As a sample project he recommended that the corps be set to work on the Lower Mekong River Development Project, "provided the Vietnam war was over" (ibid.).

Hanna's proposal revealed a change in his attitude about exporting American ideas and institutions to other parts of the world. Whereas his work in the Philippines was criticized as an unreflective imposition of educational forms that had largely failed in the United States, his recommendation to expand the Peace Corps showed some cultural sensitivity. He wrote, "One immediate effect which would be noted would be to remove the stigma from the U.S. Peace Corps and every other nation using similar youth volunteers as 'nationalistic and imperialistic'" (ibid.). His concern was more than just politically superficial. The committee suggested that the Development Corps would be an improvement over the Peace Corps by "emphasizing more forcefully the economic development of the host nation within the terms of its own plan [emphasis theirs], rather than the Peace Corps' own 'self-realization' (personal image) of the current program" (ibid.). Politics would still play a part, though, because all volunteers would come from *free nations*.

CONCLUSION

Hanna's second career in international development education seemed to have occurred without plan. After he rejected the excesses of radical social reconstruction for American schools in the 1930s, he fully embraced the liberal democratic tradition and sought means through which education could instill the requisite knowledges and skills for democratic citizenship. He fixed on two solutions. The first solution was the community school, an innovative way to teach responsible, democratic citizenship through service to the community. The second solution was embodied in his textbook series and in *Building America*. Hanna designed these books to help students understand vital social science concepts and use them to analyze current conditions in their society. The community school ideal suffered in the general backlash against progressive education methods and a reemphasis on a traditional academic curriculum in American schools. The *Building America* series was scuttled by criticism from right-wing political groups. These setbacks, combined with Hanna's wartime opportunities to investigate the instrumental uses of education overseas, encouraged him to shift his focus to the uses of education as a tool of national and international development.

In fact, Hanna had been interested in the wider world from his youth. Consulting work in Europe, Asia, South America, and Africa simply allowed him to indulge this interest and expand his influence. He aided in the proliferation of American democratic ideals throughout the postwar world. His expanding communities model for organization of the social studies curriculum became a familiar fixture in dozens of foreign school systems. Expanding communities became the organizing principle in UNESCO guides on teaching social studies (Churchill 1999; Mehlinger 1981, 379). In many countries, the conscious goal of the social studies curriculum became the promotion of democratic values. In postwar Japan, social studies "was intended to serve as a means—along with other aspects of the curriculum—by which a sense of morality might be developed along democratic lines" (R. Anderson, 102).

Hanna spread his version of development education, as well, through the work of graduates from SIDEC. Many of these students went on to hold important posts in foreign governments, international organizations, and universities around the world. Douglas Foley reflected that Hanna's Filipino graduates are "now running universities in the Philippines" (Foley 1997). Hanna saw this work as a natural complement to his curriculum work. He told Martin Gill that he considered his "social studies emphases an outgrowth of that postwar experience, but also my coming back and developing the Stanford International Development Educational [sic] Center. . . . So the social studies master design and SIDEC emphasis were really one and the same" (Hanna 1974).

Hanna's work in international education also refined his curriculum work at home. His expanding communities curriculum came to include international communities of people. He said, "It wasn't until I became involved with my international work . . . [that] I began to see that we had a whole series of concentric circle communities and I was a part of every one of them . . . That came after my experiences in the war and my international experiences after the war (Hanna 1974).

As he gained deeper multicultural understandings, Hanna brought those perspectives to his work at home. The result was a greater internationalism in the American social studies curriculum than had existed before World War II. Dozens of Hanna's students had seen something of the world during their service in the war. They easily adopted his internationalism and helped it spread through their own curriculum work. The influence of their wartime experiences in developing an international consciousness and depth of understanding of the social order in the postwar generation of curriculum workers cannot be overestimated. The impact of these scholars in school systems worldwide deserves further study.

Through seemingly random circumstances, Hanna and his ideas were thrust onto the world stage in the years after World War II. The result was a new, worldwide, UNESCO-promulgated model for use of the schools as tools of national development, a cadre of highly trained educators to carry it out, the proliferation of Hanna's expanding communities model for the social science curriculum, and an increased level of international awareness in curriculum materials in the United States. Through his work in international development education, Hanna truly became a citizen of the world.

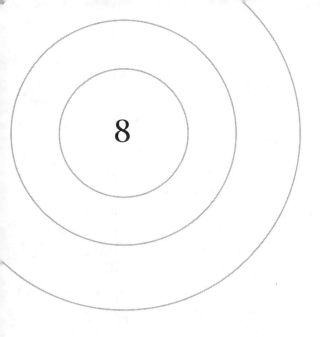

8

Conclusions

Paul Hanna embodied a unique blend of scholar and promoter. His scholarship provided the basis for the formulation of curriculum designs, concepts, and materials to help children and youth better understand their social, political, and economic environments. He employed his promotional abilities to spread his ideas and products around the world and to cause his design for the elementary social studies curriculum to become predominant (LeRiche 1987, 139). Hanna's affinity for the life of the scholar began early in his parents' home. Surrounded by books and learned visitors, he grew to love learning and ideas (Hanna 1982a, 11). This affinity only deepened as he studied philosophy at Hamline University and education at Teachers College. The promotional side of his personality developed as he persuaded classmates to initiate a debate team and a school yearbook, as he sold books door-to-door, and as he traveled with President Kerfoot to recruit students and donors for Hamline University. Without either quality, scholarship or promotional ability, Hanna would not have achieved the prominence he did as an educational leader.

HANNA'S CONTRIBUTIONS TO EDUCATION

Hanna's greatest contributions to education were in the field of social education. A critical analysis of modern culture formed the basis for much of Hanna's work. This analysis grew out of the influences of his father's Social Gospel orientation, his studies at Hamline University, and the influence of his social reconstructionist colleagues at Teachers College. He understood that industrialization and urbanization had changed profoundly the ways in which people relate to each other socially, politically, and economically. He interpreted the mission of the schools as that of helping children understand the changes their world had undergone and equipping them to effect change through the democratic system that would benefit them as individuals and benefit society as a whole. Out of this conviction, he rejected child interest as the sole basis for curriculum making, although he fully embraced interest as a tool of motivation. Together with like-minded colleagues at Teachers College, Hanna formed organizations to investigate the schools' role in society and search for an adequate basis for the school curriculum.

Hanna developed the basis for a curriculum design that would help children understand the nature of their social, political, and economic environment through his work on the Virginia Curriculum Study in the 1930s, and he spent the remainder of his life promoting it. The design centered around his conception of the basic human activities performed in all societies in all places and times. These activities constituted a scope of content that Hanna believed could portray for children the development and operations of the social, economic, and political institutions in which they lived with sufficient objectivity to provide them with deep understandings. He advocated his design in numerous articles, and it found its way into many state and local school curricula and several generations of textbooks published by Scott, Foresman and Company.

Once wedded to his concentric circles of home life, family life, school, et cetera, as a sequence of presentation, the structure became his *expanding communities* curriculum design.

The expanding communities model has been widely criticized over the years. One critique holds that because children today are exposed to world events through the electronic media prior to their first day in school, Hanna's sequence of slow progress from local communities to the state, national, and international communities is artificial (Rooze and Foerster 1972). Although this criticism may be valid, it should be noted that the electronic media were present in children's lives even before the inception of Hanna's concentric circles design. Media influence has never obviated the need for an orderly, logical sequence in the presentation of content.

Some critics of Hanna's design level their complaints against all integrated approaches to social science instruction. They prefer a return to instruction in the separate disciplines. A recent issue of *History Matters!*, the newsletter of the National Council for History Education, complained that expanding communities approaches were "here-and-now oriented, and history was nowhere to be found until Grade Four, or perhaps even Grade Five. Students had no chance whatsoever to learn about the world's past until Grade Six or beyond" (December 1997, 5). The provenance of history in the elementary school curriculum is a topic of ongoing debate. Hanna sought to integrate history along with other social sciences in his curriculum design. In any event, curriculum designers have little control over how their products are actually used in classrooms (SPAN 1982, 84).

Another critique holds that Hanna's integrated approach is "alive and well and nobody's learning anything" (Douglass 1998b). Again, this deficiency may be an issue of teacher recruitment and preparation rather than curriculum design. John Goodlad wrote, "Teachers are oriented to teaching particular things—the particular things they were taught in school. Relating these particular things to some larger purpose is not something they think about very much or have been prepared to do" (Goodlad 1984, 238). Hanna's approach attempted to integrate social science instruction within a larger framework, employing the expertise of social science scholars, for the purpose of equipping children and youth to participate as citizens in a democracy.

A critique of Hanna's design that he acknowledged as valid was that teachers were not equipped to use it as effectively as he had hoped. Hollis Caswell recognized a similar weakness with the Virginia curriculum revision from which Hanna's concept sprang. Recalling the demands of the core curriculum for Virginia, he claimed, "We couldn't find teachers who could do it" (Caswell 1978). Certainly, carrying out Hanna's vision ultimately required teachers who shared his deep understanding of the social milieu and his vision for the school's role in society. In order to share his vision, Hanna spent years directing seminars for teachers and textbook salesmen to explain his program (Gill 1974). He also included a tremendous amount of explanatory text for teachers in his Hanna Series books.

Despite the criticisms of the expanding communities curriculum design, it has predominated in elementary school social studies instruction, in part because no more compelling design has been suggested (SPAN 1982, 101). However, another factor in the spread of Hanna's design was his promotional activities for Scott, Foresman. He frequently led seminars for salesmen to help them understand the unique features of the social studies textbooks (Gill 1974). The salesmen would then promote Hanna's design to school districts across the nation. In addition, Hanna wrote about his design in scholarly journals and promoted it through his consulting work with school systems. He admitted that the distinction between promoter and scholar sometimes was narrow (Hanna 1974, 114).

Hanna knew that informing children about their social world was useful, but that simply informing them would not bring about change. Consequently, he devised ways in which children could learn about the democratic process experientially. He advocated the community school as a way for children to learn about how people provide for their needs and wants. His particular concern was that children involve themselves in community projects to improve certain aspects of life. By doing so, they would learn the practical means of change and gain confidence in their abilities to manipulate those means to advantage. He promoted his concept of the community school through numerous publications, but his most effective promotion was through his work developing community schools in the Philippines. The Philippine community schools became models for others in Southeast Asia.

Arguments similar to those Hanna advanced are used today by promoters of service learning in the schools. Fundamental to their concerns are that children develop a sense of connection to their community. Christopher Lasch articulated this concern in a description of the dilemma of today's children: "The culture at their disposal provides so little help in ordering the world that experience comes to them in [the] form of direct stimulation or deprivation" (Lasch 1989). Hanna recognized the child's need to connect to something deeper and more meaningful than the pleasures and pains of his immediate surroundings. He hoped that working as a community to build a better future would provide this connection. Late in his career, he even proposed a centralized development laboratory to provide a common curriculum for the schools. He hoped that common understandings might help develop a sense of community.

Hanna also believed that social critique was a necessary precursor of change. He developed the *Building America* series to raise children's consciousness of needs beyond the local community. Thousands of classrooms used these magazines on a monthly basis to stimulate discussion of important social, political, and economic issues facing the United States.

Both the community school movement and *Building America* were negatively affected by the post-World War II backlash against

progressive education, so Hanna turned his attention to consulting
work overseas. He helped develop community schools in the Philippines and elsewhere, and he continued to argue that schools
should help children understand the changing social, political, and
economic worlds in which they live so that they can mold those
worlds to their own needs. Hanna became a prominent figure in
international education circles, and he used his prominence to promote his ideas through educational consulting in many nations. He
also founded the Stanford International Development Education
Center to prepare others to do similar work.

Hanna's international work came under criticism by those who
saw it as an instrument of Western cultural imperialism, and the
criticism is valid to an extent. Hanna was an unabashed booster of
Western models of democratic development. In the early phase of
his international career he joined wholeheartedly in the cold war
struggle against communism, at least rhetorically. Nevertheless, he
was critical of the damage Western imperialism had done to educational, political, and economic systems abroad. His educational
proposals for foreign countries were directed at empowering the
common people in the same way as his efforts at home had. For
Hanna, using the foreign schools as a tool of economic development
was a logical extension of using domestic schools for the same
purpose during the Depression. He legitimately may be accused of
naiveté, but not of collusion with the worst aspects of imperialism.

Despite Hanna's many and varied contributions to education
in America and abroad, he is largely ignored by educational historians. Several factors stand out as possible reasons for this neglect.
First, Paul Hanna moved from Teachers College, Columbia University, to Stanford at a time when leadership in American education was centered in universities and major school systems on the
east coast and in the midwest. For example, the John Dewey Society,
organized in 1934 to investigate the crucial role of schools in society,
included in its membership many of the leaders in curriculum study

at the time, but only eleven of the 67 founding members were from institutions in places other than the East Coast or the Midwest (Harap 1970). Patricia Graham described the leadership of the Progressive Education Association in its first four decades as coming primarily from the same two regions (Graham 1967). The West had yet to mature as a leading influence in American education, and when Hanna chose to remain there rather than return to Teachers College in 1937, some of his colleagues dismissed him.

Another possible cause for the neglect of Hanna is the diversity of his interests. Although many of his contemporaries remained rather narrowly focused, teaching in universities and writing mostly for scholarly publications, Hanna's career took distinctly different paths. His textbook writing demanded time and energy, and quite likely it distracted him from purely academic publishing. Furthermore, Hanna was an entrepreneur as well as an educator. Some historians of education attribute little importance to curriculum change that comes through schools' relationships with individuals and institutions who author instructional materials. Thus, a bias exists in favor of ideas generated by theorists in universities or government agencies, a bias that discriminates against and marginalizes individuals who contribute to and profit from their contributions to routine practice. Still, through his textbooks and related consulting work, Hanna directly influenced the curriculum and the role of the school in society on as grand a scale as any of his contemporaries, and—quite likely—with more practical value.

Hanna may be neglected, too, because he focused primarily on elementary education. Paul Hanna had to fight the bias among academics that young children were incapable of understanding key concepts from the social sciences (Hanna 1973a). Only recently have major figures in elementary education such as Alice Miel (Yeager 1995) and Maycie K. Southall (Brown 1981) been accorded the prominence they deserve.

Historians of progressive education in America have encountered difficulty reconciling Hanna's early career as a *social fron-tiersman* with his later efforts to duplicate American models of schooling overseas. Certainly, Hanna grew more conservative over time, but attempts to categorize him in traditional political terms fail. Education is an inherently political endeavor; what and how we teach children shapes their thought about political theory and all else. Hanna developed a uniquely pragmatic approach in order to survive in the potentially hazardous arena of curriculum making.

INTERPRETING HANNA'S POLITICAL VIEWS

The fact that Hanna was labeled as an imperialist by critics of his work in international development education and as a radical by the critics of *Building America* illustrates the difficulty of assigning any political label to him. Those who perceive Hanna to be a polit-ical and social conservative have good reason. A lifelong Republi-can, he supported Richard Nixon's candidacy for Governor of Cal-ifornia in 1962 and for President of the United States in 1968. Much of his work overseas in the 1950s and 1960s was done in conjunction with the United States Government—and, by proxy, the United Nations—in support of American cold war foreign policy. He was also an active member of several old-line conservative men's clubs, such as San Francisco's Bohemian Club, and his final academic post was as a senior fellow at the Hoover Institution, an organization with a distinctly conservative reputation (Lowen 1997, 207). Taken together, these factors are evidence of Hanna's political conserva-tism.

On the other hand, he had been part of the network of social reconstructionists addressing education issues in the 1930s, and had espoused collectivist views. Even late in life, Hanna made no attempt to dissociate himself from those beliefs. He aligned himself with his old colleagues and their work when he proudly included himself as being instrumental in publications that voiced social reconstructionist views. Indeed, he served on the editorial board of *The Social Frontier*, a journal for the most progressive educational thinkers, in the mid-1930s.

Hanna included himself among the *social frontiersmen* because he did not consider them to be as far left as some today assume. Responding to the charge that George Counts was a radical, Hanna declared,

> If you mean by radical getting to the root of the problem, he was.
> . . . But I wouldn't call that a radical in the way it is used today.
> He was really a conservator, a conservator of the basic principles
> of democracy . . . It is truly radical if you know what radical means.
> But it was not radical in that he was a rabble-rouser, a revolu-
> tionary. He was nothing of the sort, truly. He was going back to
> the fundamental principles of democracy as laid out by the early
> French and British and the early Americans (Hanna 1973, 72–
> 73).

In Hanna's own view, revolutionary methods of instigating change were necessary "only in the rarest and most extreme conditions. Typically, advances are made by the slower but much sounder evolutionary process . . . The goals are to improve the democratic open pluralistic society, and to do it by constitutional or accepted methods" (Hanna 1974, 109–110).

Although his views on the social utility of the schools underwent change over time, his belief in the power of education to effect positive change in society did not. Hanna sought social improvement through many of his professional endeavors, but improvement within the parameters of democratic philosophy. Simplistic labels such as *radical* and *conservative* are too restrictive to describe adequately his educational philosophy or approach. If any label fit this student of John Dewey, it was *pragmatist*.

Hanna was pragmatic, too, in choosing when to refrain from defending his beliefs. For example, when the *Building America* series came under attack by right-wing forces, Hanna did not vigorously defend it, although the magazine was his brainchild and he had spent more than a decade on its editorial board. In a telling exchange, Hanna related to an interviewer that Stanford President Ray Lyman Wilbur once told him, "I have been able to achieve the things I have [because I have] . . . let the image develop and fed it that I was a conservative man" (ibid., 109). In Hanna's mind, that echoed earlier advice from Jesse Newlon to "Never behave in such a way that you have the platform from which you speak jerked out from under you. If you speak in such a way that you are no longer given the platform, you are dead" (ibid., 108). Hanna took this advice to heart, and it allowed him to advocate dramatic changes in the social education of children at home and abroad without suffering undue personal criticism.

CONCLUSION

Ultimately, none of the problems Hanna identified and on which he labored has been solved. Children and youth at home and abroad still need to understand their social, political, and economic milieus and learn to effect change through democratic means. For instance, recent studies indicated that high school students from widely diverse backgrounds share common misunderstandings about the economic systems in which they live (Stallones, McCants, and Watkins 1997; Sweeney, Foster, and Stallones 1996). However, scholastic knowledge alone—no matter how deep—may not be adequate to bring about the sense of community and the dedication to its improvement that Hanna sought to develop in children. Fundamental to the type of community that Hanna envisioned is a universal mutual respect based on the worth of each individual. Unfortunately, the mechanistic theory of social evolution upon which all his work was based provided no adequate basis for appreciating individual worth. In fact, the same theory of social evolution has led to individual worth being tied to ethnicity in fascist states, to usefulness to the state apparatus in Marxist states, and to economic productivity in market economies.

Historically, American society avoided these instrumental views of human beings by appealing to higher law. The Declaration of Independence attributes to all men an inherent equality and "unalienable rights" endowed by a creator. The Constitution is more subtle than the Declaration, but it relies throughout on the legal principle of constitutionalism, which assumes immutable, universal principles underlying positive law. By contrast, Hanna viewed values such as the worth of the individual as changeable social constructs. He wrote that a task of education is to take part in "designing social arrangements and value systems which will facilitate the basic human satisfactions" (Hanna 1939a, 14). In other words, social structures, values, and all else were subject to the whims of "basic human satisfactions." In the end, the philosophical foundation of Hanna's work was at odds with some of his practical goals, although he never dealt with that inconsistency.

Perhaps due in part to that inconsistency, Paul Hanna's success in redesigning social science instruction failed to enact his vision for American society. Americans are less community-oriented today than in the past. In fact, many look to decades past as a golden age of community life. Architects and homebuilders are experimenting with new forms of housing development that place homes closer together and focus on common areas, all within walking distance of stores and shops, to rekindle the spirit of community from the imagined past. Americans today are not any more politically active in efforts to build a better life than they were in Hanna's day. In fact, in the face of political scandals, lackluster candidates, and increasingly complex policy issues, voters express their apathy through declining levels of voting and other forms of political participation. Students in today's schools are not any better adjusted to their social milieu than in Hanna's time. In fact, the increasing alienation and isolation of children has been expressed in incidents of school violence that Hanna could not have imagined. However, these mounting social problems are not so much a repudiation of Hanna's work as an invitation to revisit it more thoughtfully.

Hanna's diagnoses of the problems in American culture are still valid. The rapid pace of change in the modern world breeds individual and social alienation, fragmentation, and isolation. These forces conflict with human longings for integration and community. Nor is postmodernism a solution. That mindset simply surrenders to the "fragmentary and chaotic currents of change as if that is all there is" (Harvey 1989, 44). Some of the solutions still lie where Paul Hanna saw them—in a sound curriculum designed to help children understand the political, social, and economic forces swirling about them, coupled with experiences in democratic problem solving to build a sense of empowerment and community in each child. A new look at the work of Paul Hanna, enhanced by careful reconsideration of the sources of universal mutual respect, will help develop new insights for social education as the schools and society move together into the twenty-first century.

Appendix A

Chronological Bibliography of Published Works by Paul R. Hanna

Barry, Mary Elizabeth, and Paul R. Hanna, eds. 1930. *Wonder flights of long ago*. New York: D. Appleton and Company.

Hanna, Paul R. 1930. Methods of arithmetic problem solving. *The Mathematics Teacher* 23 (November): 442–450.

———. 1931. Arithmetic problem solving. *Teachers College Record* 32 (May): 746–747.

———. 1932. The activity program in the intermediate grades, part III: Its development in Lincoln School intermediate grades. *Education* (April): 483–488.

Carey, Alice E., and Paul R. Hanna. 1932. *Catalog: Units of work, activities, projects, et cetera to 1932*. New York: Bureau of Publications of Teachers College.

Hanna, Paul R. 1933. Adjusting the home economics program to the present economic situation. *Teachers College Record* 34 (February): 386–397.

Newlon, Jesse H., and Paul R. Hanna. 1933. *Newlon-Hanna Speller*. Boston: Houghton Mifflin.

Hanna, Paul R. 1934. Social studies in the new Virginia curriculum. *Progressive Education* 11 (January-February): 129–134.

Hanna, Paul R., and others. 1935. Opportunities for the use of arithmetic in an activity program. In *The teaching of arithmetic: Tenth yearbook of the National Council of Teachers of Mathematics*. New York: Teachers College Bureau of Publications, 85–120.

Hanna, Paul R. 1935. *Peter's family*. Chicago: Scott, Foresman and Company.

———. 1935. A proposal for a social studies curriculum for the secondary schools. *California Journal of Secondary Education* (October): 412–428.

———. 1935. Romance or reality: A curriculum problem. *Progressive Education* 12 (May): 318–323.

———. 1936. *David's friends at school*. Chicago: Scott, Foresman and Company.

———. 1936. Developing a "sequence" with social rootage. *California Journal of Secondary Education* (October): 375–379.

———. 1936. New developments in kindergarten–primary curriculum. *NEA Proceedings*. Washington, D.C.: NEA, 270–271.

———. 1936. *Susan's neighbors at work*. Chicago: Scott, Foresman and Company.

———. 1936. *Youth serves the community*. New York: D. Appleton-Century Co.

———. 1937. The challenge of educational leadership. *Education Digest* 2 (February): 45–47.

———. 1937. Social education for childhood. *Childhood Education* 14 (October): 74–77.

Hanna, Paul R., Genevieve Anderson, and William S. Gray. 1937. *Susan's neighbors at work*. Chicago: Scott, Foresman and Company.

———. 1938. *Centerville*. Chicago: Scott, Foresman and Company.

Hanna, Paul R. 1938. Social education through cooperative community service. In *Utilization of community resources in the social studies, ninth yearbook of the National Council for the Social Studies*. Cambridge, Mass.: NCSS, 137–143.

———. 1938. Teacher participation in curriculum making. *The National Elementary Principal* (April): 142–146.

———. 1939. The problem of social education. In *Social Education: Pro-*

ceedings of the Stanford School of Education conference summer, 1938. New York: Macmillan, 1–18.

———. 1939. The school: Looking forward. In *Democracy and the curriculum: The life and program of the American school.* New York: D. Appleton-Century Co., 381–405.

———. 1939. Organization for curriculum development. *Curriculum Journal* (March): 104–107.

———. 1939. Providing significant experiences in science. *Childhood Education* (April): 339.

Hanna, Paul R., and others. 1939. *The role of education in utilizing regional resources.* New York: PEA.

Hanna, Paul R. 1939. *Without machinery.* Chicago: Scott, Foresman and Company.

Hanna, Paul R., and Harold C. Hand. 1940. Education for the wise utilization of resources. *Frontiers of Democracy* 6 (15 March): 176–179.

Hanna, Paul R. 1940. *Pioneering in ten communities.* Chicago: Scott, Foresman and Company.

———. 1940. *Ten communities.* Chicago: Scott, Foresman and Company.

———. 1941. Educational relations in the western hemisphere. *NEA proceedings, seventy-ninth annual meeting.* Washington, D.C.: NEA, 124–125.

———. 1941. Pertinent problems in school–community relationships. *Childhood Education* (November): 101–104.

———. 1941. *This useful world.* Chicago: Scott, Foresman and Company.

———. 1942. A new bill of rights; Objectives for post-war planning developed by the National Resources Planning Board. *Frontiers of Democracy* 8 (May): 243–245.

———. 1942. The classroom—a defense unit. *The Journal of Educational Sociology* (February): 369–376.

———. 1942. Capitalizing educational resources of the community. *The National Elementary Principal* (April): 162–166.

———. 1942. *Cross-Country.* Chicago: Scott, Foresman and Company.

———. 1942. This hemispheric problem. *School and Society* 55 (April): 457–462.

————. 1942. *Peter's family (revised)*. Chicago: Scott, Foresman and Company.

————. 1942. Toward a world community. *Childhood Education* (September): 3–4.

————. 1942. National seminar on after war—what? *NEA Proceedings*. Washington, D.C.: NEA, 76–77.

Hanna, Paul R., and Floyd Reeves. 1942. Post-war planning for children and youth. In *National Resources Development Report for 1942*. Washington, D.C.: U.S. Government Printing Office, 113–130.

Hanna, Paul R. 1943. The attack on the three R's. *Educational Leadership* (December): 173–174.

Hanna, Paul R., I. James Quillen, and Paul B. Sears. 1943. *Making the goods we need*. Chicago: Scott, Foresman and Company.

Hanna, Paul R., and Edward A. Krug. 1943. *Marketing the things we use*. Chicago: Scott, Foresman and Company.

Hanna, Paul R. 1943–1944. Our changing world. *Educational Leadership* (October–May).

————. 1944. *Hello, David*. Chicago: Scott, Foresman and Company.

————. 1946. *Aviation education sourcebook*. Stanford: SUSE.

————. 1946. Education for the larger community. *Educational Leadership* (October): 27–33.

————. 1947. Techniques for utilizing community resources. In *The elementary school in the community, nineteenth yearbook of the California Elementary School Principals Association*. CESPA, 81–87.

————. 1948. *Cross-Country, teacher's edition*. Chicago: Scott, Foresman and Company.

————. 1948. *Hello, David, teacher's edition*. Chicago: Scott, Foresman and Company.

————. 1948. *New Centerville*. Chicago: Scott, Foresman and Company.

————. 1948. *New Centerville, teacher's edition*. Chicago: Scott, Foresman and Company.

————. 1948. *Peter's family, teacher's edition*. Chicago: Scott, Foresman and Company.

————. 1948. *Someday soon*. Chicago: Scott, Foresman and Company.

————. 1948. *Tom and Susan*. Chicago: Scott, Foresman and Company.

———. 1948. *Tom and Susan, teacher's edition*. Chicago: Scott, Foresman and Company.

———. 1949. *Peter's family (revised)*. Chicago: Scott, Foresman and Company.

Hanna, Paul R., and Clyde F. Kohn. 1950. *Cross-Country (revised)*. Chicago: Scott, Foresman and Company.

Hanna, Paul R. 1950. The educational outlook at mid-century. *The Texas Outlook*. (February): 10–13.

———. 1952. Needed research on textbooks. *Phi Delta Kappan* (January): 298–299.

Hanna, Paul R., and James T. Moore Jr. 1953. Spelling—from spoken word to written symbol. *Education Digest* 18 (May): 16–19.

Hanna, Paul R., and Robert A. Naslund. 1953. The community school defined. In *The community school: Fifty-second yearbook of the National Society for the Study of Education, part two*. Chicago: University of Chicago Press, 49–63.

Hanna, Paul R. 1954. We teach both subject matter and children—An indispensable blend for a sound elementary school curriculum. *NEA Journal* (May): 273–275.

Hanna, Paul R., Genevieve Anderson Hoyt, and William S. Gray. 1956. *At home*. Chicago: Scott, Foresman and Company.

Hanna, Paul R. 1956. *Beyond the Americas*. Chicago: Scott, Foresman and Company.

Hanna. Paul R., and Sidney C. High Jr. 1956. Education in the Far East. *Phi Delta Kappan* (June): 426–438.

Hanna, Paul R. 1956. Give thanks unto our critics. *The National Elementary Principal* (December): 15–20.

———. 1956. *In all our states*. Chicago: Scott, Foresman and Company.

———. 1956. *In city, town, and country*. Chicago: Scott, Foresman and Company.

———. 1956. *In the Americas*. Chicago: Scott, Foresman and Company.

———. 1956. *In the neighborhood*. Chicago: Scott, Foresman and Company.

———. 1956. Philippine educators show the way. *Education* (June): 601–610.

————. 1956. Social studies for today. *NEA Journal* (January): 36–38.

Hanna, Paul R., and Genevieve Anderson Hoyt. 1957. *At school.* Chicago: Scott, Foresman and Company.

Hanna, Paul R., and Jean S. Hanna. 1957. *Building spelling power.* Boston: Houghton Mifflin.

————. 1957. *Building spelling power, teacher's manual and key.* Boston: Houghton Mifflin.

Hanna, Paul R. 1957. Generalizations and universal values: Their implications for the social studies program. In *Social studies in the elementary school: Fifty-sixth yearbook of the National Society for the Study of Education.* Chicago: University of Chicago Press, 27–47.

————. 1957. We practice conservation. *CTA* (California Timbermans' Association) *Journal* (November): 8–10.

Hanna, Paul R, and others. 1958. Arithmetic used in an activity program. In *Research in the three R's.* C. W. Hunnicut and William J. Iverson, eds. New York: Harper and Brothers, 427–429.

Hanna, Paul R. 1958. Design for a national curriculum. *The Nation's Schools* 67 (September): 43–45.

Hanna, Paul R., and Jean S. Hanna. 1959. Psychology of spelling. *Education Digest* 25 (October): 50–52.

————. 1959. Spelling as a school subject: A brief history. *The National Elementary Principal* 38 (May): 8–23.

Hanna, Paul R. 1960. A national curriculum commission? *NEA Journal* (January): 25–28.

Hanna, Paul R., and Jean S. Hanna. 1960. Spelling today. *The Instructor* (November): 6, 106.

Hanna, Paul R. 1961. Proposed: A national curriculum commission. *Phi Delta Kappan* (May): 331–338.

————, ed. 1962. *Education: An instrument of national goals.* New York: McGraw-Hill.

————. 1963. Curriculum and instruction: A proposal concerning the NEA's future role in these areas. *NEA Journal* (January): 52–54.

Hanna, Paul R., and Jean S. Hanna. 1963. *First steps. A speller for beginners.* Boston: Houghton Mifflin.

———. 1963. *First steps. A speller for beginners. Teacher's edition.* Boston: Houghton Mifflin.

———. 1963. How a great Frank Lloyd Wright house changed, grew, came to perfection. *House Beautiful* 105 (January): 55–110.

Hanna, Paul R. 1963. The social studies program in the elementary school in the twentieth century. In *The social studies*, G. Wesly Sowards, ed. Glenview, Ill.: Scott, Foresman and Company.

Hanna, Paul R., Rose E. Sabaroff, Gordon F. Davies, and Charles R. Farrar. 1966. *Geography in the teaching of social studies: Concepts and skills.* Boston: Houghton Mifflin.

Hanna, Paul R., and Jean S. Hanna. 1966. *Power to spell.* Boston: Houghton Mifflin.

Hanna, Paul R. 1966. *Phoneme-grapheme correspondences as cues to spelling improvement.* Washington, D.C.: U.S. Office of Education.

Hanna, Paul R., and Jean S. Hanna. 1967. *The foundations of spelling and its teaching.* Boston: Houghton Mifflin.

———. 1967. *Words in your language.* Boston: Houghton Mifflin.

Hanna, Paul R. 1969. Education and the creation of multinational communities of men. In *The United States and international education: Sixty-eighth yearbook of the National Society for the Study of Education, part one.* Chicago: University of Chicago Press, 254.

———. 1970. *Investigating man's world.* Chicago: Scott, Foresman and Company.

———. 1970. *Inter-American studies.* Chicago: Scott, Foresman and Company.

———. 1971. Don't kid yourself about videorecord costs. *School Management* (July): 30–31.

Hanna, Paul R., Richard E. Hodges, and Jean S. Hanna. 1971. *Spelling: Structure and strategies.* Boston: Houghton Mifflin.

Hanna, Paul R. 1973. Research in values. *The Journal of Educational Research* (November): 1.

Hanna, Paul R., and Jean S. Hanna. 1981. *Frank Lloyd Wright's Hanna house: The clients' report.* New York: The Architectural History Foundation.

Hanna, Paul R. 1987. *Assuring quality for the social studies in our schools.* Stanford: Hoover Institution Press.

Appendix B

Partial* List of Paul R. Hanna's Doctoral Advisees at Stanford University with Dissertation Titles, Arranged Chronologically

Mann, Cecil W. 1938. The education system of the colony of Fiji.

Addicott, Irwin O., Ed.D. 1940. A study of the nature and elementary school use of free printed matter prepared as advertising media.

Willey, Roy D., Ph.D. 1940. A study of the use of arithmetic in the elementary schools of Santa Clara County, California.

Haan, Aubrey E., Ed.D. 1941. The role of the community school in educating for the use of natural and human resources of the Pacific Northwest region.

Palm, Reuben R., Ed.D. 1941. A study of the types of curriculum organization and administration of curriculum development programs in laboratory schools of state teachers colleges.

Burr, James B., Ed.D. 1942. A study of the functions and services of state elementary staffs.

Culver, Mary M., Ed.D. 1942. A study of children's interests in arithmetic as indicated by their spontaneous quantitative expressions in life situations.

* This list was compiled from available editions of *Stanford Dissertation Abstracts*. The author was unable to locate those published later than 1952.

Hunnicutt, Clarence W., Ed.D. 1942. The effect of activity teaching on children's attitudes and behavior.

Polster, Arthur H., Ed.D. 1942. Leadership in curriculum development.

Staats, Pauline, G., Ed.D. 1944. A study of the educational activities of the Intellectual Cooperation Organization of the League of Nations, 1920–1940.

Adams, Robert G., Ed.D. 1945. The behavior of pupils in democratic and autocratic social climates.

Dutton, Wilbur H., Ed.D. 1945. The child-study movement in America from its origin (1880) to the organization of the Progressive Education Association (1920).

Tonge, Frederic M., Ed.D., and August G. Jelinek, Ed.D. 1945. Forecasts of California teacher supply and demand, 1945–1960.

Freeburg, Roy E. W., Ed.D. 1946. The use of musical resources of the Pacific Southwest region for elementary education.

Morton, John A., Ed.D. 1946. A study of children's mathematical-interest questions as a clue to grade placement of arithmetic topics.

Drag, Francis L., Ed.D. 1947. Curriculum laboratories in the United States.

Giles, John W., Ed.D. 1947. A suggested plan for equalizing the costs of pupil transportation in the State of California.

Light, Jerome T., Ed.D. 1947. The development of a junior–senior high school program in a relocation center for people of Japanese ancestry during the war with Japan.

Ormsby, George W., Ed.D. 1947. The effects of extremely rapid expansion in a community on its elementary schools: A case study.

Robinson, Clark N., Ed.D. 1947. A method for obtaining occupational information of value to the school.

Sherer, Lorraine M., Ed.D. 1947. A technique in curriculum development: How to improve a curriculum — mathematics, for example.

Thompson, Maury W., Ed.D. 1947. Educational aspects of California institutions for dependent children.

Wills, Clarice D., Ed.D. 1947. Housing requirements for California nursery schools.

Drummond, Harold D., Ed.D. 1948. Appraising the elementary school language arts program.

Ormsby, Lelia T., Ed.D. 1948. Audio education in the public schools of California.

Lang, Arch D., Ph.D. 1949. The integrative process in human life and in education.

Burnett, Laurie W., Ed.D. 1949. Textbook provisions in the several states with emphasis upon California.

Byers, Loretta M., Ed.D. 1949. Teacher recruitment.

Cooper, James G., III, Ed.D., and Roland B. Lewis, Ed.D. 1949. Quantitative Rorschach factors in the evaluation of teacher effectiveness.

Langston, Roderick G., Ed.D. 1949. The ideals of American organizations and their implications for citizenship education in elementary schools.

McAulay, John D. E., Ed.D. 1949. Trends in elementary school geography, 1928–1948.

Shaftel, Fannie R., Ed.D. 1949. Role-playing in the teaching of American ideals.

Swenson, Robert E., Ed.D. 1949. A method for obtaining occupational information of value to the school.

Thompson, Emmett C., Ed.D. 1949. Leaders in selected educational associations.

Doucette, Andrew L., Ed.D. 1950. A science program for Alberta schools based on student interests.

Futter, Irwin C., Ed.D. 1950. Parent–teacher relations.

Hanson, Rita C., Ed.D. 1950. Educating elementary school children of seasonal-migrant agricultural workers in San Joaquin Valley.

Larkin, Joseph B., Ed.D. 1950. Curricular practices in selected California schools.

Patrick, Margaret E., Ed.D. 1950. The selection and adoption of textbooks in Texas—a case study.

Woodworth, Ira R., Ed.D. 1950. School building and curriculum needs of an elementary school district: 1948–1968.

Grantham, Herbert H., Ph.D. 1951. The science curriculum in British Columbia schools with an emphasis upon the secondary level.

Cowan, Audley W., Ed.D. 1951. Elementary school social studies: A research guide to sequence.

Dowley, Edith M., Ed.D. 1951. Characteristics of war-born children as revealed through mother interviews.

Fox, Robert S., Ed.D. 1951. County-level educational service through contract agreements.

Hambrick, Fitzhugh L., Ed.D. 1951. Educational problems inherent in school districts.

Ingebritson, Kaspar I., Ed.D. 1951. The induction of beginning teachers.

McCarthy, Mary C., Ed.D. 1951. The local community in third-grade social studies: A case study in San Francisco.

Moore, James T., Jr., Ed.D. 1951. Phonetic elements appearing in a three-thousand word spelling vocabulary.

Nagle, Walter E., Ed.D. 1951. A pre service course in elementary education.

Naslund, Robert A., Ed.D. 1951. The origin and development of the community school concept.

Selim, Mohamed S. A., Ed.D. 1951. Conservation education in California high schools.

Sessarego, Albert J., Ed.D. 1951. Practices for discovering individual pupil needs in selected elementary schools.

Watts, Phyllis W., Ed.D. 1951. Reading improvement through cooperative in-service education of secondary school teachers.

Bevans, Lloyd E., Ed.D. 1952. Administrative practices in California elementary school principalships 1933 and 1951 (part I).

Bradford, Henry F., Ed.D. 1952. Oral–aural differentiation among phonemes as a factor in spelling readiness.

Brown, Stanley B., Ed.D. 1952. Science information and attitudes possessed by California elementary school pupils.

Bryner, James R., Ed.D. 1952. The content of primary school experience charts.

Dandoy, Maxim A., Ed.D. 1952. Student teaching in public teacher education institutions in the Philippines.

Dobson, Marie C., Ed.D. 1952. The effect of problem-story role playing by fifth grade children.

Fisher, Robert J., Ed.D. 1952. The social participation and socio-economic status of elementary school children.

Henderson, Adin D., Ed.D. 1952. The life of Ellwood Patterson Cubberley.

Livingston, Thomas B., Ed.D. 1952. An in-service education program for teachers in a typical community.

Peralta, Crescencio G., Ed.D. 1952. Teacher education for rural Philippine life.

Scobey, Mary-Margaret, Ed.D. 1952. Industrial arts for elementary teachers.

Sowards, George W., Ed.D. 1952. Supervisory practices in California elementary school principalships 1933 and 1951 (part II).

Appendix C

Chronological List of Courses
Taught by Paul R. Hanna at the
Stanford University School of Education

Fundamental Problems in Education (1935)

Seminar in Elementary School Administration (1935 and after)

Fundamental Problems of Education—Curriculum and Guidance (1936)

Language Arts Curricula in the Elementary School (1937)

Curricula of Modern Elementary Schools (1937 and after)

Silent Reading in the Upper Elementary and Secondary Schools (1937)

Organization and Administration of Elementary Schools (1937 and after)

Individual Study in Elementary Administration (1937 and after)

Individual Study in Curriculum and Instruction (1937 and after)

Curriculum Development (1938 and after)

Social Studies Program in Elementary and Secondary Schools (1939 and after)

Natural Science in the Elementary and Junior High School Curriculum (1939)

Field Practice in Elementary Administration (1939 and after)

Arithmetic Curricula for Elementary Schools (1940)

Seminar in Education for Elementary Teachers (1940 and after)

Individual Study in Elementary Curriculum, Instruction, and Supervision
   (1940 and after)

Workshop: The Elementary School (1943 and after)

Social Studies in the Elementary School Curriculum (1943 and after)

Curriculum of the Elementary School (1942 and after)

Mathematics in the Elementary School Curriculum (1944)

Supervision in Education (1945)

Thesis Seminar (1945)

The Teachers College in America (1951)

Seminar in Elementary School Education (1951 and after)

Individual Study in Elementary Education (1954 and after)

Seminar in Elementary Education for Doctoral Candidates (1955 and
   after)

Elementary School Curriculum, Instruction, and Supervision (1960 and
   after)

Elementary School Social Studies (1960)

Seminar in Comparative and Overseas Education (1961 and after)

Seminar in the School Curriculum (1961 and after)

International Development Education Seminar (1966)

Comparative Education (1967)

Seminar in Educational Planning—the Theory and Practice (1967)

Works Cited

Adiseshiah, Malcolm S. 1955. Letter to Paul Hanna, 14 November. Typewritten letter signed (TLS). In the Hanna Collection, Hoover Institution Library, Stanford, Calif.

Alexandria High School. 1920. *Commencement exercises*. Hanna Collection.

Alexandria Public Schools. 1920. Report card. Hanna Collection.

Annandale Public Schools. 1911. Report card. Hanna Collection.

Anderson, Genevieve. 1938. Telegram to Paul Hanna, 18 March. Hanna Collection.

Anderson, Ronald Stone. 1959. *Japan: The three epochs of modern education* U.S. Dept. of HEW Bulletin, no.11. Washington, D.C.: U.S. Government Printing Office.

Andrus, J. Russell. 1952. Letter to Paul Hanna, 25 February. Hanna Collection.

Bagley, William C. 1935. Editorial. *Educational administration and supervision*, 21.

Barry, Mary Elizabeth, and Paul R. Hanna, eds. 1930. *Wonder flights of long ago*. New York: Teachers College Press.

Bergman, Walter G. 1947. Memo to Chief, E&RA, OMGUS, 16 June. In

James F. Tent, *Mission on the Rhine*. Chicago: University of Chicago Press, 262.

Bernardino, Vitaliano. 1958. *The Philippine community school*. Quezon City: Phoenix Press.

Bodet, J. Torres. 1948. Letter to Paul Hanna, 18 December. Hanna Collection.

Brown, Dorothy Louise. 1981. Maycie Katherine Southall, her life and contributions to education. Ph.D. diss., George Peabody College.

Burlbaw, Lynn M. 1989. Hollis Leland Caswell's contributions to the development of the curriculum field. Ph.D. diss., University of Texas.

Burleigh, Clara M. 1977. Letter to Paul Hanna, 20 December. TLS. Hanna Collection.

Butts, R. Freeman. 1999. Letter to author, 5 March.

California Library Association. 1948. Letter to Paul Hanna, 15 April. Typewritten document (TD). Hanna Collection.

California State Board of Education. 1945. *Call for bids for textbooks in history and geography and related studies*, 1 October.

———. 1946. *Minutes of special meeting*. July 30. California State Senate. 1947. SB 1029.

———. 1947. SB 97.

Carr, Edward H. 1967. *What is history?* New York: Random House.

Castilleja School. 1982. Newsletter, May. Hanna Collection.

Caswell, Hollis. 1935. *Curriculum development*.

———. 1961. Annual report to the trustees, 1960–1961, Teachers College, Columbia University. Reprinted in Paul R. Hanna. *Assuring quality for the social studies in our schools*. 1987. Stanford, Calif.: Hoover Institution Press, 55–64.

———. 1964. Letter to Paul R. Hanna, 20 June. Autograph letter signed (ALS). Hanna Collection.

———. 1977. Interview by O. L. Davis Jr. Quoted in Lynn M. Burlbaw. Hollis Leland Caswell's contributions to the development of the curriculum field. 1989. Ph.D. diss., University of Texas.

———. 1978. Interview by Angela E. Fraley. Quoted in Angela E. Fraley. *Schooling and innovation: The rhetoric and the reality*. 1981. New York: Tyler Gibson Publishers, 95.

Chapin, June R., and Richard E. Gross. 1973. *Teaching social studies skills.* Boston: Little, Brown and Company.

Churchill, Terry. 1999. Interview by author, 12 March.

Clements, Millard, William R. Fielder, and B. Robert Tabachnick. 1966. *Social studies-inquiry in elementary classrooms.* Indianapolis: Bobbs-Merrill Co.

Conant, James B. 1937. Letter to Ray Lyman Wilbur, 15 February. Quoted in Rebecca S. Lowen: *Creating the cold war university: The transformation of Stanford.* 1997. Berkeley: University of California Press, 47.

Conference on policies and strategy for strengthening the curriculum of the American public school. 1959. TD. Hanna Collection.

Counts, George S. 1932. *Dare the school build a new social order?* New York: John Day Co.

Cremin, Lawrence A. 1961. *The transformation of the school: Progressivism in American education, 1876–1957.* New York: Alfred A. Knopf.

Cremin, Lawrence A., David A. Shannon, and Mary Evelyn Townsend. 1954. *A history of Teachers College, Columbia University.* New York: Columbia University Press.

Crunden, Robert M. 1982. *Ministers of reform: The progressives' achievement in American civilization.* New York: Basic Books.

Cuban, Larry. 1993. *How teachers taught: Constancy and change in American classrooms, 1890–1990, second edition.* New York: Teachers College Press.

Cubberley, Elwood P. 1938. Letter to Ray Lyman Wilbur, 16 March. Hanna Collection.

Davidson, William J. 1921. Letter to Paul Hanna, 3 June. TLS. Hanna Collection.

Davis, Margo, and Roxane Nilan. 1989. *The Stanford album: A photographic history, 1885–1945.* Stanford: Stanford University Press.

Davis, O. L., Jr. 1997. The personal nature of curricular integration. *Journal of Curriculum and Supervision* 12 (Winter): 95–97.

Davis, Paul. 1943. Letter to Ray Lyman Wilbur, 1 January. In Lowen, 56.

deLima, Agnes. 1932. A communication. *The New Republic* 71 (3 August): 317–318.

Dewey, John. 1897. My pedagogic creed. *The School Journal* 54 (January 16): 77–80.

———. 1913. *The school and society*. Chicago: University of Chicago Press. (Original edition, 1900).

———. 1928. Progressive education and the science of education. *Progressive Education* 5 (Summer): 201.

———. 1930. How much freedom in the schools? *New Republic* 63 (July 9): 204–206.

Douglass, Malcolm. 1998a. Presentation at the National Council for the Social Studies Annual Meeting held in Anaheim, Calif., 20–22 November, 1998.

———. 1998b. Interview by author, 6 December.

Drummond, Harold. 1997. Letter to author, 5 June.

Embree, E. R. 1935. In order of their eminence, an appraisal of American universities. *Atlantic Monthly* (June): 652–664.

Evans, Ronald W. 1998. Turf wars as a way of life: A framework for understanding the history of social studies. (A paper presented at the annual meeting of the American Educational Research Association, April 15.) San Diego, California.

Foley, Douglas. 1984. "Colonialism and Schooling in the Philippines, 1898–1970." In *Education and the Colonial Experience, 2nd revised edition*. Philip G. Altbach and Gail P. Kelly, eds. New Brunswick, N.J.: Transaction Books, 35.

Foley, Douglas. 1997. Interview by author, 17 June.

Foster, Donald M. 1975. Letter to Paul Hanna, 24 April. Hanna Collection.

———. 1998a. Letter to author, 19 November.

———. 1998b. Letter to author, 24 November.

Fraley, Angela E. 1981. *Schooling and innovation: The rhetoric and the reality*. New York: Tyler Gibson Publishers.

Gill, Martin. 1974. Paul R. Hanna: The evolution of an elementary social studies textbook series. Ph.D. diss., Northwestern University.

———. 1975. Letter to Paul Hanna, 31 October. Hanna Collection.

Glenwood Schools. 1916. Report card. Hanna Collection.

———. 1917. Report card. Hanna Collection.

———. 1918. Report card. Hanna Collection.

———. 1919. Report card. Hanna Collection.

Golden, Arthur. 1997. *Memoirs of a geisha*. New York: Random House.

Goodlad, John. 1984. *A place called school*. New York: McGraw-Hill.

Graham, Patricia A. 1967. *Progressive education from arcady to academe: A history of the P.E.A., 1919–1955*. New York: Teachers College Press.

Greater Hamline Liner. 1924. Hanna Collection.

Griffin, W. F. 1974. Interview by Martin Gill, 21 February. Quoted in Gill Martin. 1974. Paul R. Hanna: The evolution of an elementary social studies textbook series. Ph.D. diss., Northwestern University.

Gross, Richard. 1998. Interview by author, 9 August.

Hamline University. 1975. *Financial Planner*, Summer. Hanna Collection.

———. 1999. Brochure.

Hand, Harold. 1938(?). Letter to Paul Hanna, undated. Hanna Collection.

Hanna, Aurelia. 1999. Interview by author, 28 February.

Hanna, Jean. 1938(?). Note to Paul Hanna, undated. Hanna Collection.

Hanna, John. 1998. Interview by author, 11 August.

Hanna, Paul R. 1921. Letters to R. C. Barnum Company. Hanna Collection.

———. 1925. Typescript. Hanna Collection.

———. 1932a. Typescript. Hanna Collection.

———. 1932b. Readings in methods of social change. TD. Hanna Collection.

———. 1932c. The activity program in the intermediate grades, part three: Its development in Lincoln School intermediate grades. *Education* (April): 483–488.

———. 1933. Adjusting the home economics program to the present economic situation. *Teachers College Record* 34 (February): 386–397.

———. 1934. Social studies in the new Virginia curriculum. *Progressive Education* 11 (January–February): 129–134.

———. 1935a. Romance or reality: A curriculum problem. *Progressive Education* 12 (May): 318–323.

———. 1935b. A proposal for a social studies curriculum for the secondary schools. *California Journal of Secondary Education* (October): 412–428.

———. 1935c. Education 256/Education 331. TD (mimeograph). Hanna Collection.

———. 1936a. *Youth serves the community*. New York: D. Appleton-Century Co.

———. 1936b. Developing a "sequence" with social rootage. *California Journal of Secondary Education* (October): 375–379.

———. 1936c. New developments in kindergarten–primary curriculum. *NEA: Proceedings of the seventy-fourth annual meeting*. Washington, D.C.: NEA, 270–271.

Hanna, Paul R., ed. 1936(?) General comments. TD. Hanna Collection.

———. 1937a. Education 256. TD (mimeograph). Hanna Collection.

———. 1937b. The challenge of educational leadership. *Education Digest* 2 (February): 45–47.

———. 1937c. Social education for childhood. *Childhood Education* 14 (October): 74–77.

———. 1938a. Social education through cooperative community service. In *Utilization of community resources in the social studies: Ninth yearbook of the National Council for the Social Studies*. Cambridge, Mass.: NCSS, 137–143.

———. 1938b. Teacher participation in curriculum making. *The National Elementary Principal* (April): 142–146.

———. 1939a. The problem of social education. In *Social education: Proceedings of the Stanford School of Education conference, summer, 1938*. New York: Macmillan, 1–18.

———. 1939b. The school: Looking forward. In *Democracy and the curriculum: The life and program of the American school*. New York: D. Appleton-Century Co., 381–405.

———. 1939c. Organization for curriculum development. *Curriculum Journal* (March): 104–107.

———. 1939d. Providing significant experiences in science. *Childhood Education*. (April): 339.

———. 1941a. Pertinent problems in school–community relationships. *Childhood Education* (November): 101–104.

———. 1941b. Educational relations in the western hemisphere. *NEA pro-*

ceedings, seventy-ninth annual meeting. Washington, D.C.: NEA, 124–125.

———. 1942a. A new bill of rights: Objectives for post-war planning developed by the National Resources Planning Board. *Frontiers of Democracy* 8 (May): 243–245.

———. 1942b. The classroom—a defense unit. *The Journal of Educational Sociology* (February): 369–376.

———. 1942c. Capitalizing educational resources of the community. *The National Elementary Principal* (April): 162–166.

———. 1942d. This hemispheric problem. *School and Society* 55 (April): 457–462.

———. 1942e. Toward a world community. *Childhood Education* (September): 3–4.

———. 1942f. National seminar on After war—what? *NEA Proceedings.* Washington, D.C.: NEA, 76–77.

———. 1942g. Proposed curriculum procedures for Japanese relocation centers. TD (mimeograph). Hanna Collection.

———. 1942(?). *Confidential Report to Council of National Defense, Coordinator of Commercial and Cultural Relations Between the American Republics.* Typewritten document signed (TDS). Hanna Collection.

———. 1943. *Programs of training, research, and service for the Pacific, Asia, and Latin American regions.* TD. Hanna Collection.

———. 1944. Letter to Donald Tressider, 29 March. TLS. Hanna Collection.

———. 1945. Stanford Pacific Institute. TD. Hanna Collection.

———. 1946. Education for the larger community. *Educational Leadership* (October): 27–33.

———. 1947a. Techniques for utilizing community resources. In *The elementary school in the community: Nineteenth yearbook of the California Elementary School Principals Association.* No place: CESPA, 81–87.

———. 1947b. "Excerpts from *Report on Germany.*" Autograph manuscript signed (AMsS). Hanna Collection.

———. 1948. Letter to Frances Foster, 29 February. TLS. Hanna Collection.

——. 1950. The educational outlook at mid-century. *The Texas Outlook*. (February): 10–13.

——. 1951. Letter to A. John Bartky, 19 December. Typewritten letter (TL). Hanna Collection.

——. 1952a. "Educating the Economic Man." Address to the Third Biennial Conference of the Philippine Association of Christian Schools and Colleges, April. Hanna Collection.

——. 1952b. Needed research on textbooks. *Phi Delta Kappan* (January): 298–299.

——. 1953. *The Educational Program*. TDS. Hanna Collection.

——. 1954. We teach both subject matter and children—An indispensable blend for a sound elementary school curriculum. *NEA Journal* (May): 273–275.

——. 1955. Letter to Malcolm Adiseshiah, 16 December. TLS. Hanna Collection.

——. 1956a. Social studies for today. *NEA Journal* (January): 36–38.

——. 1956b. Philippine educators show the way. *Education* (June): 601–610.

——. 1957a. Generalizations and universal values: Their implications for the social studies program. In *Social studies in the elementary school: Fifty-sixth yearbook of the National Society for the Study of Education*. Chicago: University of Chicago Press, 27–47.

——. 1957b. Letter to Gordon Hullfish, 30 December. TLS. Hanna Collection.

——. 1957c. Memo to Harry Brenn (?), February. Typewritten manuscript signed (TMsS). Hanna Collection.

——. 1957d. We practice conservation. *California Timber Association Journal* (November): 12–14.

——. 1958a. Design for a national curriculum. *The Nation's Schools* 67 (September): 43–45.

——. 1958b. Social studies: Curriculum in the elementary school. TD. Hanna Collection.

——. 1960. A national curriculum commission? *NEA Journal* (January): 25–28.

———. 1961a. Proposed: A national curriculum commission. *Phi Delta Kappan* (May): 331–338.

———. 1961b. Letter to Bailey K. Howard, 14 March. TLS. Hanna Collection.

———. 1961c. Letter to Geneva Hanna, 23 February. TLS. Hanna Collection.

———. 1961d. Memo, July. TD. Hanna Collection.

———. 1962a. Letter to J. E. Wallace Sterling, 20 July. TLS. Hanna Collection.

———. 1962b. Letter to Bailey K. Howard, 26 June. TLS. Hanna Collection.

———. 1963a. Curriculum and instruction: A proposal concerning the NEA's future role in these areas. *NEA Journal* (January): 52–54.

———. 1964a. The university and the government. TMsS. Hanna Collection.

———. 1964b. Letter to Donald Ludgin, 3 July. TLS. Hanna Collection.

———. 1966. *Report of the Binational Advisory Commission for Long-Term Planning of Educational, Scientific-Technical, and Cultural Cooperation between the Socialist Federal Republic of Yugoslavia and the United States of America*. TD. Hanna Collection.

———. 1967a. Letter to R. Freeman Butts, 23 November. TLS. Hanna Collection.

———. 1967b. *Report on Tour of Duty in Four African Nations*. TDS. Hanna Collection.

———. 1968a. Typewritten manuscript (TMs). 3 March. Hanna Collection.

———. 1968b. TMs. 27 March. Hanna Collection.

———. 1968c. Letter to H. Thomas James, 24 April. TL. Hanna Collection.

———. 1969. Education and the creation of multinational communities of men. In *The United States and international education: Sixty-eighth yearbook of the National Society for the Study of Education, part one*. Chicago: University of Chicago Press, 254.

———. 1970. Investigating man's world. Chicago: Scott, Foresman and Company.

———. 1973a. Interview by Martin Gill, 5 September. Hanna Collection.

———. 1973b. Research in values. *The Journal of Educational Research* (November): 1.

———. 1974. Interview by Martin Gill, 19 June. Hanna Collection.

———. 1976. I recall. TMs. Hanna Collection.

———. 1977. *Campus Report*, 5 October. Hanna Collection.

———. 1982a. Interview by Gerald Dorfman, 10 November. Transcript. Hanna Collection.

———. 1982b. Hanna's participation in Stanford University fund-raising. TMs. Hanna Collection.

———. 1986. Interview by Rebecca S. Lowen, 26 March. In Lowen, Rebecca S. 1997. *Creating the cold war university: The transformation of Stanford*. Berkeley: University of California Press.

———. 1987. *Assuring quality for the social studies in our schools*. Stanford: Hoover Institution Press.

———. Undated. Why Frank Lloyd Wright? TMs. Hanna Collection.

Hanna, Paul R., and others. 1935. Opportunities for the use of arithmetic in an activity program. In *The teaching of arithmetic: Tenth yearbook of the National Council of Teachers of Mathematics*. New York: Teachers College Bureau of Publications, 85–120.

Hanna, Paul R., Genevieve Anderson, and William S. Gray. 1937. *Susan's neighbors at school*. Chicago: Scott, Foresman and Company.

———. 1938. *Centerville*. Chicago: Scott, Foresman and Company.

Hanna, Paul R., and Colba F. Gucker. 1930. Hobbies for parents. *Parents Magazine* (29 April): 66–67.

Hanna, Paul R., and Jean S. Hanna. 1959. Psychology of spelling. *Education Digest* 25 (October): 50–52.

———. 1960. A national curriculum commission? *NEA Journal* (January): 25–28.

———. 1963. How a great Frank Lloyd Wright house changed, grew, came to perfection. *House Beautiful* 105 (January): 55–110.

———. 1981. *Frank Lloyd Wright's Hanna house: The clients' report*. New York: The Architectural History Foundation.

Hanna, Paul R., Genevieve Anderson Hoyt, and William S. Gray. 1956. *At home*. Chicago: Scott, Foresman and Company.

Hanna, Paul R., and Sidney C. High Jr. 1956. Education in the Far East. *Phi Delta Kappan* (June): 426–438.

Hanna. Paul R., and Genevieve Anderson Hoyt. 1957. *At school*. Chicago: Scott, Foresman and Company.

Hanna, Paul R., and Clyde F. Kohn. 1950. *Cross-Country*. Chicago: Scott, Foresman and Company.

Hanna, Paul R., and Edward A. Krug. 1943. *Marketing the things we use*. Chicago: Scott, Foresman and Company.

Hanna, Paul R., and James T. Moore Jr. 1953. Spelling—from spoken word to written symbol. *Education Digest* 18 (May): 16–19.

Hanna, Paul R., and Robert A. Naslund. 1953. The community school defined. In *The community school: Fifty-second yearbook of the National Society for the Study of Education, part two*. Chicago: University of Chicago Press, 49–63.

Hanna, Paul R., I. James Quillen, and Paul B. Sears. 1943. *Making the goods we need*. Chicago: Scott, Foresman and Company.

Hanna, Paul R., and Floyd Reeves. 1942. Post-war planning for children and youth. In *National Resources Development Report for 1942*. Washington, D.C.: U.S. Government Printing Office, 113–130.

Hanna, Paul R., Rose E. Sabaroff, Gordon F. Davies, and Charles R. Farrar. 1966. *Geography in the teaching of social studies: Concepts and skills*. Boston: Houghton Mifflin.

Harap, Henry. 1970. The beginnings of the John Dewey Society. *Educational Theory* 20 (Spring): 157–163.

———. Undated. Spring conference: A brief history. TD. In Caswell folder, University of Texas Oral History Collection.

Harvard University. 1959. *Advanced Administrative Institute*. TD. Hanna Collection.

Harvey, David. 1989. *The condition of postmodernity*. Oxford: Basil Blackwell.

Hayse, Michael. 1997. Education among the ruins: Proposals for institutions of higher learning in American occupied Germany, 1945–1949. Presentation to the History of Education Society annual meeting, 24 October. Philadelphia, Pa.

Henderson, Adin D. 1952. The life of Ellwood Patterson Cubberley. Ed.D. diss., Stanford University.

Hoover Institution. Undated. *The Paul and Jean Hanna archival collection on the role of education in the twentieth century.* Stanford: Hoover Institution Press.

Howard, Bailey K. 1962. Letter to Paul R. Hanna, 25 June. TLS. Hanna Collection.

Improving the Philippine Educational System: Report of the Joint Congressional Committee on Education to the Congress. 1951. Manila: Bureau of Printing.

International Cooperation Agency. 1957. *The sixth milestone.* Manila: AID.

———. 1962. *The tenth milestone.* Manila: AID.

James, Thomas. 1987. *Exile within: The schooling of Japanese Americans 1942–1945.* Cambridge: Harvard University Press.

Johnson, Henry C., Jr. 1977. Reflective thought and practical action: The origins of the John Dewey Society. *Educational Theory* 27 (Winter): 65–75.

Kandel, Isaac. 1933. Education and social disorder. *Teachers College Record* 24 (February): 359–367.

Kaub, Verne P. 1953. *Communist-socialist propaganda in American schools.* No place: American Council of Christian Laymen.

Kefuaver, Grayson. 1938. Letter to Paul R. Hanna, March. Hanna Collection.

Kilpatrick, William H. 1934. Editorial. *Progressive Education* 11.

———. 1935. Diary for 24 February. Quoted in Beineke, John A. 1998. *And there were giants in the land: The life of William Heard Kilpatrick.* New York: Peter Lang, 1998, 218.

———. 1939. The promise of education. *The New Republic* 101 (8 November): 57.

King, Irving. 1913. *Education for social efficiency.* New York: D. Appleton-Century Co.

Kliebard, Herbert M. 1986. *The struggle for the American curriculum 1893–1958.* Boston: Routledge and Kegan Paul.

Klous, Major D. Donald. 1946. Letter to Paul Hanna, 20 December. TLS. Hanna Collection.

von Kreisler-Bomben, Kristin. 1984. So who's retired? *The Stanford Magazine.* Winter.

Lasch, Christopher. 1989. A life of pain in an empty culture. *Raleigh News and Observer* (31 December), 7J. Quoted in Nord, Warren A. *Religion and American education: Rethinking a national dilemma*. 1995. Chapel Hill: University of North Carolina Press, 321.

LeRiche, Leo W. 1987. *Theory and Research in Social Education* 15 (Summer): 137–154.

Light, Jerome T. 1947. The development of a junior–senior high school program in a relocation center for people of Japanese ancestry during the war with Japan. Ed.D. diss., Stanford University.

Livingston, William B. 1958. Letter to Paul Hanna. TLS. Hanna Collection.

Lowen, Rebecca S. 1997. *Creating the cold war university: The transformation of Stanford*. Berkeley: University of California Press.

Ludgin, Donald. 1964. Letter to Paul Hanna, 23 June. TLS. Hanna Collection.

Manalang, Prishla S. 1977. *A Philippine rural school: Its cultural dimension*. Quezon City: University of the Philippines Press.

Mayhew, Lewis B. 1974. *Educational leadership and declining enrollments*. Berkeley: McCutchan.

McKenzie, Gary R. 1998. Rise, stagnation and decline of elementary social studies and a successful defense. A paper presented at the annual meeting of the American Educational Research Association, April 15. San Diego, Calif.

McMurry, Charles A. 1903. *Special method in history*. New York: Macmillan.

Mehlinger, Howard D., ed. 1981. *UNESCO handbook for the teaching of social studies*. Paris: UNESCO.

Miller, Norman. 1967. Structured social studies content for elementary schools: The emerging Atlantic community. Ph.D. diss., Stanford University.

Moore, Frank J. 1973. Letter to Paul Hanna, 24 April. TLS. Hanna Collection.

Moore, James T., Jr. 1951. Phonetic elements appearing in a three thousand word spelling vocabulary. Ph. D. diss., Stanford University.

Nash, George H. 1988. *Herbert Hoover and Stanford University*. Stanford: Hoover Institution Press.

Naslund, Robert A. 1953. The impact of the power age on the community-school concept. In *The community school: Fifty-second yearbook of the National Society for the Study of Education*. Chicago: University of Chicago Press, 251–264.

The Nation. 1935. Editorial, 13 March: 293.

National Council for American Education. 1948a. *Building America condemned as unfit for use in American public schools*. New York: NCAE.

———. 1948b. *Series of textbooks designed for junior high schools sponsored by the National Education Association and titled Building America condemned as unfit for use in American public schools by the Senate Investigating Committee on Education*. New York: NCAE.

———. 1950. *Red-ucators at University of California, Stanford University, California Institute of Technology*. New York: NCAE.

National Education Association. 1932. Report of the Committee on Resolutions: *Proceedings of the Seventeenth Annual Meeting*. Washington, D.C.: NEA.

Nelson, Murry R. 1988. Paul Hanna: 1902–1988. *Social Education* 52 (October): 413.

Newlon, Jesse. 1934. Letter to Henry Harap, 11 January. Quoted in Johnson, Henry C., Jr. 1977. Reflective thought and practical action: The origins of the John Dewey Society, 70. *Educational Theory* 27 (Winter), 1977.

———. 1938a. Letter to Paul Hanna, 29 April. TLS. Hanna Collection.

———. 1938b. Letter to Paul Hanna, 18 May. TLS. Hanna Collection.

Newlon, Jesse, and Paul R. Hanna. 1933. *The Newlon-Hanna speller*. Boston: Houghton Mifflin.

Newman, Robert E., Jr. 1961. History of a civic education project implementing the social problems technique of instruction. Ph.D. diss., Stanford University.

Newman, Robert E. 1969. Letter to Dr. Frederick Wilhelms, 9 December. TLS. Hanna Collection.

Noonan, Richard B. 1984. The emergence of the professional curriculum specialist: A historical interpretation of the Society for Curriculum Study. Ed.D Report, Teachers College, Columbia University.

Ord, John E. 1972. *Elementary social studies for today's children.* New York: Harper and Row.

Paynesville Public Schools. 1913–1915. Report cards. Hanna Collection.

Perkins, James A. 1967. Letter to Paul Hanna, 10 June 10. TLS. Hanna Collection.

Progressive Education 15 (November) 1938.

Progressive Education Association. 1938. *Report of the Resolutions Committee.* Columbus, Ohio: American Education Press.

Progressive Education Association Advisory Board. 1932. Minutes, April 29–May 1. In Graham, 67.

Ragan, William B. 1958. Letter to Paul Hanna, 19 November. TLS. Hanna Collection.

Reich, Cary. 1996. *The life of Nelson A. Rockefeller: Worlds to conquer 1908–1958.* New York: Doubleday.

Reinhartz, Judy, and Don M. Beach. 1997. *Teaching and learning in the elementary school: Focus on curriculum.* Upper Saddle River, N.J.: Merrill.

Report of the Mission to the Philippines. 1950. Paris: UNESCO.

Report of the President of Stanford University, 1933–34. In Lowen, 23.

Report of the U.S. Education Mission to Germany. 1946. Washington, D.C.: U.S. Government Printing Office. Hanna Collection.

Rooze, Gene E., and Leona M. Foerster. 1972. *Teaching elementary social studies — a new perspective.* Columbus: Charles E. Merrill.

Roxas, Manuel A. 1947. Message to the Philippines Association of Colleges and Universities, 14 June. In *Improving . . . ,* 58.

Rugg, Harold, ed. 1939. *Democracy and the curriculum: The life and program of the American school.* New York: John Dewey Society.

——. 1941. *That men may understand: An American in the long armistice.* New York: Doubleday, Doran and Co.

——. 1952. *The teacher of teachers: Frontiers of theory and practice in teacher education.* New York: Harper.

——. 1958. Letter to Paul Hanna, 12 December. TLS. Hanna Collection.

Rugg, Harold, and Ann Shumaker. 1928. *The child-centered school: An appraisal of the new education.* Yonkers-on-Hudson, N.Y.: World Book Co.

Russell, William F. 1938. Letter to Paul Hanna, April. TLS. Hanna Collection.

Rusteika, George. 1998. Interview by author, 16 August.

Santa Barbara City Schools. 1935. *A curriculum at work*. Santa Barbara: Schauer Printing.

Sargent, Aaron. 1947. Complaint, 21 February. TD. Hanna Collection.

Saxe, David Warren. 1991. *Social studies in schools: A history of the early years*. Albany: SUNY Press.

Saylor, J. Galen. 1986. ASCD and its beginnings. In *ASCD in retrospect: Contributions to the history of the Association for Supervision and Curriculum Development*. Alexandria: ASCD, 5–14.

Scott, Foresman and Company. 1950. *Agreement*, a contract between Scott, Foresman and Paul R. Hanna, Genevieve Anderson Hoyt, and Fannie Shaftel, 15 December. TD. Hanna Collection.

———. 1966. *Agreement*, a contract between Scott, Foresman and Paul R. Hanna. TD. Hanna Collection.

———. 1969. *Rationale of the program*, a promotional brochure. Hanna Collection.

Scott, Willis. 1938. Letter to Paul Hanna, 19 March. TLS. Hanna Collection.

Seguel, Mary L. 1966. *The curriculum field: Its formative years*. New York: Teachers College Press.

Shaftel, Fannie R., and George Shaftel. 1967. *Role-playing for social values: Decision-making in the social studies*. Englewood Cliffs, N.J.: Prentice-Hall.

Shelley, Bruce L. 1995. *Church history in plain language*, second edition. Dallas: Word.

Simpson, Roy E. 1948. Letter to Ellis A. Johnson, 16 December. TLS. Hanna Collection.

Smith, B. Othanel, William O. Stanley, and J. Harlan Shores. 1957. *Fundamentals of curriculum development*, revised edition. New York: Harcourt, Brace, 259–260.

Social Frontier 1. 1934. Editorial, 4.

Society for Curriculum Study. 1932. *News Bulletin* III (25 March).

———. 1935a. *Building America*. Promotional brochure. New York: Society for Curriculum Study.

———. 1935b. Teachers' guide for the housing issue of *Building America*. New York: SCS.

———. 1935c. *Curriculum Journal* 6 (January): 3.

———. 1940. *Curriculum Journal* 11 (September): 3.

Southeast Asian Ministers of Education Secretariat. 1971. *Director's Annual Report*. No place. Hanna Collection.

SPAN. 1982. *The current state of social studies: A report of Project SPAN*. Boulder: Social Science Education Consortium.

Stallones, Jared, Stephen McCants, and Brian Watkins. 1997. Attitudes of American teenagers toward the U.S. economy. Cincinnati: National Council for the Social Studies.

Stanford Daily 14 February 1938.

Stanford Daily 10 December 1941.

Stanford International Development Education Center. 1967. TD. Hanna Collection.

Stanford University. 1935. *Catalog of courses*. Stanford University.

———. 1936. *Catalog of courses*. Stanford University.

———. 1938. *Catalog of courses*. Stanford University.

———. 1941. *Catalog of courses*. Stanford University.

———. 1942. *Catalog of courses*. Stanford University.

———. 1952. *Abstracts of dissertations* (1936–1952). Stanford University Press.

———. 1961. *School of Education Bulletin*. Stanford University.

———. 1962. *School of Education Bulletin*. Stanford University.

———. 1963. *School of Education Bulletin*. Stanford University.

———. 1964. *School of Education Bulletin*. Stanford University.

———. 1966. *School of Education Bulletin*. Stanford University.

Stanford University News Service. 7 May 1969. TD. Hanna Collection.

Strayer, George D. 1925. Professional training for superintendents of schools. *Teachers College Record* 26: 815–826.

Sweeney, Jo Ann, Stuart Foster, and Jared Stallones. 1996. How do teenagers from different socio-economic and ethnic backgrounds value, understand, and interact with the American economic system? Washington, D.C.: National Council for the Social Studies.

Tanner, Daniel. 1991. *Crusade for democracy: Progressive education at the crossroads*. Albany: SUNY Press.

———. 1998. Letter to author, 22 August.

Tanner, Daniel, and Laurel Tanner. 1990. *History of the school curriculum*. New York: Macmillan.

Tent, James F. 1982. *Mission on the Rhine: Reeducation and denazification in American-occupied Germany*. Chicago: University of Chicago Press.

Thornton, Stephen J. 1996. NCSS: The early years. In *NCSS in retrospect*. Washington, D.C.: NCSS, 1–7.

Time. 1931. 8 June.

———. 1943. Commerce for children. 15 November.

The Tournament. 1926. West Winfield, N.Y.: privately printed.

———. 1927. West Winfield, N.Y.: privately printed.

Tupas, Isabelo, and Vitaliano Bernardino. 1955. *Philippine rural problems and the community school*. Manila: Jose C. Velo.

Tyack, David. 1974. *The one best system*. Cambridge, Mass.: Harvard University Press.

Van Til, William. 1983. My way of looking at it. Terre Haute, Ind.: Lake Lure Press.

———. 1986. *ASCD in retrospect: Contributions to the history of the Association for Supervision and Curriculum Development*. Alexandria, Va.: ASCD.

Walker, Frank F. 1942. Memo to Ray Lyman Wilbur, 13 February. In Lowen, 49.

Weiler, Hans. 1973. 14 February. TD. Hanna Collection.

West, Allan M. 1980. *The National Education Association: The power base for education*. New York: The Free Press.

Who's Who in America. 1968. Hanna, Paul Robert. New York: Who's Who.

Williams, Forbes. 1998. Interview by author, 16 July.

Wright, Frank Lloyd. 1931. *Modern architecture*. Princeton: Princeton University Press.

———. 1938. *The Architectural Forum* (January). New York: American Institute of Architecture.

Yeager, Elizabeth Anne. 1995. Alice Miel's contributions to the curriculum field. Ph.D. diss., University of Texas.

Index